Must Corporate Income
Be Taxed Twice?

Studies of Government Finance: Second Series

TITLES PUBLISHED

Must Corporate Income Be Taxed Twice?

CHARLES E. McLURE, JR.

A report of a conference sponsored by the Fund for Public Policy Research and the Brookings Institution

Studies of Government Finance

THE BROOKINGS INSTITUTION

WASHINGTON, D.C.

Library of Congress Cataloging in Publication Data:

McLure, Charles E
 Must corporate income be taxed twice?
 (Studies of government finance: Second series)
 Includes bibliographical references and index.
 1. Income tax. 2. Corporations—Taxation.
3. Dividends—Taxation. I. Title. II. Series.
HJ4639.M32 336.2′43′0973 78-27905
ISBN 0-8157-5620-8
ISBN 0-8157-5619-4 pbk.

9 8 7 6 5 4 3 2 1

THE BROOKINGS INSTITUTION is an independent organization devoted to nonpartisan research, education, and publication in economics, government, foreign policy, and the social sciences generally. Its principal purposes are to aid in the development of sound public policies and to promote public understanding of issues of national importance.

The Institution was founded on December 8, 1927, to merge the activities of the Institute for Government Research, founded in 1916, the Institute of Economics, founded in 1922, and the Robert Brookings Graduate School of Economics and Government, founded in 1924.

The Board of Trustees is responsible for the general administration of the Institution, while the immediate direction of the policies, program, and staff is vested in the President, assisted by an advisory committee of the officers and staff. The by-laws of the Institution state: "It is the function of the Trustees to make possible the conduct of scientific research, and publication, under the most favorable conditions, and to safeguard the independence of the research staff in the pursuit of their studies and in the publication of the results of such studies. It is not a part of their function to determine, control, or influence the conduct of particular investigations or the conclusions reached."

The President bears final responsibility for the decision to publish a manuscript as a Brookings book. In reaching his judgment on the competence, accuracy, and objectivity of each study, the President is advised by the director of the appropriate research program and weighs the views of a panel of expert outside readers who report to him in confidence on the quality of the work. Publication of a work signifies that it is deemed a competent treatment worthy of public consideration but does not imply endorsement of conclusions or recommendations.

The Institution maintains its position of neutrality on issues of public policy in order to safeguard the intellectual freedom of the staff. Hence interpretations or conclusions in Brookings publications should be understood to be solely those of the authors and should not be attributed to the Institution, to its trustees, officers, or other staff members, or to the organizations that support its research.

To my parents

Foreword

IN THE United States, the earnings of corporations are taxed twice: once as corporate income and again, after distribution to shareholders, as personal income. The 1970s have seen a remarkable rise of interest in what is called integration of the personal and corporate income taxes—a technical term meaning relief from the present practice of double taxation.

Much discussion of integration has focused on policy issues such as the economic distortions caused by double taxation and the effects of integration on corporate financial policy, capital accumulation, income distribution, and economic growth. Until recently little attention was given to how integration could be brought about. This book examines the administrative problems that integration presents and discusses the approaches that might be taken in dealing with them.

The author first summarizes the arguments that have been made for and against integration and describes the various systems of relief from double taxation of dividends that have been adopted in Canada, France, West Germany, and the United Kingdom. He then deals with tax preferences, an issue largely ignored in most discussions of the policy implications of integration in the United States, and demonstrates the crucial importance of the treatment of tax preferences to any proposal for integration or dividend relief.

Those who argue for integration of the income taxes have long favored the partnership method, under which corporations would pay no income tax, and all their equity income, whether distributed or retained, would be taxed to shareholders. McLure reexamines and confirms the traditional view that integration by the partnership method, if applied with conceptual purity, would be virtually impossible to administer. Moreover, he finds that even a conceptually impure application of the partnership method would be plagued by formidable administrative problems.

Finally, McLure considers how integration ought to affect the tax treatment of foreign-source income and income attributable to foreign ownership—an issue that has assumed great importance owing to the proliferation of multinational corporations and vastly increased international flows of capital income.

A substantial portion of this book was prepared as a background paper for a conference at the Brookings Institution on October 13 and 14, 1977, that brought together public finance economists, tax specialists, and government officials. Because the conference was organized to assess the administrative feasibility of integration, policy issues were not discussed extensively. The conference focused instead upon the feasibility of full integration, alternative approaches to dividend relief, the treatment of tax preferences, the impact on tax-exempt organizations, and international aspects of integration. As the final chapter suggests, little agreement was reached in any area, probably because the administrative problems of integration have only recently started to receive serious consideration in the United States. Hence McLure concludes that the United States should neither rush into integration nor reject it as infeasible pending the results of future study—a conclusion that European experience seems to corroborate.

Charles E. McLure, Jr., is vice president of the National Bureau of Economic Research and Allyn R. and Gladys M. Cline Professor of Economics and Finance at Rice University. In preparing his manuscript for the conference and in revising it afterwards, he received valuable assistance from many persons, including William D. Andrews, Hugh J. Ault, Richard M. Bird, David F. Bradford, Gerard M. Brannon, Martin S. Feldstein, J. S. Flemming, Martin D. Ginsburg, Harry G. Gourevitch, Frederic W. Hickman, Daniel M. Holland, Mervyn A. King, William A. Klein, Michael E. Levy, George

Mundstock, Peggy B. Musgrave, Joseph A. Pechman, Carl S. Shoup, Emil M. Sunley, Jr., Stanley S. Surrey, Willard B. Taylor, A. J. van den Tempel, John Wadsworth, and Bernard Wolfman. Contributions made during the conference are described without attribution in the summary of conference proceedings. Mary Jane Chisholm is to be commended for her unusual care in typing several drafts of the book. The manuscript was checked for accuracy by Evelyn P. Fisher and edited by Caroline Lalire. The index was prepared by Florence Robinson. The author's biggest debt is to his wife, Patsy, who bore even more than the usual hardship inflicted on spouses of authors while the book was in progress.

The project was supported with funds provided by the Fund for Public Policy Research, Washington, D.C. This is the tenth volume in the second series of Brookings Studies of Government Finance. Both series are devoted to examining issues in taxation and public policy.

The views expressed in this book are those of the author and the conference participants and should not be ascribed to the Fund for Public Policy Research or to the trustees, officers, or other staff members of the Brookings Institution.

BRUCE K. MACLAURY
President

January 1979
Washington, D.C.

Contents

Figure

CHAPTER ONE

Introduction

INTEGRATION of the corporate and individual income taxes—a policy long favored by some public finance economists, but few others in the United States—has suddenly moved to the forefront in discussions of tax policy. It was raised on two different occasions by the Ford administration, it was expected to be the key proposal in the Carter administration's 1978 tax reform package, and Chairman Al Ullman of the House Committee on Ways and Means proposed it in early 1978.[1] Yet to most Americans, and perhaps even to most economists, lawyers, accountants, politicians, and public offi-

1. William E. Simon, Testimony in *Tax Reform* (*Administration and Public Witnesses*), Hearings before the House Committee on Ways and Means, 94 Cong. 1 sess. (Government Printing Office, 1975), pt. 5, pp. 3846–61, and U.S. Department of the Treasury, *Blueprints for Basic Tax Reform* (GPO, 1977), especially pp. 68–75 and 194–200; "Tax Reform Option Papers Prepared by Treasury Department, September 2, 1977, for the White House," Bureau of National Affairs, *Daily Report for Executives* (Special Supplement), DER 196 (October 7, 1977), especially pp. 48–53; and *Congressional Record*, daily ed., February 2, 1978, pp. H 640–42, and ibid., March 22, 1978, pp. H 2337–38. The Simon proposal, the anticipated Carter proposal, and the Ullman proposal were for relief from double taxation of dividends, while the "proposal" in *Blueprints* (which strictly speaking was not an official proposal, though it is generally considered one) was for full integration (this distinction is explained below). It should be noted that the present study was basically completed before the expected Carter proposals were leaked to the press in early September 1977.

1

cials, integration is so novel that they would have considerable diffi-
culty in answering such questions as: What is integration? What are
its advantages? Why the sudden interest in integration? Not to men-
tion: How is integration achieved? What are the issues of tax policy
it involves? Are there any unusual practical problems? This book is
primarily devoted to the second group of questions. But for back-
ground it will be useful to answer the first three questions briefly and
give some indication of the importance of the others, as well as to
consider some terminology.[2]

What Is Integration?

Under U.S. federal income tax law, income earned on investments
in corporate stock is subjected to two distinct tax regimes. First, the
income is taxed at the corporate level at a rate of 46 percent, once in-
come exceeds $100,000 in a given year.[3] Then, to the extent that the
net income (that is, income after corporate income tax) is distrib-
uted to shareholders as dividends it is taxed as ordinary personal in-
come at rates up to 70 percent. Thus, under this so-called classical
system, such distributed income from corporate sources is subject to
"double taxation of dividends." One objective of integration is to
eliminate, or at least to reduce, this double taxation. It can be
achieved essentially in one of two ways: (1) by treating (all or part
of) the corporate income tax as a mere withholding tax to the extent

2. For more extensive discussion of the arguments for and against integration,
see chapter 2; Charles E. McLure, Jr., "Integration of the Personal and Corporate
Income Taxes: The Missing Element in Recent Tax Reform Proposals," *Harvard
Law Review,* vol. 88 (January 1975), pp. 532–82; and George F. Break and Joseph
A. Pechman, *Federal Tax Reform: The Impossible Dream?* (Brookings Institution,
1975), chapter 4, which was reprinted, with a few changes, in George F. Break and
Joseph A. Pechman, "Relationship between the Corporation and Individual Income
Taxes," *National Tax Journal,* vol. 28 (September 1975), pp. 341–50. For further
explanation of terms relating to integration, see the glossary of this book.

3. The statutory rates range from 17 percent on the first $25,000 of income to 40
percent on the amount of income between $75,000 and $100,000. Of even greater
importance, various tax preferences (accelerated depreciation, investment tax credits,
firms operating as domestic international sales corporations, and so on) reduced the
average effective rate of tax collected on economic income of corporations to 36–38
percent in recent years. Despite the overriding importance of these qualifications
(especially the investment tax credits) for the implementation of integration, I am
ignoring them at this point to facilitate explanation of the basic nature of integration.
(Nor do I consider state income taxation.) The treatment of tax preferences is,
however, the subject of chapter 4.

that it applies to distributed income of the corporation (the imputation method), or (2) by allowing the corporation a deduction for (all or part of) the dividends it pays similar to the deduction for interest paid on corporate debt (the dividend-paid deduction method), or, equivalently, by applying different rates of corporate tax to distributed and undistributed corporate income (the split-rate method). Or these two approaches can be combined, as in the West German system.

More far-reaching than the schemes for *dividend relief* just outlined is true *integration*. Under integration the income earned at the corporate level, whether distributed or not, would be attributed to shareholders, as in a partnership, and taxed only at the rates applicable to the incomes of the various shareholders. Advocates of this approach point out that dividend relief is defective because it provides integration for only that portion of corporate income that is distributed, whereas a major source of inequity and distortion in the U.S. tax system is the interplay of the corporate income tax and the provisions of the personal income tax law relating to long-term capital gains. That is, once the 46 percent corporate tax is paid, high-income taxpayers can let corporate earnings accumulate and produce preferentially taxed long-term capital gains, instead of having to pay the personal tax rates that are levied on ordinary income (for example, wages and salaries, interest income, and income from unincorporated businesses), which can be as high as 70 percent.[4] Full integration would eliminate this possibility.

Types of Integration

The following table shows the alternative approaches to integration of the corporate and individual income taxes.[5] Case 1 involves

4. Tax preferences make this practice even more favorable to the high-income taxpayer, and, some would argue, more inequitable from society's point of view than a simple comparison of statutory rates would suggest. On the other hand, most of the tax preferences available to shelter corporate-source income are also available for investment made under other forms of business organization.

5. It is not intended that the table provide a complete list of countries providing dividend relief. Moreover, it should be noted that the table (and the entire book) omits what many would take to be the most promising approach to overcoming the inequities and distortions generated by an unintegrated corporate income tax. Carl Shoup, for example, has strongly advocated eliminating the corporate income tax and taxing capital gains as ordinary income, using constructive realization of gains every several years to prevent indefinite postponement of tax on gains. See, for ex-

Scope of relief	*Degree of relief*	
Dividends only	1. Partial dividend relief France United Kingdom Canada	2. Total dividend relief West Germany
Dividends and retained earnings	3. Partial integration None extant None proposed	4. Total integration None extant Proposed in Canada and West Germany

partial relief from double taxation of dividends; the systems of France, the United Kingdom, and Canada are examples of this approach. In case 2 dividend relief is complete, as in West Germany. In case 4 integration is extended to the entire amount of corporate-source income, whether distributed or retained; the proposal of the Royal Commission on Taxation in Canada is the best-known example of this case, though West Germany also considered full integration before adopting dividend relief. Case 3 does not exist in practice and, to my knowledge, has not been proposed, and is probably not a workable alternative.[6]

Unfortunately, there has been considerable confusion over terminology. Many economists refer to case 4 as "total integration" and to case 2 as "partial integration." Under this convention, case 1 becomes "partial partial" and, even worse, case 3 would be "partial total." But at least one group of authors has called case 4 "complete integration" and case 3 "partial integration,"[7] much to the dismay

ample, Carl S. Shoup, *Facing the Tax Problem: A Survey of Taxation in the United States and a Program for the Future* (Twentieth Century Fund, 1937), pp. 464–91, for an early statement of this position. Detailed appraisal of the technical feasibility of this approach would require an entire book and is beyond the scope of the present study. A second alternative not examined here is that for an annual tax on undistributed profits; see William Vickrey, *Agenda for Progressive Taxation* (Roland Press, 1947; reprinted, Kelley, 1972), pp. 151–53, 156–61.

6. For an elementary exposition of the Canadian Royal Commission's proposal for integration, the dividend-paid deduction, and the shareholder credit approach to dividend relief, see McLure, "Integration." For further details on the systems as actually implemented, see chapter 3 and references given there. Case 3 is explored more fully in the appendix to this chapter.

7. See Martin Feldstein and Daniel Frisch, "Corporate Tax Integration: The Estimated Effects on Capital Accumulation and Tax Distribution of Two Integration Proposals," *National Tax Journal*, vol. 30 (March 1977), pp. 37–52.

of some observers. All things considered, it seems best in this book to refer to cases 1 and 2 as partial and total (or complete) dividend relief and to cases 3 and 4 as partial and total (or full or complete) integration. Sometimes "integration" is used in its broad sense, to include all four cases; the context will make clear which meaning is intended.[8]

Finally, such inherently defective schemes as excluding dividends from personal taxable income, providing a credit for dividends received (without gross-up), eliminating the corporate income tax without allocating retained earnings to shareholders, and allowing corporations a deduction for some standard percentage of equity capital are not called either integration or dividend relief (unless preceded by the term "unacceptable" in the latter case) in order to avoid confusing them with legitimate schemes for providing integration or dividend relief.[9]

Comparison of Integration with the Classical System

Integration and dividend relief can perhaps most easily be understood by comparing them with the more familiar "classical," or separate, system. Table 1-1 therefore presents the tax picture for corporate-source income attributable to shareholders in the classical and fully integrated systems under a variety of assumptions about dividend payout rates. (It is assumed throughout that capital gains resulting from retained earnings are realized so long after accrual that the present value of taxes paid on them can be ignored. A more accurate description of the tax treatment of such gains would lead too far from the central theme of this discussion.) Under the classical system, of course, the excess taxation of dividends is greater the lower the marginal tax bracket of the shareholder and the higher the dividend payout rate. Under total integration, on the other hand, all

8. In the interest of diversification I have occasionally used such terms as "relief from double taxation of dividends" and "integration for dividends only." They are to be understood to be synonymous with "dividend relief," which, in turn, is intended to be merely descriptive, not pejorative. The first of these terms is, however, not really descriptive, and in fact can lead to confusion, for the problem with an unintegrated tax is not that dividends are taxed twice, but that corporate-source income is subject to taxation that can, in the aggregate, be too light or too heavy. In this book "partial integration" is never used to refer to dividend relief.

9. For a description of the faults of these schemes, see McLure, "Integration."

Table 1-1. Tax Burdens under Classical and Fully Integrated Income Tax Systems, by Alternative Marginal Personal Tax Rates and Payout Rates[a]

Rates in percent; other data in monetary units

Item[b]	Classical system						Fully integrated system	
	(1)	(2)	(3)	(4)	(5)	(6)	(7)	(8)
1. Marginal personal tax rate	20	20	20	70	70	70	20	70
2. Dividend payout rate	100	50	0	100	50	0
3. Corporate-source income	100	100	100	100	100	100	100	100
4. Corporate income tax [50% of 3]	50	50	50	50	50	50	50	50
5. Net corporate income [3 − 4]	50	50	50	50	50	50	50	50
6. Cash dividends	50	25	0	50	25	0
7. Gross-up [from 4]	50	50
8. Taxable personal income[c,d]	50	25	0	50	25	0	100	100
9. Gross personal tax[d] [1 × 8]	10	5	0	35	17.5	0	20	70
10. Shareholder credit [from 7]	50	50
11. Net personal tax[d] [9 − 10]	10	5	0	35	17.5	0	−30	20
12. Total taxes [4 + 11]	60	55	50	85	67.5	50	20	70

... Not applicable to this system.
a. Terms relating to integration systems are explained in the glossary.
b. Except for percentages, the numbers in brackets refer to the lines of this table.
c. Classical system [from 6]; fully integrated system [5 + 7].
d. Shareholder taxes on capital gains resulting from retained earnings are ignored.

corporate-source income is taxed at the marginal rate of the shareholder. Under dividend relief the shareholder's marginal tax rate is applied to distributed corporate-source income, as in columns 7 and 8. But retained corporate-source income is taxed at the corporate rate, so that for that part of income column 3 or 6 is relevant. Thus the aggregate tax burden on corporate-source income depends on the dividend payout rate and the marginal tax rates of shareholders.[10]

10. It depends, as well, on the extent to which tax preferences reduce the effective tax rate of the corporation.

Pros and Cons of Integration

Those who object to the pattern of taxation resulting from the separate, unintegrated income taxes on income originating in investments in corporate shares argue that the separate taxation of corporate-source income is logically indefensible, that it creates both horizontal and vertical inequities, that it distorts the allocation of investment between the corporate sector and the noncorporate sector, that it encourages corporations to rely too heavily on debt financing and retain too great a share of net corporate income, and that it depresses the nation's rates of capital accumulation and economic growth. Against this rather impressive list of indictments, it is countered that the separate taxation of corporate income *can* be defended on basic tax principles, especially because it adds significantly to the progressivity of the income tax; that the distortions of resource allocation and corporate financial policy have not been firmly documented and would not be very important, in any event; and that integration of the income taxes, because it would encourage distribution of corporate profits, is likely to increase the rates of private capital accumulation and economic growth only if the substantial loss of revenue it would entail were made up in a distinctly regressive way—or not made up at all. Furthermore, say the skeptics, full integration, having never been tried in any country and having been rejected explicitly in at least two, involves considerable practical problems, and even dividend relief, which they view as inequitable, raises many problems, as European experience shows.

Interest in Integration

Interest in integration, which had largely been dormant in the United States since the penalty tax on undistributed profits was repealed in 1939, can be traced to the confluence of several forces.[11] Perhaps the most visible of these has been the much-discussed capital

11. From 1954 to 1965 there had, of course, been a credit for a fixed percentage of dividends received by shareholders, and shareholders still retain the right to exclude $100 of dividends per taxpayer. But these approaches to relieving the double taxation of dividends are sufficiently defective—as explained in McLure, "Integration," pp. 550–54—to need no further discussion.

shortage.[12] Businessmen (and some economists) have argued that the tax system in general, and the double taxation of corporate dividends in particular, is responsible for what they take to be an undesirable shortfall in capital formation.[13] Relief from double taxation of dividends, they argue, would go far in relieving the capital shortage.

A second important reason for the recent American interest in integration is the increased tendency for other developed countries to provide at least partial dividend relief.[14] In 1965 France began to allow shareholders credit for half the corporate tax attributable to dividends, and in 1973 the United Kingdom returned to a system of partial relief from double taxation of dividends after using a classical system from 1965 to 1973. Finally, on January 1, 1977, West Germany, which since 1953 had applied a lower rate of tax to dividends than to retentions, became the first member of the European Community to provide complete relief from the double taxation of dividends. And of perhaps even greater ultimate importance, in its

12. This is not the place to attempt to judge whether the "capital shortage" is real or imaginary (or indeed what the term is intended to mean). Among attempts to do so are: Leonall C. Andersen, "Is There a Capital Shortage: Theory and Recent Empirical Evidence," *Journal of Finance,* vol. 31 (May 1976), pp. 257–68; Barry Bosworth, James S. Duesenberry, and Andrew S. Carron, *Capital Needs in the Seventies* (Brookings Institution, 1975); Allen Sinai and Roger E. Brinner, *The Capital Shortage: Near-Term Outlook and Long-Term Prospects* (Lexington, Mass.: Data Resources, Inc., 1975); Paul Wachtel, Arnold Sametz, and Harry Shuford, "Capital Shortages: Myth or Reality?" *Journal of Finance,* vol. 31 (May 1976), pp. 269–85; and New York Stock Exchange, *The Capital Needs and Savings Potential of the U.S. Economy: Projections Through 1985* (New York Stock Exchange, 1974). See also Joint Committee on Taxation, *Tax Policy and Capital Formation,* prepared for the Task Force on Capital Formation of the House Committee on Ways and Means by the Staff of the Joint Committee on Taxation (GPO, 1977); and Eli Shapiro and William L. White, eds., *Capital for Productivity and Jobs* (Prentice-Hall, 1977).

13. For further references, see chapter 2.

14. Much of the descriptive information on foreign systems has appeared in International Bureau of Fiscal Documentation, *European Taxation* (Amsterdam), various issues, and in International Fiscal Association, *Cahiers de Droit Fiscal International* (Rotterdam), various issues. In addition, for details of integration schemes used in other countries, see Organisation for Economic Co-operation and Development, *Company Tax Systems in OECD Member Countries* (Paris: OECD, 1973); Richard M. Hammer, "The Taxation of Income from Corporate Shareholders: Review of Present Systems in Canada, France, Germany, Japan and the U.K.," *National Tax Journal,* vol. 28 (September 1975), pp. 315–34; and Hugh J. Ault, "Germany: The New Corporation Tax System," *Intertax: European Tax Review* (August 1976), pp. 262–75. These are reviewed in chapter 3.

1975 proposal for a directive on the harmonization of company income taxes, the Commission of the European Communities suggested that all nine member countries should eventually provide relief for from 45 to 55 percent of the double taxation of dividends.[15] This suggestion was not approved by the European Parliament.[16]

A final factor contributing to the upsurge in interest in integration was the suggestion by a Canadian Royal Commission on Taxation that total integration, long held to be a convenient conceptual norm that was infeasible, might indeed be feasible.[17]

Policy Issues in Integration

The three most obvious issues in the debate over integration are whether or not to have some kind of integration; if so, whether it should involve all corporate income or only distributed income; and whether integration or dividend relief should be complete or only partial. But positions on these basic issues depend crucially on how less obvious questions are resolved.

First, corporations, like other business taxpayers, benefit from an array of tax preferences that reduces the effective rate of taxation of corporate economic income—to an average rate of only about 36 to 38 percent. The proper treatment of tax preferences, usually overlooked in elementary discussions of integration and dividend relief, permeates any detailed discussion of dividend relief, and it can do so for integration, too, if a decision is not made at an early stage to eliminate all preferences from the tax code. Among the policy questions that must be settled are whether tax preferences should be

15. Commission of the European Communities, "Proposal for a Council Directive Concerning the Harmonization of Systems of Company Taxation and of Withholding Taxes on Dividends," *Bulletin of the European Communities,* Supplement 10/75: *Harmonization of Systems of Company Taxation* (Luxembourg: Office for Official Publications of the European Communities, 1975), article 3.

16. *Intertax* (January 1978), p. 1.

17. See *Report of the Royal Commission on Taxation,* vol. 4 (Ottawa: Queen's Printer, 1967), chap. 19. Though it has been customary to refer to this commission as the "Carter Commission," here the term "Canadian Royal Commission" will be used to avoid confusion. For analyses of the commission's integration proposals, see George F. Break, "Integration of the Corporate and Personal Income Taxes," *National Tax Journal,* vol. 22 (March 1969), pp. 39–56, and George F. Break, "Integrating Corporate and Personal Income Taxes: The Carter Commission Proposals," *Law and Contemporary Problems,* vol. 34 (Autumn 1969), pp. 726–35; and McLure, "Integration," pp. 558–61, 569–74.

eliminated so far as corporate-source income is concerned, passed through to shareholders on all corporate-source income, or passed through only on income that is not distributed; and, beyond that, whether exclusion preferences (such as interest on municipal bonds) and deductible preferences (such as the excess of accelerated depreciation over economic depreciation) should be treated differently from creditable preferences (such as the investment tax credit). Additional questions that must be addressed, especially in the case of dividend relief, include whether preference income is to be assumed to be paid out, or "stacked," first (so that dividends are attributed initially to tax-preferred income) or last (so that dividends are attributed initially to fully taxed income) or to be split proportionately between dividends and retentions. Whereas economic reasoning may point to certain answers to some of these questions, administrative realities may point elsewhere.

Chapter 4 examines the implications of tax preferences for integration in greater detail. Here it is sufficient to note that decisions on the treatment of preferences (especially rules for stacking and washout) involve serious questions of economic policy and not mere technical details. Commercial banks and regulated public utilities, for example, would be hit hard by a system that washed out tax preferences (especially if the foreign tax credit were treated as a preference), even if preference income were stacked last. Considerations such as this may help to explain the adoption of liberal stacking and transition rules in Europe.

Second, some 20 to 25 percent of all corporate stock is held by tax-exempt organizations, including pension funds, foundations, and educational and religious organizations.[18] Should the burden of the corporate income tax be removed from these otherwise tax-exempt organizations if the income taxes are integrated? The revenue consequences of doing so is enormous (for example, some $12 billion [1976 dollars] under total integration).[19]

Third, any scheme involving integration of the corporation and personal income taxes will have important implications for other

18. This estimate is based on figures for the receipt of dividends contained in Marshall E. Blume, Jean Crockett, and Irwin Friend, "Stockownership in the United States: Characteristics and Trends," *Survey of Current Business*, vol. 54 (November 1974), pp. 16–40.

19. See Simon, *Tax Reform*, pp. 3856–57, and Break and Pechman, *Federal Tax Reform: The Impossible Dream?* p. 103.

components of the income tax system. In some cases the relation will be direct; full integration necessarily involves reconsideration of the tax treatment of long-term capital gains and losses on corporate shares. In other instances the tie will be less direct, but still very strong; full integration, for example, may be unacceptable without a withholding tax levied at the corporate level at a rate that is coordinated with the top marginal rate under the personal income tax. Furthermore, whether any form of integration is politically acceptable will depend on the tax reforms that accompany it. Dividend relief, for example, would substantially reduce the distributional progressivity of the tax system and would be acceptable among liberals only if packaged with a large reduction of the tax preferences currently enjoyed by high-income households; total integration, by comparison, because it would reach retained earnings on a current basis, might be acceptable to this group even if accompanied by less extensive tax reform.

Fourth, any form of integration involves incredibly complicated questions about the proper taxation of international flows of corporate earnings. How, for example, should dividends flowing between two countries that provide dividend relief be taxed? Should the relief be granted by the source country or the residence country? Does it matter whether direct or portfolio investment is involved? What if the two countries employ different means of providing dividend relief? What if only one country allows dividend relief and the other has a classical system? A fully integrated system? These basic questions must be settled—and the answers agreed upon by the countries—before it is possible to proceed to technical problems of implementation.

Some Technical Issues

There are also a number of technical questions that must be answered for any integration proposal, as well as others that are specific to given approaches. Though some are questions that determine whether a particular variant of a basic method is feasible, without consideration of whether the basic method should be adopted, this is not true in most cases.

If full integration is to be adopted, it is necessary to decide whether (and how) to try to preserve the character of the various components

of corporate income in the hands of the shareholder. For example, should interest income from tax-exempt securities remain tax-exempt once it is attributed to shareholders? How should adjustments to corporate income resulting from audits be handled under full integration? How could corporations provide shareholders with the timely information needed to prepare their tax returns if the filing dates were the same for both? Since it has been asserted that West Germany shied away from attempting full integration because of such practical problems,[20] they should not be taken lightly. This is especially true in that the effects of full integration and of dividend relief could be quite different (see chapter 2), so that many who would favor, or at least would tolerate, integration would oppose dividend relief. (The converse is also true.) Thus, if full integration were found to be technically infeasible, dividend relief might not be the "half loaf" that is midway between the present system and integration, either economically or politically.

But even if dividend relief were a viable alternative, technical considerations—as, for example, the treatment of tax preferences—would affect the desirability and form of dividend relief.[21] Some would favor an assumption that dividends are paid first from fully taxed income, while others would wish to treat dividends as coming first from tax-preferred income and wash out the preference on dividends. Given the distributional and allocational implications of some of these choices, and the strength of feelings attached to them, more than mere technical detail would be involved.

International Considerations

One of the few subjects commonly encountered by tax economists that is more complicated than integration is the tax treatment of income flowing across international boundaries; unfortunately the

20. See Harry G. Gourevitch, *Integration of Corporate and Shareholder Taxes on Income: The European Experience* (Library of Congress, Congressional Research Service, 1977), pp. 48–54.

21. Transition measures could also affect the desirability of various approaches. An example would be the treatment of dividends paid out of earnings accumulated before the adoption of relief from double taxation of dividends. Some would favor the assumption that dividends are paid first from such earnings (first in, first out, or FIFO), while others would prefer to treat dividends as resulting first from income of the current period (last in, first out, or LIFO).

proper tax treatment of such income poses major problems for either integration or dividend relief. Clearly, international tax relations are simplest if all countries employ classical systems. But the United States' most important trading partners use tax systems that provide at least partial relief from the double taxation of dividends; therefore, it may become increasingly difficult to negotiate tax treaties if the United States retains an unintegrated classical system. Yet international considerations, as well as administrative difficulties, tend to militate against the adoption of full integration. Given the present interpretation of "reciprocity" in double taxation conventions, the difficulty of not allowing the benefits of integration to foreign shareholders in U.S. firms might dictate against the use of the dividend-paid deduction method of dividend relief, which many observers find to be the most natural and most easily administered approach if appraised only in terms of its domestic attributes. Thus the very choice between the shareholder credit approach and the dividend-paid deduction might be in large part predetermined by U.S. treaty obligations and foreign practices. Unless the United States could persuade other major countries to change from the shareholder credit approach to the dividend-paid deduction (or the equivalent split-rate system), use of the second approach might be effectively foreclosed.[22]

It would also be necessary to decide how to treat income from foreign investments in applying any U.S. system of integration or dividend relief. Should the foreign tax credit be treated like a tax preference and therefore washed out on distributed earnings, as in Europe, or should shareholders be granted credit against personal tax for foreign corporate taxes paid? If the latter choice were made, should (and could) the limitation on the use of the foreign tax credit be applied at the shareholder level? Or would it be necessary to abolish the limitation or apply it at the corporate level? Should the United States allow relief to foreign shareholders in U.S. firms? Again, these issues (which are the topic of chapter 6) involve important questions of policy and are not mere minor technical questions.

22. The split-rate system has been combined with the imputation system in West Germany. But foreign tax considerations played an important role in Germany's decision not to use just the split-rate approach and in the rejection of it by the United Kingdom. Such considerations seem to be growing less important, however, since the British have, in effect, agreed to allow most foreign shareholders the benefits they would enjoy under the split-rate approach.

Plan of the Book

Chapter 2 presents the basic arguments for and against integration, noting especially that the term means different things (true integration or just dividend relief) to different people. Readers who are familiar with this debate may want to skip over this chapter—though they may find it interesting that dividend relief was adopted in Europe for reasons that bear little resemblance to the arguments for integration commonly heard in the United States.

Those who are familiar with foreign systems of dividend relief may find little that is new in chapter 3, which outlines foreign practice. But those unfamiliar with foreign experience should find acquaintance with foreign systems useful in understanding what follows. And the reasons for the particular form dividend relief has taken in Europe (involving problems in negotiating double taxation treaties) is relevant to an appraisal of U.S. options.

Chapters 4 through 7 constitute the primary contribution of the book. Although the proper tax treatment of tax preferences has been discussed at length in Europe and Canada, much of the discussion is largely inaccessible to U.S. audiences because of language barriers, and even what is accessible is generally unfamiliar. Moreover, the entire concept of tax preferences seems not to be as well developed in Europe as in the United States. In chapter 4, therefore, I have tried to describe the problems tax preferences create for integration and dividend relief, beginning with a discussion of conceptual issues, proceeding to a consideration of practical problems of implementation, and ending with tentative conclusions about the administrative feasibility of various alternatives. That the general approach commonly followed in Europe seems to be the easiest to administer, even if not the best conceptually, helps to explain the attention devoted to foreign experience in chapter 3.

Though questions of the proper treatment of tax preferences permeate the discussion of integration, they are not the only practical problems. Chapter 5 discusses the administrative problems that would arise if integration were attempted in a closed economy, and chapter 6 discusses the treatment of income crossing national borders. In chapter 5, after concluding that the pure partnership method of integration would probably be administratively impossible

and that the modified form of integration proposed by the Canadian Royal Commission and by the U.S. Department of the Treasury in *Blueprints for Basic Tax Reform* would be difficult to implement, I discuss problems that would occur even if only dividend relief were attempted. Among these are the proper ways to handle intercorporate dividends and tax-exempt organizations.

International treaty obligations and economic realities demand that choices about integration cannot be made as if the United States were a closed economy. Although the "international tail" should not be allowed to wag the "domestic dog" of integration, the tail cannot prudently be ignored. A realistic consideration of the likely reaction of other major industrial nations suggests that the dividend-paid deduction may not be a workable short-run alternative. Moreover, the reaction of developing countries, which are for the most part "source" rather than "residence" countries, may limit the way dividend relief is provided under the shareholder credit approach. Finally, traditional American concern for worldwide efficiency may dictate that certain policies are preferable to others. But no matter what policies are adopted, administrative problems are particularly complex in the international sphere.

Chapter 7 summarizes the discussion at the Brookings conference in October 1977. Among the issues discussed were the following: Is full integration feasible? Would it be much more difficult than dividend relief? Could most of its advantages be achieved by adopting only dividend relief? Is one of the means of providing dividend relief to be preferred? How should tax preferences be handled? How should tax-exempt organizations be treated? How would they respond to various ways of treating them? What is the proper treatment of international flows of corporate-source equity income? There was a disquieting lack of agreement on almost all these questions—and on others. This may reflect the relative novelty of the idea of integration in the United States and the consequent lack of in-depth study of it. One possible conclusion is that more analysis is required before integration or dividend relief is accepted—or rejected.

Appendix: Partial Integration

Since no one has given much attention to defining and analyzing partial integration, I shall attempt to do so here.

Table 1-2. Tax Burdens under Partial Integration, by Alternative Assumptions about Marginal Personal Tax Rates and Percentage Gross-up and Credit[a]

Rates in percent; other data in monetary units

Item[b]					Degree of gross-up and credit[c]			
					20 per-cent	20 per-cent	50 per-cent	50 per-cent
	Zero	Zero	Zero	Zero				
1. Marginal personal tax rate	20	20	70	70	20	70	20	70
2. Dividend payout rate	100	0	100	0	d	d	d	d
3. Net corporate income	50	50	50	50	50	50	50	50
4. Gross-up [relevant % of 3]	0	0	0	0	10	10	25	25
5. Taxable personal income [3 + 4]	50	50	50	50	60	60	75	75
6. Gross personal tax [1 × 5]	10	10	35	35	12	42	15	52.5
7. Shareholder credit [from 4]	0	0	0	0	10	10	25	25
8. Net personal tax [6 − 7]	10	10	35	35	2	32	−10	27.5
9. Total taxes[e]	60	60	85	85	52	82	40	77.5
10. Corresponding total taxes for other systems								
a. Classical[f]	60	50	85	50	g	g	g	g
b. Fully integrated[h]	20	20	70	70	20	70	20	70
11. Overtaxation								
a. Classical system [10a − 10b]	40	30	15	−20	g	g	g	g
b. Partial integration [9 − 10b]	40	40	15	15	32	12	20	7.5

a. Terms relating to integration systems are explained in the glossary.
b. Except for percentages, the numbers in brackets refer to the lines of this table.
c. If the corporate tax rate is 50 percent, a gross-up and credit of 100 percent of dividends and allocated retentions produces total integration.
d. The dividend payout rate is irrelevant to the partial integration system. For the case of zero gross-up and credit, this is demonstrated in the first four columns.
e. Corporate tax of 50 percent of 100 of economic income plus line 8.
f. Columns 1 and 3: corporate tax of 50 percent of 100 of economic income + (marginal personal tax rate × 50); columns 2 and 4: corporate tax of 50 percent of 100 of economic income.
g. Depends on dividend payout rates; see note d.
h. Marginal personal tax rate × 100 of economic income.

Consider the pattern of tax burdens shown in table 1-2, which is constructed under the assumption that all retained earnings are attributed to shareholders but only some fraction (less than one) of such retained earnings and dividends received are employed in cal-

culating gross-up and credit.[23] Several things are immediately apparent. First, the attribution of retained earnings results in their being taxed exactly as dividends are taxed, rendering the dividend payout rate irrelevant so far as tax consequences are concerned. (This is shown only for the first set of columns.) Second, the overtaxation of both dividends and retentions falls as the degree of integration (gross-up and credit) increases. Finally, by combining these two results, one sees that it is the attribution of the after-tax retentions to shareholders that increases the tax burden on retentions; given the allocation of after-tax retentions for tax purposes, gross-up and credit reduces the tax burden, and by a greater amount the higher the percentage of gross-up and credit.

Stated still differently, integration, whether partial or full, involves two distinct steps: (1) the attribution of retained earnings to shareholders (together with write-up of basis for calculating capital gains), and (2) the gross-up and credit for both dividends and allocated retained earnings.[24] In contrast, dividend relief involves only

23. Since a corporate tax rate of 50 percent is assumed, a gross-up and credit equal to the amount of dividends and allocated retentions provides complete integration, and therefore a convenient benchmark. It is also assumed that allocation of retained earnings results in a write-up of the cost basis of stock by the amount of the retentions, which, in turn, is assumed to equal the capital gains realizable on sale of the shares. Thus allocation, as in complete integration, would eliminate taxable capital gains so far as the latter can be traced to retained earnings. The tax consequences for retained earnings are the same as in the case of a classical system in which there is no significant tax in present value terms because capital gains are postponed indefinitely or appreciated property is transferred at death. (But lock-in would be reduced because there would be no tax incentive for postponement.) Of course, under the classical system there would be some capital gains tax not reflected in table 1-2, to the extent that gains are realized.

24. Implicit in this discussion is a specific definition of partial integration, namely, the *complete* allocation of retentions and *partial* gross-up and credit for both dividends and retentions. But another definition could reasonably be proposed. Under it, 50 percent integration would involve gross-up and credit for 50 percent of dividends together with allocation of half of retained earnings but gross-up and credit for the full amount of the *allocated* earnings. Since such an approach would involve less allocation of retained earnings, but the same amount of gross-up and credit, it would be more favorable to retained earnings than the approach described in the text. Thus there is little reason to believe that a road whose beginning was marked "integration" might not eventually pass by such a way station. But this is something of a conceptual monstrosity that would probably involve severe administrative problems. All things considered, it seems best to define the term "partial integration" as I do in the text. Even so, the existence of this alternative meaning highlights the difficulty of arriving at clear-cut definitions in this field.

the second step, which is limited in that case to dividends.[25] Naturally enough, given the results outlined above, businessmen tend to be interested in dividend relief, not in integration. And given the taxation of all corporate-source income at marginal personal rates that complete allocation of retained earnings entails, there is no reason to resist full gross-up and credit from a conceptual point of view, though some might prefer the progressive distributional consequences of not going all the way to full integration. In short, partial integration has little to recommend it at the conceptual level, but it has all the administrative complexities of full integration.[26]

25. But failure to tax dividends and retentions equally may necessitate a concept such as earnings and profits to differentiate between dividends and other distributions.

26. Partial integration is particularly vulnerable to one of the criticisms often leveled against full integration: liquidity problems for those whose marginal personal tax rates exceed the corporate withholding rate. This can be seen by considering the case of the high-income shareholder in a firm that distributes no earnings in the context of a 50 percent corporate tax and only 50 percent gross-up and credit. Such a shareholder in the 70 percent tax bracket would have a net personal tax liability of 27.5 on 100 of corporate-source income attributed to him, whereas under full integration the net liability would be only 20. Of perhaps equal interest, reducing the top personal rate to equal the corporate rate does not eliminate the problem, as it does in the case of complete integration. (If the personal rate is reduced to 50 percent, the net personal tax is 12.5.) The reason is, of course, that under integration retained earnings are taxed like dividends. Under partial integration liquidity problems can be avoided with certainty only if the marginal personal tax rate is no higher than the gross-up and credit expressed as a percentage of the grossed-up income (33⅓ percent in this case).

The Pros and Cons
of Integration

OVER THE PAST several years the presentation of the cases for and against integration and dividend relief in the United States has evolved into a more or less standard format. Yet, rather surprisingly, the arguments used to support dividend relief in the European countries where it is actually practiced are usually quite different from the arguments commonly heard in the United States. This chapter briefly reviews the U.S. debate and then shows how it differs from the European version.[1] Whether the United States should adopt integration (or dividend relief) depends upon at least two types of infor-

1. Rather than give both the pros and the cons on each question in sequence, I present the argument for integration (broadly defined to include dividend relief), the argument against, and the reply, to give some continuity and integrity to the arguments on each side and to facilitate comparisons with the rationale for dividend relief as it has developed in Europe. Of course many objective observers can see valid points on both sides of the integration issue; thus the division into two opposing camps is not as clear-cut as I have made it appear. At times arguments made by proponents of integration are used to buttress the case against integration, and vice versa. (Ordinarily this is noted.) Finally, though an effort has been made to present the two sides of the debate in a balanced and unbiased manner, the reader should be aware that I have been an advocate of full integration and, with less enthusiasm, of dividend relief.

mation: the economic effects of integration (or dividend relief) and whether integration (or dividend relief) is administratively feasible. Economists are far from unanimous in appraising the economic effects in such areas as equity, neutrality, and the amount, quality, and financing of capital formation. Though in this chapter I try to raise most of the economic issues that must be addressed, I do not settle them, nor do I attempt to do so in the remainder of the book.

The Case for Integration: The Conduit View

Central to the U.S. case for integration is the view that the corporation has no independent taxpaying ability and should be seen as a conduit through which earnings pass on the way to shareholders.[2] The "conduit" theory of the corporation is important because it has implications for the form integration should take, and especially for the meaning of full integration and the proper treatment of tax preferences. Once the conduit view is accepted, it is natural to calculate the aggregate (corporate and personal) tax rates paid on corporate-source equity income at various points in the personal income distribution (as indicated by marginal personal tax rates) and compare them to the rates that would be paid on ordinary income. Table 2-1 presents one such set of comparisons; it assumes that the corporation income tax is borne by corporate shareholders, that is, that it is not shifted to other owners of capital or to consumers or workers.[3] (The implications of shifting are described below.)

2. The conduit view is most often used to justify full integration, but can be used to argue for dividend relief. For recent statements of the conduit view, see Richard A. Musgrave and Peggy B. Musgrave, *Public Finance in Theory and Practice,* 2d ed. (McGraw-Hill, 1976), pp. 291–301; and Charles E. McLure, Jr., "Integration of the Personal and Corporate Income Taxes: The Missing Element in Recent Tax Reform Proposals," *Harvard Law Review,* vol. 88 (January 1975), pp. 532–82. For a particularly provocative essay on the relation between corporations and shareholders, see William A. Klein, "Income Taxation and Legal Entities," *UCLA Law Review,* vol. 20, issue 1 (1972–73), pp. 13–74.

3. For a more detailed discussion of such a table, see McLure, "Integration," pp. 537–42. Implicit in the construction of table 2-1 and in much of the discussion of equity issues that follows is the assumption that, though capital gains and losses may occur for reasons unrelated to retentions of earnings, there is a tendency for retained earnings to be reflected initially in share prices, and hence in capital gains, on a dollar-for-dollar basis. For evidence of the validity of this assumption, see George F. Break, "Integration of the Corporate and Personal Income Taxes," *National Tax Journal,* vol. 22 (March 1969), pp. 44–49, and references cited there. Of course, it can be expected that corporate financial policies will adjust to the implied difference in costs of various sources of capital.

Table 2-1. Taxation of $100 of Corporate-Source Income under U.S. Law, 1979

Rates in percent; other data in dollars

	Dividend payout rate					
Item[a]	*Zero*			*100 percent*		
1. Shareholder's marginal tax rate[b]	0	20	70	0	20	70
2. Corporate-source income[b]	100.0	100.0	100.0	100.0	100.0	100.0
3. Corporate income tax [46% of 2]	46.0	46.0	46.0	46.0	46.0	46.0
4. Net corporate income [2 − 3]	54.0	54.0	54.0	54.0	54.0	54.0
5. Dividends [from 4]	54.0	54.0	54.0
6. Retained earnings (= capital gains)[c] [from 4]	54.0	54.0	54.0
7. Personal tax on dividends [1 × 5]	0	10.8	37.8
8. Tax on long-term capital gains						
a. Maximum[d] [6 × 40% of 1]	0	4.3	15.1
b. Minimum[e]	0	0	0
9. Total tax						
a. With maximum capital gains tax [3 + 7 + 8a][d]	46.0	50.3	61.1	46.0	56.8	83.8
b. With minimum capital gains tax [3 + 7 + 8b][e]	46.0	46.0	46.0	46.0	56.8	83.8
10. Overtaxation						
a. Maximum tax on capital gains [9a − (1 × 2)]	46.0	30.3	−8.9	46.0	36.8	13.8
b. Minimum tax on capital gains [9b − (1 × 2)]	46.0	26.0	−24.0	46.0	36.8	13.8
11. Percentage overtaxation[f]						
a. Maximum tax on capital gains [10a ÷ 1]	∞	151.5	−12.7	∞	184.0	19.7
b. Minimum tax on capital gains [10b ÷ 1]	∞	130.0	−34.3	∞	184.0	19.7

a. Except for percentages, the numbers in brackets refer to the lines of this table.

b. The shareholder's marginal tax rate is assumed invariant with regard to inclusion of corporate-source income and throughout the taxpayer's life. The statutory corporate rate is assumed to be the effective marginal rate.

c. Assumes that, on the average, retained earnings give rise to capital gains on a dollar-for-dollar basis.

d. Assumes that gain is realized after the passage of a one-year holding period, but within the year in which it accrues. Short-term gains are taxed like dividends.

e. Assumes that the appreciated asset is held indefinitely or transferred at death.

f. The percentage of overtaxation of the zero-bracket taxpayer is infinite.

The combination of corporate and personal income taxes produces aggregate tax rates that are grossly inequitable compared to the statutory personal rate structure.[4] The overtaxation of dividends is greater at the bottom of the income scale than at the top. This is true whether overtaxation is measured by the number of percentage points by which the aggregate tax burden exceeds the statutory marginal tax rates at various income levels or by the excess expressed as a percentage of the statutory rate. Moreover, because of the preferential tax treatment accorded long-term capital gains, retained corporate-source income may actually be taxed at lower aggregate rates at the top of the income scale than ordinary income is.[5]

Indicative of the extra burden created at various income levels by the separate corporate income tax are figures calculated by Break and Pechman and reported in table 2-2. These show that corporate-source income is overtaxed by some 1½ percentage to 3 percentage points at the bottom of the income scale, but undertaxed by some 1 percentage to 2 percentage points at the top of the scale.[6]

4. For an alternative analysis of these effects, see the discussion of the "ACID test statistic," in Mervyn King, *Public Policy and the Corporation* (London: Chapman and Hall, 1977), pp. 57–58.

5. This is especially the case when relatively small, closely held corporations are concerned. It has been estimated, for example, that the 91.4 percent of corporations with less than $1 million of assets showing net income for 1974 paid an aggregate effective tax rate of only 21.5 percent. Many of these corporations would probably have qualified for subchapter S treatment (taxation as partnerships), but at most only 16 percent elected it. This suggests that tax saving motivated the choice to be taxed as regular corporations. Further evidence in support of this hypothesis is the relatively low percentage of net income (before tax) distributed to shareholders by these firms (14.1 percent, compared to 42.3 percent for firms with net income and assets in excess of $250,000,000 in 1974). See Dennis J. Gaffney and James E. Wheeler, "The Double Taxation of Corporate-Source Income: Reality or Illusion?" *Tax Adviser,* vol. 8 (September 1977), pp. 523, 526. Of course, this argument is not fully persuasive, since by increasing salaries and bonuses to shareholder-employees, the closely held corporation can reduce taxable income at the corporate level and thereby avoid one layer of the double tax while achieving most of the benefits of dividends.

There has been an unfortunate tendency in some quarters to focus on the double taxation of dividends; unfortunate, because it obscures (1) the fact that at the top of the income scale retained corporate income can be taxed at effective rates well below those on ordinary income, and (2) the fact that tax-exempt organizations and individual shareholders with incomes below levels at which personal tax liability begins pay only *one* tax, the relatively high corporate tax. The real issue is not the number of times corporate source income is taxed, but that (except by accident) it is not taxed in aggregate at the marginal tax rates of shareholders.

6. See George F. Break and Joseph A. Pechman, *Federal Tax Reform: The Impossible Dream?* (Brookings Institution, 1975), p. 93, whose calculations were

Table 2-2. Extra Tax Burdens of the Corporation Income Tax, by Adjusted Gross Income Class, 1976

Adjusted gross income class (*thousands of dollars*)	Extra burden as a percent of adjusted AGI[a]	
	With no capital gains tax from retained earnings	*With 7 percent capital gains tax from retained earnings*
0–3	2.2	2.4
3–5	2.8	3.1
5–10	1.3	1.5
10–15	0.7	0.8
15–20	0.7	0.8
20–25	0.6	0.7
25–50	0.6	0.8
50–100	−0.6	0.1
100–200	−2.0	−1.1
200–500	−3.5	−2.2
500–1,000	−3.4	−1.7
1,000 and over	−1.2	0.6
Total[b]	0.6	0.9

Source: George F. Break and Joseph A. Pechman, *Federal Tax Reform: The Impossible Dream?* (Brookings Institution, 1975), p. 93.
a. Adjusted AGI equals AGI plus retained corporate earnings plus corporate profits tax.
b. Includes negative incomes not shown separately.

In a related exercise, Feldstein and Frisch have calculated the distributional effects that integrating the income taxes would have at different income levels. They find that the proportion of "full income" (adjusted gross income plus corporate-source income) taken by taxes on corporate-source income would drop by 2 percentage points in the lowest income class ($0–$5,000) and by 1 percentage point for families with annual incomes as high as $30,000–$50,000, while it would rise by over 5½ percentage points for households with annual incomes in excess of $500,000.[7] Their conclusion that

based on the 1972 Brookings tax file. In the first column any capital gains tax resulting from retained corporate income is ignored; in the second column a uniform tax rate of 7 percent is applied to such retentions. The 7 percent rate is consistent with the estimate that higher-income shareholders probably paid an average effective rate (in present value terms) of only about 7 percent on gains realized over the period from 1926 to 1961. See Martin J. Bailey, "Capital Gains and Income Taxation," in Arnold C. Harberger and Martin J. Bailey, eds., *The Taxation of Income from Capital* (Brookings Institution, 1969), p. 37.

7. See Martin Feldstein and Daniel Frisch, "Corporate Tax Integration: The Estimated Effects on Capital Accumulation and Tax Distribution of Two Integration Proposals," *National Tax Journal*, vol. 30 (March 1977), pp. 37–52. In this exercise, which does not involve recoupment of revenue lost in integration, tax

"integration would reduce taxes relatively more for low income individuals and would actually raise taxes for high income individuals" is entirely consistent with that of Break and Pechman.[8]

Some descriptions of the inequities of an unintegrated income tax system go little further than the presentation and discussion of a table such as 2-1. But to stop there is wrong, since cursory inspection of the figures in table 2-1 indicates that the situation shown there is one of disequilibrium. That is, at all levels of income, distributed corporate income is taxed more heavily than ordinary income, and retained corporate earnings are effectively taxed at rates that (in present-value terms) can be either greater or (for high-income shareholders) less than the rates applied to ordinary income. It would be strange, indeed, if the shareholder viewed the corporation as a conduit and yet did not respond to the indicated differences in the taxation of ordinary (corporate interest and noncorporate) income, corporate-source income resulting in dividends, and undistributed corporate-source income. Rather, it is generally assumed, especially by advocates of integration, that these differentials in taxation can be expected to lead to a number of adjustments, all of which are held to be socially undesirable.[9]

First, the tendency for retained earnings to be undertaxed at the top of the income scale induces the ownership of firms with low dividend payout rates to be concentrated in the hands of the wealthy and, together with the relatively heavy taxation of dividends at all income levels, produces strong incentives to reduce dividend payout rates.[10]

falls as a percentage of income of all households by a 0.84 percentage point. Under an alternate scheme that leaves revenue essentially unchanged, the only substantial reductions are in the bottom two income classes ($0–$10,000), and the increase in burden at the top of the income scale is 8½ percentage points.

8. See Feldstein and Frisch, "Corporate Tax Integration," p. 49, and Break and Pechman, *Federal Tax Reform*, p. 94. Both these studies ignore investors' adjustments to changes in tax policy.

9. These arguments are presented in somewhat greater detail in McLure, "Integration," pp. 537–46.

10. Feldstein has estimated that a 10 percent increase in the opportunity cost of retained earnings, in terms of forgone dividends, results in the reduction of retentions by some 9 percent. See M. S. Feldstein, "Corporate Taxation and Dividend Behaviour," *Review of Economic Studies,* vol. 37 (January 1970), pp. 57–72. These estimates have been the subject of further exchange between Feldstein and M. A. King in subsequent issues of the *Review of Economic Studies* (for example, vol. 38 [July 1971], pp. 377–86, and vol. 39 [April 1972], pp. 231–40). Even if one accepts King's somewhat lower point estimate of the relevant elasticity, Feldstein's

Artificially high retention rates have several adverse effects. For one thing, they allow profitable firms to reinvest without passing the test of the marketplace.[11] Besides resulting in investment in projects that do not yield the highest social rate of return, this may give rise to mergers, thereby worsening competitive conditions in the economy.[12] Moreover, the tax premium on retained earnings is often said to place newer, smaller firms at a disadvantage in competing with larger established firms.[13] Relief from double taxation of dividends would reduce the tax stimulus for retention of earnings and full integration would eliminate it.[14]

basic conclusion that tax policy has an important impact on dividend policy seems to hold up. Furthermore, after reviewing several studies that try to determine the tax effect on dividend policy, J. Wiseman and M. Davenport in an OECD report conclude that Feldstein's results should be accepted. For a review of this and other literature relevant to the integration debate, see Organisation for Economic Co-operation and Development, *Theoretical and Empirical Aspects of Corporate Taxation* (Paris: OECD, 1974), especially pp. 38–56.

11. It allows, in the words of one British critic, the "survival of the fattest"; quoted in Organisation for Economic Co-operation and Development, *Company Tax Systems in OECD Member Countries* (Paris: OECD, 1973), p. 14, and in Harry G. Gourevitch, *Integration of Corporate and Shareholder Taxes on Income: The European Experience* (Library of Congress, Congressional Research Service, 1977), p. 15. One piece of evidence consistent with this view is found in William J. Baumol and others, "Earnings Retention, New Capital and the Growth of the Firm," *Review of Economics and Statistics,* vol. 52 (November 1970), pp. 345–55. The authors concluded that

the rate of return on equity capital ranged from 14.5 per cent to 20.8 per cent. The rate of return on ploughback, however, ranged from 3.0 to 4.6 per cent; while the rate of return on debt ranges from 4.2 to 14 per cent. Thus, it appears that the rate of return on new equity is substantially higher than the rate of return on ploughback; while the rate of return on new debt is somewhere between the rates of return to ploughback and equity [p. 353].

Yet they do not attribute the differences in rates of return to tax influences, which could go far in explaining them.

12. This would occur, for example, if acquisitions of other firms appeared more attractive to firms with excess retained profits than acquisition of physical assets, as has apparently been the case recently.

13. Of course, this argument cuts both ways. Smaller firms may be more dependent on retained earnings for expansion, especially since larger established firms are likely to have better access to capital markets.

14. If dividend relief were complete and were accompanied by reduction of the top personal marginal tax rate to the level of the corporate rate, the discrimination in favor of retaining earnings could actually be reversed. Preliminary survey evidence on the effect that dividend relief would have on dividend payout rates is in Marshall E. Blume, Jean Crockett, and Irwin Friend, *Financial Effects of Capital Tax Reforms* (New York University, Salomon Brothers Center, 1978). It is often asserted that dividend relief has had little effect on either debt-equity ratios or dividend policy in Europe. But the statistical basis for such assertions is weak.

Second, despite the attraction that retained earnings hold for some investors, the return to equity capital in the corporate sector is taxed more heavily, on the average, than interest on debt and income earned in the noncorporate sector. As a result, corporate debt-equity ratios tend to be distorted in the direction of overreliance on debt finance, and too little investment occurs in the corporate sector. It has been estimated that the annual welfare loss resulting from the differentially heavy fiscal burden on the return to corporate equity may be on the order of 0.5 percent of gross national product.[15] Although the corresponding loss that results from tax-induced increases in leverage has not been estimated—indeed it is difficult even to conceive how it would be quantified—the increased vulnerability of American corporations to bankruptcy induced by the unintegrated corporate tax should not be taken lightly.[16] Consider, for example,

15. The pioneering articles on the misallocation of resources caused by the corporate income tax are Arnold C. Harberger, "The Incidence of the Corporation Income Tax," *Journal of Political Economy,* vol. 70 (June 1962), pp. 215–40, and Arnold C. Harberger, "Efficiency Effects of Taxes on Income from Capital," in Marian Krzyzaniak, ed., *Effects of Corporation Income Tax* (Wayne State University Press, 1966), pp. 107–17. Subsequent contributions to the refinement of estimates of excess burdens (welfare losses) are Leonard Gerson Rosenberg, "Taxation of Income from Capital, by Industry Group," in Harberger and Bailey, *Taxation of Income from Capital,* pp. 123–84, and John B. Shoven, "The Incidence and Efficiency Effects of Taxes on Income from Capital," *Journal of Political Economy,* vol. 84 (December 1976), pp. 1261–83. Note that in this literature there is an assumption (often implicit) that certain activities (producing steel, automobiles, and so on) require such large amounts of capital that the limited liability afforded by the corporate form is essential, whereas other activities exhibit considerable flexibility in their form of business organization. The important distortion is against inherently corporate *activities,* not against the use of the corporate *form* of business organization.

16. For preliminary attempts to model the corporate financial decision and response to the tax differentials described above, see Martin Feldstein, Jerry Green, and Eytan Sheshinski, "Corporate Financial Policy and Taxation in a Growing Economy," *Quarterly Journal of Economics* (forthcoming, 1979), and J. Gregory Ballentine and Charles E. McLure, Jr., "Corporate Tax Integration: Incidence and Effects on Financial Structure," *Quarterly Journal of Economics* (forthcoming, 1979). These papers have the disadvantage that neither includes a progressive personal income tax, and the paper by Feldstein and coauthors assumes that all economic activity occurs in the corporate sector. The comment in that paper about the difficulty of defining a measure of incidence in a world with risk premiums (a problem also encountered by Ballentine and McLure) is also relevant for the measurement of the economy-wide risk of bankruptcy: "A more complete analysis of risk and risk aversion would be required to provide a precise welfare measure." Finally, an attempt to include progressive personal taxes (but not the corporate financial decision) in the so-called Harberger model of general equilibrium incidence analysis is made in Martin Feldstein and Joel Slemrod, "Personal Taxation,

the recent orgy of takeovers by the go-go conglomerates of the 1960s (which was financed in large part by borrowing) and the experience of the real estate investment trusts.

Finally, it has been argued that the extraordinary tax burden on capital, which can be traced in large part to the two-tier levy on corporate-source income, reduces the rates of capital formation and economic growth.[17] To the extent that capital-labor ratios are adversely affected, labor may share in the burden of the corporation income tax in the long run.[18] Moreover, whether or not capital formation and economic growth are affected, the extraordinarily heavy taxation of capital income creates an undesirable distortion in choices between present and future consumption.[19] For all these reasons it has been argued that the U.S. income taxes should be integrated.[20]

Portfolio Choice, and the Effect of the Corporation Income Tax," working paper 241 (National Bureau of Economic Research, 1978). Blume and others, *Financial Effects of Capital Tax Reforms,* report survey evidence that suggests that dividend relief would have little impact on debt-equity ratios. But British experience suggests otherwise; see King, *Public Policy,* pp. 222–27.

17. Among the important academic expressions of views of this type are: Marian Krzyzaniak, "The Long-Run Burden of a General Tax on Profits in a Neoclassical World," *Public Finance,* vol. 22, no. 4 (1967), pp. 472–91; Martin Feldstein, "The Welfare Cost of Capital Income Taxation," *Journal of Political Economy,* vol. 86 (April 1978), pt. 2, pp. S29–S51; and Michael J. Boskin, "Taxation, Saving and the Rate of Interest," *Journal of Political Economy,* vol. 86 (April 1978), pt. 2, pp. S3–S27. Note, however, that Feldstein, for example, though an advocate of integration, does not argue that integration will necessarily increase saving. See Feldstein and Frisch, "Corporate Tax Integration." Less cautious statements have been made by public officials and businessmen about the positive effects integration or dividend relief would have on capital formation. See, for example, William E. Simon, Testimony in *Tax Reform (Administration and Public Witnesses),* Hearings before the House Committee on Ways and Means, 94 Cong. 1 sess. (Government Printing Office, 1975), pt. 5, pp. 3846–61. For an expression of this view by a particularly vocal business spokesman, see Reginald H. Jones, "The Need for Capital," *National Tax Journal,* vol. 28 (September 1975), pp. 265–81. Jones also decries the tax-induced tendency toward higher debt-equity ratios.

18. See especially Krzyzaniak, "Long-Run Burden of a General Tax"; Martin Feldstein, "Incidence of a Capital Income Tax in a Growing Economy with Variable Savings Rates," *Review of Economic Studies,* vol. 41 (October 1974), pp. 505–13; and Martin S. Feldstein, "Tax Incidence in a Growing Economy with Variable Factor Supply," *Quarterly Journal of Economics,* vol. 88 (November 1974), pp. 551–73.

19. Feldstein, "The Welfare Cost of Capital Income Taxation."

20. But, as is noted in greater detail in the next section, "integration" has not meant the same thing to all its advocates, and various advocates are not uniformly concerned about all the alleged ills of an unintegrated system.

The Case against Integration:
The Separate Entity View

Opponents of integration argue that, though the conduit theory
of the corporation may be relevant for closely held corporations, in
which the interests of the shareholders and those of the firm are
closely identified, it has virtually no relevance for the large widely
held corporations that dominate the U.S. business scene and pay the
great bulk of corporate income taxes.[21] As has been noted in the lit-
erature, because of the separation of ownership and control the inter-
ests of the corporation may be quite different from those of its
shareholders, and indeed the interests of various groups of stock-
holders may be in conflict, especially when dividend policy is in-
volved.[22] Thus, Surrey has said, preference for the conduit theory
and integration is no more than "tax theology" and therefore a mat-
ter about which agreement is not to be expected. In his view, the
choice between integration and separate treatment "should be cast
in terms of the desired overall effects of the entire tax system, taking
into account the distribution of the tax burden, growth, savings,
investment, and other fiscal and social aspects."[23]

Once the conduit view is rejected, the conceptual case for integra-
tion is weakened considerably. Under the separate entity view the
existence, nature, and level of the corporate income tax is essentially
irrelevant for the appraisal of the personal income tax, and the pri-
mary structural problem that remains is the preferential treatment
of long-term capital gains, interest on state and local securities, ex-

21. For a strong statement of the "separatist" case against integration, see Rich-
ard Goode, *The Corporation Income Tax* (Wiley, 1951), pp. 24–43.

22. See Commission of the European Communities, "Proposal for a Council
Directive Concerning the Harmonization of Systems of Company Taxation and of
Withholding Taxes on Dividends," *Bulletin of the European Communities,* Supple-
plement 10/75: *Harmonization of Systems of Company Taxation* (Luxembourg:
Office for Official Publications of the European Communities, 1975), p. 8. Note,
however, that this point is used in the European context to justify integration for
dividends, even though dividend relief can actually accentuate such conflicts.

23. Stanley S. Surrey, "Reflections on 'Integration' of Corporation and Individual
Income Taxes," *National Tax Journal,* vol. 28 (September 1975), p. 335. For ex-
pression of a generally similar view by the German Ministry of Finance, see page
44 below. That there is relatively little recent literature opposing integration is
probably indicative of the suddenness with which the policy debate has arisen,
rather than the absence of opposition. Moreover, "integration" has so many mean-
ings that most groups can find a version they like.

tractive industries, and so forth, under the individual income tax. The "double taxation of dividends" has no meaning in such a context, since each tier of the two-tier system of taxing corporate-source income has independent significance.

A second line of opposition to integration is based on theoretical reasoning and empirical evidence that the corporation income tax might be shifted to consumers or to workers, rather than be borne by shareholders or even by all owners of capital.[24] If the tax is shifted, this argument goes, then it cannot have the effects usually attributed to it, including especially the double taxation of dividends. Instead, the tax is more like a payroll or sales tax than an income tax, and such shifting, Musgrave has argued, implies that a deduction should be granted for the corporation tax, not that the tax should be abolished or integrated into the personal tax.[25]

A third argument against integration, and the one that probably has the most popular and political appeal, accepts the incidence of the tax as falling on shareholders, but decries the reduction in progressivity that dividend relief would entail. Because ownership of corporate equities is concentrated in upper income families, the corporate income tax adds greatly to the overall distributional progressivity of the tax system.[26] Full integration at existing rates would, it

24. This is not the place to review the theory and evidence on the incidence of the corporation income tax. For such a review, and references to other literature, see George F. Break, "The Incidence and Economic Effects of Taxation," in Alan S. Blinder and others, *The Economics of Public Finance* (Brookings Institution, 1974), pp. 119–237, especially pp. 138–54.

25. R. A. Musgrave, "The Carter Commission Report," *Canadian Journal of Economics,* supplement 1 (February 1968), pp. 163–64.

26. Indicative of this is the incidence pattern that results if the corporation tax is allocated to shareholders in proportion to their receipt of corporate dividends. Allocating one-half of the tax to dividend recipients and one-half to recipients of capital income in general (which reduces the estimated progressivity), Pechman and Okner report the following effective rates (tax as a percentage of income) at various points in the income scale:

Population decile	Effective rate
First	1.7
Second	2.1
Third	2.2
Fourth	1.9
Fifth	1.7
Sixth	1.5
Seventh	1.6
Eighth	1.8
Ninth	2.2
Tenth	8.1

is admitted, increase progressivity even further because it would reduce the tax shelter that high-income households currently find in retained earnings. But full integration might be accompanied by reduction of the top-bracket rate under the personal tax; in that case much of any increase in progressivity integration might cause would be lost.[27] Moreover, as a political matter, it is quite conceivable that dividend relief, not full integration, might be enacted. Since it lacks the compensating closure of the capital gains loophole that advocates of full integration find so attractive, dividend relief is likely to reduce rather than increase progressivity. Feldstein and Frisch have estimated, for example, that under dividend relief tax reductions as a percentage of "full income" would range from less than 1 percent at the bottom of the income scale to some 3 percent to 5 percent at the top of the scale.[28]

Stanley S. Surrey has elaborated on this theme:

economists are talking—almost in a dreamlike world—about "full integration," which means treating the corporation like a partnership or conduit. But the business groups pushing integration are talking in terms of "partial integration," which in simple terms means tax relief for dividends. Each is thus seeking a different goal, but in the world of reality I believe the economists are being used to make "integration" a respectable issue . . . while . . . a fast shuffle quickly makes partial integration the path to follow if "integration" is to be pursued.[29]

Given the likelihood that neither full integration nor significant tax reform will occur, the adverse distributional implications of dividend relief, and the political difficulty of obtaining full integration once dividend relief is on the books, Surrey and others oppose even considering the issue of full integration.[30]

See Joseph A. Pechman and Benjamin A. Okner, *Who Bears the Tax Burden?* (Brookings Institution, 1974), p. 61. On annual income above $500,000 the effective rate nears 25 percent; see ibid., p. 59. Note that these figures relate to the burden of the corporate tax, not to the extra burden that tax imposes over and above what would be levied under an integrated system.

27. See Break and Pechman, *Federal Tax Reform,* p. 94, for an expression of this fear.

28. From unpublished tables accompanying Feldstein and Frisch, "Corporate Tax Integration"; the exact effect depends upon the response of dividend payout policy.

29. Surrey, "Reflections," p. 335. "Partial integration," as used by Surrey, means, of course, dividend relief.

30. Taking a somewhat different tack, McLure and Surrey have suggested that the outcome of any legislative consideration of integration is so uncertain that none

Concern over the distributional implications of integration is heightened by a consideration of the role of corporate tax preferences in reducing the effective rates of tax actually paid by corporations. Whereas the statutory marginal rate for firms paying the great bulk of corporate taxes has been 48 percent, and the average rate would have been almost as high if tax were paid on book income, the effective rate actually paid has been only about 36 to 38 percent, and differs both between and within industries.[31] It would be inequitable, some have argued, to allow integration or dividend relief at the statutory rate when in fact the effective tax does not approach that figure in many cases.[32]

Yet another equity argument against integration and dividend relief takes as its basic premise the prior capitalization of the corporate tax. If indeed the tax has been capitalized in the form of lower prices for corporate shares, present owners of such shares may not, in fact, bear the burden of the tax. Moreover, integration or dividend relief would be inequitable because it would result in windfall gains (and losses) to present owners of corporate shares.

A fourth line of reasoning against integration questions the importance of the presumed losses of welfare resulting from use of a classical system. Wiseman and Davenport argue, for example, that "it is difficult to take seriously Harberger's estimates of the loss in output resulting from the double-taxation of dividends in the corporate sector. . . . Clearly tax discrimination against particular legal

of the interested parties in the debate—corporate executives, investors, managers of pension funds and other tax-exempt organizations, labor unions, professional tax reformers, and public interest groups—may "want to push integration into the legislative arena and risk the roll of the legislative dice." See Charles E. McLure, Jr., and Stanley S. Surrey, "Integration of Income Taxes: Issues for Debate," *Harvard Business Review*, vol. 55 (September–October 1977), p. 181.

31. See various issues of *Tax Notes*, and particularly Richard L. Kaplan, "Disparity in Corporate Rates Raises Questions About Underlying Tax Policy," Tax Analysts and Advocates, *Tax Notes*, vol. 3 (November 17, 1975), pp. 13–37; and U.S. Department of the Treasury, *Effective Income Tax Rates Paid by United States Corporations in 1972* (GPO, 1978).

32. See Gerard M. Brannon, "Dividend Relief and Tax Reform," Tax Analysts and Advocates, *Tax Notes*, vol. 3 (August 11, 1975), pp. 3–7. In the article, Brannon, an advocate of full integration, criticized the 1975 proposal of the U.S. Treasury Department, which would have used the statutory rate in calculating dividend relief, thereby providing overly generous relief. Though Canada does so, European countries do not generally allow relief for dividends paid in excess of income on which corporate tax has been paid.

forms of enterprise or particular asset classes must involve a cost in the misallocation of capital. The cost takes the form of a loss in output, but to attempt to quantify that cost, even in the crudest sense, may result in a totally misleading impression."[33] Surrey adopts a particularly strong viewpoint on this issue:

As to efficiency and allocation of resources between corporate and non-corporate capital, it is here that the economists plant their flag of integration. . . . But if this is so, the issue of integration turns on the extent of the seriousness of those allocative effects weighed against the consequences of integration. . . . While economists may plant their integration flag on the uncertain terrain of allocation of resources, the Congress should not follow in their path. . . . The uncertainties surrounding the effects on allocation of resources of the various forms of corporate taxation are hardly the base to support a major change in the United States tax system with all the known serious and adverse consequences of such a change.[34]

In addition, the claim that tax-induced tendencies to retain earnings leads to inferior investment decisions has also been questioned.[35] Kaldor, for example, argues that only firms that have retained earnings really have access to external capital markets.[36] Moreover, it can be argued that dividend relief could lead to stratification of the market for corporate equities if it were not accompanied by reduction in the top personal tax rate—a reduction that most opponents of dividend relief would probably not welcome. That is, low-income shareholders would prefer stocks of firms with high dividend payout rates, in order to take advantage of the shareholder credit (or analogous relief under a dividend-paid deduction). But shareholders with marginal rates above the corporate rate might prefer to invest in shares

33. Organisation for Economic Co-operation and Development, *Theoretical and Empirical Aspects,* pp. 43, 44.

34. Surrey, "Reflections," p. 340. Surrey is discussing integration in the broad sense.

35. See, for example, Irwin Friend and Frank Husic, "Efficiency of Corporate Investment," *Review of Economics and Statistics,* vol. 55 (February 1973), pp. 122–27, and G. Whittington, "The Profitability of Retained Earnings," *Review of Economics and Statistics,* vol. 54 (May 1972), pp. 152–60. Both papers are summarized in Organisation for Economic Co-operation and Development, *Theoretical and Empirical Aspects,* pp. 41–42.

36. Nicholas Kaldor, "The Economic Effects of Alternative Systems of Corporation Tax," in *Report from the Select Committee on Corporation Tax, Together with Minutes of Proceedings of the Committee, Minutes of Evidence, Appendices and Index, Session 1970–71* (London: Her Majesty's Stationery Office, 1971), Appendix 15, pp. 248–56.

of firms retaining substantial portions of their earnings, in order to take advantage of the exclusion and deferral benefits of the taxation of long-term capital gains. Furthermore, tax-exempt organizations might effectively be driven from the market for corporate equities if they were not allowed the benefits of integration or dividend relief. These results, it could be argued, would not appear to improve the effectiveness of the nation's capital markets as allocators of resources.

Opponents of integration also argue that claims that integration will relieve the capital shortage are grossly exaggerated, or at least incomplete. As two proponents of integration have stated, "Corporate tax integration is not an effective instrument for achieving the goal of capital accumulation,"[37] and "It seems likely that the effects on saving would be minimal if the lost revenue were made up through tax reform that left the existing pattern of tax burdens essentially unchanged. . . . Maintenance of progressivity and raising the saving rate seem to be in direct conflict."[38]

Yet another conceptual reason for opposing integration has been provided by Stiglitz, writing in the tradition of the Modigliani-Miller literature[39] on the irrelevance of corporate financial structure.[40] Stiglitz argues that in a world without taxes or the risk of bankruptcy there is no optimal debt-equity or dividend policy and that firms sub-

37. Martin Feldstein, "Corporate Tax Integration and Capital Accumulation," discussion paper 437 (Harvard University, Harvard Institute of Economic Research, 1975), p. 32. For a more detailed elaboration of this position, see Feldstein and Frisch, "Corporate Tax Integration." Feldstein's conclusion is based on his earlier econometric work in Britain in which he found that the transferral of one pound of corporate net income from retained earnings to dividends would reduce total private saving by from 0.15 to 0.50 pound. See Martin Feldstein and George Fane, "Taxes, Corporate Dividend Policy and Personal Savings: The British Postwar Experience," *Review of Economics and Statistics*, vol. 55 (November 1973), pp. 399–411. For a similar analysis in the United States, see Martin S. Feldstein, "Tax Incentives, Corporate Saving, and Capital Accumulation in the United States," *Journal of Public Economics*, vol. 2 (April 1973), pp. 159–71.

38. Charles E. McLure, Jr., "Integration of the Income Taxes: Why and How," *Journal of Corporate Taxation*, vol. 2 (Winter 1976), pp. 458, 463. Preliminary survey evidence that supports this conclusion is reported in Blume and others, *Financial Effects of Capital Tax Reforms*.

39. For example, Franco Modigliani and Merton H. Miller, "The Cost of Capital, Corporation Finance and the Theory of Investment," *American Economic Review*, vol. 58 (June 1958), pp. 261–97.

40. See especially Joseph E. Stiglitz, "Taxation, Corporate Financial Policy, and the Cost of Capital," *Journal of Public Economics*, vol. 2 (February 1973), pp. 1–34.

ject to a corporate income tax would never pay dividends and would
finance marginal investments from debt rather than with equity.
However, far from drawing the conclusions that integrationists draw
from qualitatively similar results about tax effects on dividend pay-
out rates and debt-equity ratios, Stiglitz reasons that at the margin
the corporation income tax affects neither corporate financial deci-
sions nor the cost of capital and is therefore neutral; that is, it has
none of the adverse effects on the allocation of resources attributed
to it by Harberger.[41]

David Bradford has recently presented a theoretical analysis of
the effects of business income taxation which can be interpreted as
implying that the unintegrated corporation income tax does not
necessarily have all the adverse effects on corporate financial struc-
tures commonly attributed to it.[42] In Bradford's analysis there is a tax
only on distributions—with no corporate tax or capital gains tax.
The essence of his argument is that such a system would not favor
retention over distribution, because the present value of tax liabilities
is the same whether distribution occurs currently or with a lag. In
fact, the taxation of retained earnings would involve distortion
against retentions and in favor of current distribution.[43] Moreover,
the tax on distributions is best thought of as a lump-sum levy on those
who own corporate equities at the time the tax is imposed. Thus
neither debt-equity ratios, dividend payout, nor sectoral allocation
of capital will be distorted. In short, the tax is completely neutral.

41. If, by assumption, bankruptcy is impossible, an all-debt financial policy can
do no harm.

42. David F. Bradford, "The Incidence and Allocation Effects of a Tax on
Corporate Distributions," discussion paper 7738 (Louvain, Belgium: Université
Catholique de Louvain, Center for Operations Research and Econometrics, August
1977).

43. It may be useful to consider the analogy of the expenditure tax. As is com-
monly recognized, if future consumption is discounted by the market rate of inter-
est, a tax on expenditures is neutral between present and future consumption. In
contrast, an income tax discriminates against future consumption, while a tax on
saving—the difference between income and consumption—is clearly distorting. If
one thinks of dividends as being analogous to consumption, corporate income
(dividends plus retained earnings) as being analogous to income in the debate over
income versus expenditure taxation, and retained earnings as being analogous to
saving, then given his very limiting assumptions, Bradford's propositions follow.
Of course, more than analogy is involved: retained earnings *are* saving, and so
forth.

The step from Bradford's model, which is based on the assumption of a single tax on distributions levied in a world of rational expectations, to policy conclusions about the corporate income tax is not a small and simple one. Bradford does, however, suggest that "the partial integration approach may have gotten the matter just backwards . . . insofar as partial integration amounts to eliminating a tax on distributions it may result primarily in windfall wealth redistributions, reversing the by now irrelevant wealth changes that occurred when the tax was introduced, while leaving the features of the tax system giving rise to inefficiency."[44]

A final set of objections against integration is practical rather than conceptual, theoretical, or distributional. Any form of integration would involve difficult problems in tax administration and in the taxation of international flows of corporate-source income. For full integration, the complications might be so severe as to doom any proposal. Since assessment of these problems is the focus of the bulk of this book, only a brief outline of them can be given here.

The conduit theory has implications for the nature of integration that have not been generally recognized. If the corporation and its shareholders are seen to be distinct, then there is no question that the income the corporation receives from various sources should be merged and that the different components of corporate income should lose their identities when distributed to shareholders or retained in their behalf. But the conduit theory says that the corporation has no separate existence from a fiscal point of view; thus the various components of corporate income should retain their separate characteristics in the hands of shareholders. That is, interest on tax-exempt securities held by the corporation should be received free of tax when attributed to the shareholder; long-term capital gains should be taxed as such to the shareholder, rather than as ordinary income; investment tax credits should be passed through to shareholders; and so on. It takes little imagination to realize that imple-

44. Bradford, "Incidence and Allocation Effects," pp. 2, 6–7. Bradford uses the term "partial integration" for what I call dividend relief. That the forces for and against integration are not monolithic can again be demonstrated by noting that Bradford, as deputy assistant secretary of the treasury for tax policy, was largely responsible for the proposal for full integration in U.S. Department of the Treasury, *Blueprints for Basic Tax Reform* (GPO, 1977).

mentation of such a pure partnership approach would be administratively difficult.[45]

Of course, if the conduit theory is not taken quite so literally, it is possible to have a system of full integration in which components of income do not retain their character in the hands of shareholders; this is essentially the approach suggested by the Canadian Royal Commission and by the U.S. Department of the Treasury in *Blueprints for Basic Tax Reform*. But even under such an impure scheme for full integration, difficult problems would have to be surmounted. How, for example, would corporate earnings be allocated to shareholders who had owned stock for less than a year? Presumably it would be necessary to choose a date of record rather than attempt day-by-day allocations to shareholders.[46] Moreover, how would operating losses be treated? Would they be passed through to shareholders or would they merely be available for carry-forward to profitable years? (Carry-back of losses, like audit adjustments of shareholder incomes for prior years, is not satisfactory, because the ownership of shares may have changed; furthermore, audit adjustments and carry-back would necessitate the reopening of the returns of prior shareholders, in any case.) What if some portfolio shareholders were corporations? What should be done if corporate-source income initially taxed to holders of common stock is subsequently distributed to owners of preferred shares? As mentioned in chapter 1, these problems should not be taken lightly. (Administrative difficulties of integration and dividend relief are considered further in chapter 5.)

Finally, even if one is willing to be less ambitious and strive for relief from double taxation of dividends only, difficult problems still arise, as can be seen from European experience. Since many of these involve the tax treatment of international capital flows, I mention only a few here. (See also chapters 3 and 6.) First, there is no doubt

45. See also chapter 5. It is of interest to note that, though this approach underlies the taxation of partnerships, it does not form the basis of the taxation of closely held corporations under subchapter S, the clearest case of integration of personal and corporate taxes extant in the U.S. tax code. This point is made in Edwin S. Cohen, "Possible Solutions to Practical Problems in Integration of the Corporate and Shareholder Income Tax," *National Tax Journal,* vol. 28 (September 1975), p. 361. For further discussion, see also Klein, "Income Taxation and Legal Entities."

46. The U.S. Department of the Treasury, in *Blueprints for Basic Tax Reform,* p. 70, would choose the first day of the tax year to prevent trafficking in shares of firms with losses. See also chapter 5.

that the neutral taxation of international capital flows is simplest if all nations adopt the classical, or separate, system of taxing corporate-source income.[47] The principles that have traditionally governed U.S. tax relations with other nations (primacy of source-country taxation, limited foreign tax credits in capital-exporting country, nondiscrimination, and reciprocity) are most appropriate in a world of separate corporate income taxes; in a world of integrated domestic tax systems the analogous rules are far more complex and less likely to command agreement. Of more immediate relevance, the fact that many European countries have already adopted dividend relief conditions U.S. policy choices, but does not necessarily imply that achieving neutrality will be easier if the United States adopts dividend relief than if it does not.[48] Even though dividend relief may be provided most simply in the domestic sphere through the deduction of dividends at the corporate level, a combination of preexisting tax treaties and revenue and competitive effects may effectively preclude use of that method by the United States. Thus if dividend relief is to be granted, it will probably be through the imputation method.

Finally, whether integration is provided only for dividends or is extended to retained earnings, it will be necessary to decide how tax preferences should be treated. Among the options are (1) to eliminate them entirely, (2) to eliminate them only for the corporate sector, (3) to allow them, but only if preference income is retained, (4) to allow them, but only if preference income is distributed, or (5) to allow them whether preference income is retained or distrib-

47. Categorical statements such as this are hazardous, since capital-import neutrality (not a particularly important goal) may be more easily achieved than capital-export neutrality (an important goal), especially in the absence of foreign tax credits. Moreover, what is true for direct investment may not be true for portfolio investment. Yet the statement in the text seems reasonable. This is affirmed in Richard M. Hammer, "The Taxation of Income from Corporate Shareholders: Review of Present Systems in Canada, France, Germany, Japan and the U.K.," *National Tax Journal*, vol. 28 (September 1975), pp. 315–16, and Mitsuo Sato and Richard M. Bird, "International Aspects of the Taxation of Corporations and Shareholders," International Monetary Fund, *Staff Papers*, vol. 22 (July 1975), p. 412. Note, however, that Sato and Bird argue that "the attempt to discourage integration because it fails to achieve nondiscriminatory treatment of resident and nonresident investors does not appear to be a realistic alternative. . . . There is no case for concluding that the international tail (nondiscrimination) should wag the domestic dog (integration)" (p. 425).

48. For more on this, including a definition of neutrality, see Sato and Bird, "International Aspects of Taxation," pp. 411–17, and chapter 6 below.

uted. In cases 3 and 4 it is necessary to have arbitrary rules for the determination of the order in which distributions are assumed to come from fully taxed and preference income. No matter which of the alternatives (other than eliminating preferences) is chosen, important technical difficulties and distortions of choices are likely to result.[49]

The Integrationists' Reply

The integrationists have at least two lines of response to Surrey's claim that preference for the conduit view is a matter of tax theology. One is to reply that integration and broad-based tax reform are cut from the same cloth, namely the Haig-Simons definition of income;[50] to favor the latter but not the former seems to them to be logically inconsistent.[51] The other is to argue that whether or not one accepts the conduit view of the corporation, one must contend with the effects the corporation tax has on the allocation of resources and corporate financial structures, for those effects are quite independent of how the corporation is viewed.

Economists who favor integration also question the highly influential views of Stiglitz on the irrelevance of the corporate tax in determining marginal choices on resource allocation.[52] They argue that, as Stiglitz himself has acknowledged, in a world in which bankruptcy

49. Many opponents of integration also dislike tax preferences. If they cannot have preferences eliminated they are likely to opt for ordering rules and tax treatment that would minimize the value of preferences.

50. The Haig-Simons definition of income is discussed in Richard Goode, "The Economic Definition of Income," in Joseph A. Pechman, ed., *Comprehensive Income Taxation* (Brookings Institution, 1977), especially pp. 7–20.

51. The integrationist would question the logical foundation of part of the so-called tax-expenditure budget, which is closely linked to Surrey's name. Instead of treating the exemption from the corporate surtax as a tax expenditure, the integrationist would argue that the Haig-Simons definition of income makes sense only when applied to tax burdens of individuals. Thus he would treat the corporation as a conduit in calculating tax expenditures and would therefore treat much of the corporate income tax (the excess over what would be paid under full integration) as a negative tax expenditure (and hence come full circle to "tax penalty").

52. See, for example, Feldstein and others, "Corporate Financial Policy," and Ballentine and McLure, "Corporate Tax Integration." On the effects taxation has on the optimal debt-equity ratio of the firm, see James H. Scott, Jr., "A Theory of Optimal Capital Structure," *Bell Journal of Economics,* vol. 7 (Spring 1976), pp. 33–54.

is possible and costly there *is* an optimal debt-equity ratio, and the firm's debt-equity ratio is distorted away from that optimal level by differential taxation of debt and equity.[53] Moreover, this distortion of financial decisions does have effects on resource allocation and implications for tax incidence.

Integrationists have not yet provided a full-fledged answer to the implications of the Bradford analysis, since the latter has appeared only recently. But it can be expected that an answer would proceed on several fronts. First, to the extent that Bradford's analysis relies on the theory of rational expectations, its relevance to the real world might reasonably be questioned. But since some of the most vocal advocates of integration live rather conspicuously in glass houses of economic theory, this approach could be ill advised. A more promising line of theoretical attack might be to question Bradford's other assumptions. Bradford assumes no risk of bankruptcy and the presence of an untaxed alternative investment. As is true of Stiglitz's theory, Bradford's theory cannot survive the relaxation of the no-bankruptcy assumption. And the result is quite different if the tax on distributions is only one part of a personal tax system, one part of which is levied on interest income and returns from noncorporate investment. Perhaps even more persuasive is an attack based in empiricism. The theory of rational expectations aside, businessmen seem to behave as if the extraordinarily heavy taxation of dividends encouraged retentions.[54]

As the adjustments to differential taxation inherent in an unintegrated system occur, the extreme differences in net rates of return on alternative investments implicit in table 2-1 diminish, or even vanish, at the margin.[55] As a result of these adjustments the burden of the

53. Thus Stiglitz has written ("Taxation," p. 23): "The tax advantages of debt would increase the debt equity ratio from what it would have been otherwise, but would not result in the firm going to an 'all debt' position." This qualification throws doubt on the relevance of Stiglitz's elegant proof.

54. See note 10 for the discussion of the work on this issue by Feldstein, "Corporate Taxation and Dividend Behaviour."

55. As Bailey has stated, "Apparent horizontal inequities as a rule shake out in competitive resource allocation and translate into misuse of resources." Martin J. Bailey, "Progressivity and Investment Yields under U.S. Income Taxation," *Journal of Political Economy*, vol. 82 (November–December 1974), p. 1174. See also Martin Feldstein, "On the Theory of Tax Reform," *Journal of Public Economics*, vol. 6 (July–August 1976), pp. 77–104.

corporate income tax is diffused to owners of capital other than corporate shares, instead of burdening only shareholders.[56] Since the ownership of capital in general is less concentrated in the hands of high-income families than stock ownership, this diffusion of burden reduces the distributional progressivity of the corporate income tax and the regressivity of dividend relief, but it does not diminish the equity argument for integration.[57]

The progressivity of the corporate tax may be further reduced by another relatively unnoticed influence. Since the differentially heavy corporate tax induces firms to want to rely more heavily on debt than they would under a neutral tax regime, the risk of bankruptcy increases, and it is likely that increased risk premiums must be offered to attract investors from noncorporate investments to both corporate debt and equities.[58] This being the case, investors in corporate securities experience less of a reduction in their income as a result of the corporation tax than even the Harberger diffusion result would suggest, and full integration is more progressive and dividend relief less regressive than under the hypothesis of diffusion.[59]

Further responses to the equity arguments against integration take at least five forms. First, in theory, almost any degree of progressivity can be achieved, whether or not full integration or dividend relief is adopted, by changing marginal rate schedules. Thus integration and dividend relief should be appraised primarily for their effects on horizontal equity, resource allocation, and corporate financial policy rather than on vertical equity. Second, because the tax relief is included in personal income for tax purposes, integration is the most progressive of the commonly discussed ways to cut business taxes,

56. This is the key conclusion of Harberger, "The Incidence of the Corporation Income Tax." For attempts to convert the burdens on shareholders and on capitalists in general into burdens by income classes, see Pechman and Okner, *Who Bears the Tax Burden?* chap. 4.

57. For a more detailed statement of this argument, see McLure, "Integration," pp. 543–46.

58. For a persuasive statement of this proposition, see Luigi Tambini, "Financial Policy and the Corporation Income Tax," in Harberger and Bailey, *Taxation of Income from Capital*, pp. 185–222.

59. This line of reasoning is developed more fully in Ballentine and McLure, "Corporate Tax Integration." Note that incidence is a matter of effects on income under the Harberger and Ballentine-McLure theories. Whether holders of corporate securities are better off just because they receive higher risk premiums cannot be known, for the reasons mentioned by Feldstein and others, "Corporate Financial Policy," and quoted in note 16 above.

and even dividend relief is more progressive than such standard approaches as the investment tax credit and accelerated depreciation. Third, either integration or dividend relief *could* be combined with taxation of capital gains as ordinary income. Fourth, although it is true that the corporate tax may have been capitalized and that removing it would create windfall gains and losses, an improved system of dealing with capital gains and losses would go a long way in overcoming this defect. Moreover, adherence to the fiscal doctrine of original sin—that old taxes are good taxes—has as its price the continued welfare loss resulting from tax-induced misallocations of resources. Finally, low-income shareholders may hold few corporate shares precisely because of the tax disadvantages of doing so. It is thus misleading to employ arguments against integration or dividend relief that are based on the pattern of stock ownership found under the classical system. Acceptance of such arguments would tend to perpetuate the absence of low-income taxpayers from the markets for corporate equities. On the other hand, an increase in stock ownership by low-income groups would increase the perceived progressivity of integration or dividend relief.

Though such generalizations are certain to run afoul of counterclaims, it seems fair to say that most advocates of integration are more likely to believe that the corporate tax is diffused to owners of noncorporate capital than that it is borne by shareholders or shifted in the short run to consumers or labor. But even granting the existence of short-run shifting, integrationists would not generally accept the proposition that it justifies retention of the separate corporation income tax.[60] Though a shifted tax may resemble a sales or payroll

60. One response of the separatists to the view that short-run shifting is irrelevant is that a shifted tax might not be "unshifted" once integration occurs. Failure to unshift, they would argue, would be most likely under the imputation system, since corporate management might view the creditable tax on distributed earnings not as a simple withholding tax on shareholder income, but as a classical tax. From a cash flow standpoint such a characterization of the tax is not without merit; the creditable tax is a form of forced dividend to shareholders that constitutes a cost of the firm's output. (See Surrey, "Reflections," p. 336.) Unshifting might be more likely if dividend relief took the form of the deduction for dividends paid or a split rate. Those worried that the tax might not be unshifted argue that relief should follow the latter approach, to assure unshifting and thereby minimize the risk of creating an unnecessary windfall for shareholders. For such a view, see Musgrave, "The Carter Commission Report," pp. 163–66. It should be noted that the evidence that shifted taxes are not unshifted comes primarily from Marian Krzyzaniak and Richard A. Musgrave, *The Shifting of the Corporation Income Tax* (Johns Hopkins

tax, the resemblance is only to a particularly non-uniform and capricious one; certainly no one would deliberately design such a complicated and discriminatory way to tax payrolls or sales.[61] If the corporate tax were shifted, nothing would be lost on equity grounds from substituting a uniform sales or payroll tax for it, and resource allocation would probably be improved.[62] By assumption, the present tax has no effects on the income of shareholders; thus dividends are already taxed appropriately and retained earnings are not taxed at all (except through the capital gains tax). This state of affairs would continue if the corporate tax were simply repealed. In addition, there is much to be said for not using taxes whose incidence is so uncertain that economists can reach no conclusions on who bears their burden. Finally, it can be argued (but not proved) that, though a classical corporate income tax may be shifted, it is far less likely that a fully integrated tax would be shifted; after all, if the income taxes had always been integrated, it is hard to believe that anyone would seriously suggest that the corporate part, which at most would be a withholding tax, would be shifted. Acceptance of the no-shifting view of an integrated tax would constitute another plus for the integrationists.

Dividend Relief: Integration by the Back Door

Those who believe that integration is right seem to respond in one of three ways to the assertion that any form of integration—but especially full integration—is administratively infeasible.[63]

Press, 1963). This finding is even more suspect than that of full shifting, which has been the object of considerable controversy. Moreover, the theory of efficient markets would suggest that shareholders would see through the corporate veil and that corporate managers could not neglect the fact that the creditable tax is indeed not a simple classical tax.

61. For more detailed statements of the views expressed here, see Peter Mieszkowski, "Integration of the Corporate and Personal Income Taxes: The Bogus Issue of Shifting," *Finanzarchiv,* vol. 31 (December 1972), pp. 286–97, and McLure, "Integration," pp. 542–49.

62. Strictly speaking, there is no way to be certain that a uniform sales or payroll tax would involve less loss of welfare than one in which the implicit tax rate depended on the profitability of various industries, so that, in principle, objection to the quasi-sales or quasi-payroll tax implicit in a shifted corporate tax would have to be based on equity considerations alone. But it is hard to believe that a general retail sales tax, a value-added tax, or a payroll tax would not be more neutral than a shifted corporate income tax.

63. Thus Surrey ("Reflections," p. 335) is quite right in saying that "the economists and the business groups will each accept only its own version of integra-

First, there are those who did not want full integration in the first place; they know from the European experience that relief from double taxation of dividends is feasible and do not mourn the prospective demise of full integration, with its implicit current taxation as ordinary income of long-term capital gains resulting from corporate retentions. This group tends to be composed of businessmen and conservative academic economists.

A second group, if it were convinced that full integration was not feasible, would prefer to retain the present classical system than to adopt dividend relief, which they see as a giveaway to the rich. Moreover, they suspect that dividend relief is not just a stopping point on the road to full integration; given the nature of the difference between full integration and dividend relief, it may be politically impossible to achieve full integration once dividend relief is part of the tax law. Thus this group, composed of liberal economists, would prefer no loaf to the half-loaf of dividend relief.

A third group is strongly attracted to integration and its advantages over a classical system. It would concede only reluctantly that full integration was infeasible. But it might argue that dividend relief, if properly packaged, offered an acceptable fallback position. Suppose that dividend relief were accompanied by a reduction in the top-bracket personal tax rates to about the level of the corporate tax rate.[64] No shareholder would have a strong tax incentive to prefer retentions to dividends, and most would have a fiscal reason to prefer dividends. Hence corporations could be expected to pay out nearly all their earnings as dividends. But if this were done, the equity and efficiency objectives of full integration, which depend on shareholders being taxed on corporate-source income at their own marginal tax rates, would be largely achieved.[65] Integration would, in a

tion and would reject the other's version," though there may be a third group that would prefer full integration but would accept dividend relief under the right circumstances. The widespread opinion that full integration is infeasible reveals that the integrationists are hardly a monolithic group. This would be revealed just as dramatically if it were thought that full integration *were* feasible and politically popular. In that case it would be the businessmen and conservative economists who would be seen deserting the integration ship.

64. It has been often argued that the revenue lost in dividend relief should be recouped by raising the basic tax rate on retained corporate-source income. Such an approach sacrifices one of the primary virtues of integration—intersectoral neutrality.

65. Note, however, that such an approach would not be neutral for corporate dividend payout policy. Moreover, if European practice were followed in the tax

sense, have arrived by the back door, thereby avoiding the severe administrative complications of full integration. Of course, such an approach might result in a slight drop in progressivity. But even that could be avoided if dividend relief were combined with tax reform in other areas of special advantage to upper income groups.[66]

The Foreign Rationale[67]

Though many European countries and Canada now provide at least partial relief from the double taxation of dividends, many of the arguments for integration described above are noticeably absent from the foreign discussion, and some have been explicitly rejected. For example, in the minds of many U.S. integrationists the conduit view of the corporation is central to the case for integration. But the West German government, in proposing elimination of the double taxation of dividends, stated:

The government does not subscribe to the controversial view of public finance experts that the separate taxation of legal entities is unjustified. On the contrary, the government rejects this view. Within the framework of constitutional limitations, the political decision as to the extent to which the double tax of legal entities and their shareholders should be maintained, reduced or eliminated is strictly one of expediency.[68]

treatment of preferences, it is likely that not all earnings would be distributed. See also chapter 4.

66. See, for example, "Tax Reform Option Papers Prepared by Treasury Department, September 2, 1977, for the White House," Bureau of National Affairs, *Daily Report for Executives* (Special Supplement), DER 196 (October 7, 1977), p. 49; and *Congressional Record,* daily ed., March 22, 1978, pp. H2337–38.

67. At this point I discuss only the reasons given for and against the adoption of integration or dividend relief in Canada and Europe. In the last part of chapter 3 I review the rationale for the particular choices made in Europe and Canada on various technical issues, especially imputation versus split-rate approaches and taxation of international flows of income.

68. Gesetzentwurf der Bundesregierung, Entwurf eines Dritten Steuerreformgesetzes, Bundesrat, Drucksache 700/73, p. 326, as quoted in Gourevitch, *Integration of Corporate and Shareholder Taxes,* p. 10. Similarly, the following sentence appears in "Federal Republic of Germany: Introduction of a Total Imputation System," *European Taxation,* vol. 16 (October 1976), p. 351: "Although the corporate income tax levied on the distributed profits is creditable against the shareholder's personal income tax, it cannot be said that this tax is a pre-levy of personal income tax; it does not change its character of corporate income tax in being creditable." Of course, as the discussion of international aspects of integration in chapter 6 makes clear, statements such as this may simply be intended as window dressing to be used in negotiations of foreign tax treaties.

Similarly, Gourevitch claims that "the tax credit systems adopted in France and the United Kingdom were meant to reduce the tax burden on dividends, but they did not reflect any reservations about the separate economic reality of corporate entities."[69]

Although the scheme for full integration proposed by the Canadian Royal Commission would have converted the corporation into a conduit for tax purposes, it is not clear that the conduit theory of the corporation motivated the commission's proposal for integration. Certainly the original impetus for the commission was somewhat different. In particular, the conversion of undistributed corporate earnings into untaxed capital gains by means of "surplus stripping" had become so prevalent that many believe that the commission was created to examine the matter. In the eyes of the commission the problems of taxing capital gains as ordinary income and of integration constituted an inseparable package.[70] Despite the concern for equity in taxation inherent in the desire to minimize the tax advantages of surplus stripping, the commission did not base its integration proposal on considerations of the inequity of the "double taxation" of corporate-source income. Realizing that any such inequities had long since been capitalized in the form of lower share prices, the commission based its proposal primarily on the distortions of resource allocation between the corporate and noncorporate sectors that a separate corporate tax induces.[71]

The proposals of the Royal Commission were, of course, ultimately rejected in favor of an imputation system. The rejection was undoubtedly caused in part by the objection of industry to the full taxation of capital gains that integration implied and to which it

69. Gourevitch, *Integration of Corporate and Shareholder Taxes,* pp. 65–66. On the other hand, the explanatory memorandum to the recently rejected proposal by the Commission of the European Communities for a directive on harmonizing company taxes can be interpreted as giving a slight bow to the conduit view when it says that "the classical system, by involving economic double taxation, has the effect of making shareholders whose rate of personal income tax is low subject to a tax burden which is heavier relatively than that of shareholders whose rate of personal income tax is high." Commission of the European Communities, "Proposal for a Council Directive," p. 8.

70. The discussion of Canadian experience in this section is based largely on Meyer Bucovetsky and Richard M. Bird, "Tax Reform in Canada: A Progress Report," *National Tax Journal,* volume 25 (March 1972), pp. 15–41. On this point, see especially pp. 28 and 29 and references cited there.

71. Ibid., p. 28.

was linked in the proposals. This illustrates the point made earlier in this chapter that, although business may be perfectly content to have dividend relief, it may not want full integration. In addition, integration was strongly opposed by owners of small businesses in Canada. Whereas under preexisting law these businessmen benefited from the advantages of a preferential rate of corporate tax on income up to a certain level, under integration all corporate income, including that earned in such businesses, would be taxed at the marginal tax rates of the owners.[72]

European concern about the effects of differentially heavy taxation of the return to corporate equity seems to have focused on financial effects and distortion of the form of business organization, rather than on the effects on the allocation of resources between the corporate and noncorporate sectors that are more familiar in the U.S. literature. The French, for example, are said to have been concerned primarily about increasing the yield of corporate shares and thereby improving the operation of the stock market, which was felt to be too narrow and subject to speculation. Improved capital markets, together with the reduced incentive for Frenchmen to invest abroad, would make it easier for French companies to meet capital requirements, and the increased value of corporate shares that was expected to result from dividend relief would lessen the tendency for French firms to be taken over by foreign interests.[73]

West Germany's adoption of the split-rate system in 1953 can be traced to similar considerations; that is, it was thought that a preferential rate on distributed earnings would encourage payout and reduce reliance on retained earnings. The 1971 proposal for full integration and the subsequent partial movement to the imputation method show the continuing concern about this issue: the West Germans felt that the split-rate system continued to provide an incentive for high-income shareholders to prefer retentions to dividends and,

72. Under the imputation system finally adopted a preferential rate of 25 percent is levied on the first $50,000 of income, so that the roughly 33⅓ percent gross-up and credit effectively eliminates double taxation of dividends paid from taxable corporate-source income below this level and actually lowers the aggregate marginal tax rate to below the marginal personal rate for distributed income that benefits from tax preferences. Ibid., p. 26.

73. Organisation for Economic Co-operation and Development, *Company Tax Systems,* p. 14, and Gourevitch, *Integration of Corporate and Shareholder Taxes,* pp. 5–6.

in fact, created conflicts between the interests of such shareholders and shareholders in lower tax brackets. And they also were concerned that even the split-rate system, to the extent that it failed to provide complete relief from double taxation, discriminated in favor of debt finance and against the use of the corporate form of business organization.[74]

The French and West German interest in improved capital markets and higher share prices has no counterpart in the early U.S. discussion of integration, though the concerns about effects on corporate financial policy (retention rates and debt-equity ratios) and capital formation could be interpreted as being similar. So far as the discrimination against the corporate form of business is concerned, the emphasis seems to be quite different. In the United States the discussion of the welfare costs of this discrimination takes as given and fairly inflexible the makeup of the corporate and noncorporate sectors; thus the distortion at issue is between two *sectors* producing generally different goods and services, not between two different ways of organizing to produce a given product. The European concern, on the other hand, appears to be primarily with the *form* in which a given business operation is undertaken.[75] This difference in

74. Organisation for Economic Co-operation and Development, *Company Tax Systems,* p. 14, and Gourevitch, *Integration of Corporate and Shareholder Taxes,* pp. 8–12.

75. In part this contention is based more on impressions than on concrete statements. But see the following explicit statements that run directly counter to the policy implications of the Harberger analysis of the welfare loss created by the differential taxation of corporate-source income:

This study only aims at a comparison of the nature and the consequences of the *structural* differences in the relation of corporation tax and individual income tax. . . .

In Chapters II and III of this study therefore proceed from the alternative application of the systems in *one and the same level of burden.* . . .

The most usable criterion would seem to be the *joint yield of the tax on the profit of the share company and of the tax on the dividends of the shareholder.* This approach has the advantage that *in the judgment of the relative merits of the systems the aspect of the tax proceeds can be disregarded* [emphasis added].

A. J. van den Tempel, *Corporation Tax and Individual Income Tax in the European Communities* (Brussels: Commission of the European Communities, 1970), p. 9.

The following is a later statement that expresses the same view with even greater clarity:

The Commission would consider it socially unacceptable that a change from a classical system to a system relieving the economic double taxation of dividends should lead on any substantial scale to a transfer of a taxation burden from companies and shareholders, on the one side, to wage earners or consumers on the other.

W. E. Pool, "Reply to the Special Issue on the Harmonisation of Systems of Company Taxation and of Withholding Taxes on Dividends," *European Taxation,* vol. 16 (October 1976), pp. 336–37. Any objection that Pool, who is a member of the

outlook, however, may be quite reasonable, given the differences in the national economies and laws on the two sides of the Atlantic.[76]

Moreover, when Europeans speak of the misallocation of investment resources, they are generally referring to the failure of internally reinvested funds to be subjected to the test of the marketplace and not to the misallocation of capital between the corporate and noncorporate sectors. On the other hand, the tax-induced tendency to retain earnings has been decried more in the United States for its equity implications than for its efficiency effects. And few critics of the American classical system have objected to the possibility that majority shareholders may dictate payout ratios that are lower than low-income taxpayers would prefer.

Finally, in Europe and in Canada especially, discussion has focused more on how international flows of capital income are affected by integration than it has in the United States, where, until recently, attention has been given primarily to domestic issues. This reflects in part the greater openness of the European and Canadian economies (including French concern about takeover by U.S. firms) and in part the necessity of harmonizing national tax systems if the objectives of the Treaty of Rome (which established the European Economic Community) are to be realized.[77] It would appear, how-

staff of the Commission of the European Communities, did not mean that burdens should be maintained on companies and shareholders, qua shareholders, is easily dispelled by reference to Pool's subsequent discussion (p. 337), which speaks of maintaining receipts from the corporate sector. Accuracy demands, however, that it be noted that van den Tempel wrote his report as a private consultant to the Commission of the European Communities, and that the commission does not necessarily speak for the member countries of the European Community. Moreover, as Sato and Bird have noted in "International Aspects," p. 430, van den Tempel focused on the international implications of alternative systems of taxing corporate income. Nonetheless, these statements are indicative of the way in which Europeans view the problem and the objectives of dividend relief. On the other hand, see the discussion of Harberger's attempts to measure tax-induced resource misallocation in Organisation for Economic Co-operation and Development, *Theoretical and Empirical Aspects*, pp. 42–44. Particular reference is made there to Harberger, "Efficiency Effects."

76. Because of the severe limitations on the use of subchapter S, little opportunity exists under U.S. law to combine the advantages of limited liability, taxation only at the marginal tax rates of equity owners, and widespread public ownership.

77. Uncoordinated state corporation income taxes can create similar problems in the United States, but the magnitude of any distortions is much less because of the lower rates and deduction for state taxes in calculating liability for federal income tax. Moreover, there is no tendency to try to integrate state corporate and personal income taxes.

ever, that the U.S. debate must focus increasingly on international aspects as it moves from questions of tax policy, which may be settled largely on domestic grounds, to problems of implementation, where international aspects dominate.[78]

78. Chapter 6 takes up these questions at length.

Foreign Experience

As the United States considers whether (and how) to integrate its income taxes, there is a natural tendency to ask what the experience with dividend relief has been in Europe, Japan, and Canada. The United States should not necessarily duplicate foreign practice; after all, the same policy issues may have to be resolved differently in every country, in part because of differences in legal and economic environments. But foreign experience is instructive, for it shows some of the practical problems that arise when relief from double taxation of dividends is provided and suggests possible solutions to those problems. Moreover, foreign experience is especially relevant because the problems of mitigating the double taxation of international capital flows are among the most troublesome for integration. In this chapter, therefore, I give a thumbnail sketch of the systems for dividend relief now used in France, the United Kingdom, and the Federal Republic of Germany and comment on certain features of the Canadian and pre-1977 West German systems (the latter because it provides a prototype of a different system and its problems) and on the proposals for a directive for the harmonization of corporate taxes in the European Community.[1]

1. This chapter draws extensively on material in Mitsuo Sato and Richard M. Bird, "International Aspects of the Taxation of Corporations and Shareholders," International Monetary Fund, *Staff Papers,* vol. 22 (July 1975), pp. 384–455; Rich-

Domestic Features

Foreign systems of dividend relief have certain characteristics that would prevail even if there were no international capital flows. A survey and comparison of these characteristics raise important questions that must be resolved by any country contemplating some form of integration.

France

In 1965 France instituted a system of dividend relief that gives the resident (individual and corporate portfolio) shareholder a tax credit (avoir fiscal) for half the French income tax attributed to dividends paid by resident corporations. Since the corporate rate is 50 percent, the shareholder need simply add 50 percent of cash dividends to the amount of dividends to be included in his taxable income. He then takes credit for the amount of the avoir fiscal. (An individual shareholder will receive a refund if the credit exceeds his total tax liability, but corporate shareholders cannot benefit from excess credits.) The benefits of the avoir fiscal system are available only to residents of France (except as provided by tax treaty), so that foreigners and Frenchmen holding stock through nominee accounts abroad do not share in the benefits.[2] Moreover, the benefits are not extended to charitable and educational institutions.

The essence of the French system is partial relief from the double taxation of dividends. Thus France allows the shareholder credit only for corporate taxes actually paid. Since France generally em-

ard M. Hammer, "The Taxation of Income from Corporate Shareholders: Review of Present Systems in Canada, France, Germany, Japan and the U.K.," *National Tax Journal,* vol. 28 (September 1975), pp. 315–34; Organisation for Economic Co-operation and Development, *Company Tax Systems in OECD Member Countries* (Paris: OECD, 1973); and Hugh J. Ault, "Germany: The New Corporation Tax System," *Intertax: European Tax Review* (August 1976), pp. 262–75. For a further description of European tax systems, which inexplicably fails to focus on the crucial role played by tax preferences, see Bernard Snoy, *Taxes on Direct Investment Income in the EEC: A Legal and Economic Analysis* (Praeger, 1975). Snoy's work came to my attention only after work on this book was well advanced.

2. See especially Hammer, "Taxation of Income," p. 327, on the latter point. For a description of a similar phenomenon in Italy, see Michele Soldati, "Taxing Corporate Income: European Harmonization and the Italian Experience," *American Journal of Comparative Law,* vol. 24 (Spring 1976), pp. 273–76.

ploys the territorial principle in the taxation of corporate income, income earned abroad is not ordinarily taxed to the corporation. To prevent this tax exemption from carrying over to the taxation of individuals, France levies a supplementary tax at the corporate level on any foreign-source income distributed to shareholders.[3] This equalization or advance tax, called the "précompte mobilier," or more commonly "précompte," equals one-third of dividends grossed up by the amount of the shareholder credit, or one-half of the cash dividend. Though the précompte brings the tax paid to France at the corporate level on otherwise tax-exempt income up to only 33⅓ percent when the income is distributed, compared to the statutory rate of 50 percent, the shareholder is allowed to use a uniform percentage in calculating the avoir fiscal credit on the dividends he receives, regardless of how the earnings that yield the dividends are taxed at the corporate level. The précompte is also levied on other distributed corporate-source income that would otherwise bear less than the full 50 percent corporate tax—such as long-term capital gains—and to earnings accumulated more than five years before their distribution (even if they have previously been taxed at the full rate). The general effect, in the case of income that is taxed preferentially at the corporate level, is to wash out such preferences to the extent income is distributed to shareholders. As a result, under the précompte system, distributed corporate-source income that initially is not fully taxed to the corporation is ultimately taxed at the shareholder's marginal tax rate. Thus tax preferences tend to be of benefit only to the extent that income receiving preferential treatment is not distributed.[4]

3. Under the territorial principle a country taxes only income arising within its borders. In contrast, under the worldwide principle all the income earned by the residents of a given country is taxed by that country, no matter where the income originates. For further discussion of this distinction, see Sato and Bird, "International Aspects," especially pp. 395–406. French firms can elect to be taxed on a worldwide basis, in which case the foreign tax credit is available.

4. Note that the précompte is collected only at the rate of the avoir fiscal (25 percent of corporate income from which dividends are paid), not at the statutory tax rate (50 percent). Because the avoir fiscal credit offsets the précompte, distributed preference income is taxed at the shareholder's marginal tax rate. On the other hand, when income that is taxable at the corporate level is distributed, the avoir fiscal credit falls short of the corporate tax collected and the aggregate tax exceeds the shareholder's marginal rate. Thus preference income is treated more generously than other income, even if it is distributed.

Given the difference in the treatment of tax preferences attributed to retained and distributed earnings, rules are needed for the allocation of current distributions between fully taxed and preferentially taxed categories. Likewise, rules are needed for the presumptive ordering of distributions among current income and previously retained earnings. Though some uncertainty exists, and French officials may grant the interpretation that the taxpayer chooses as being most favorable to him, the ordering rules seem to be that dividends are attributed first to fully taxed current earnings, then to fully taxed earnings of the four previous years (but on a first-in, first-out, or FIFO, basis), and then to earnings on which précompte is due.[5] This means, in effect, that there is a tendency to attribute preference income to retentions and to assume that distributed income has been subject to full corporate tax.[6]

To prevent the double taxation of intercorporate dividends between subsidiaries and parent firms requires a special system. Such dividends, net of (minus) a presumed 7.5 percent for expenses relating to the derivation of such income, are excluded from the taxable income of the parent. For purpose of this provision the parent firm must be incorporated in France and own at least 10 percent of the outstanding shares of the subsidiary.

United Kingdom[7]

In 1965 the United Kingdom abolished its long tradition of allowing partial gross-up and credit for the corporate tax and adopted a classical system. But in April 1973 the United Kingdom returned to an imputation system after considering adopting a split-rate system.[8]

5. This description is based on Hammer, "Taxation of Income," p. 329.

6. Use of a full FIFO assumption, so that dividends were assumed to come first from the fully taxed income of the previous four years before coming from current income, would, of course, reduce the likelihood of fully taxed earnings slipping into the précompte category of income accumulated more than five years previously. The ordering rules may reflect the intent to encourage current distribution. See ibid.

7. For a comprehensive examination of the British tax system, which appeared after this chapter was written, see Institute for Fiscal Studies, *The Structure and Reform of Direct Taxation,* Report of a Committee chaired by Professor J. E. Meade (London: Allen and Unwin, 1978).

8. The pre-1965 and post-1973 systems have the important difference that under the current system credit is given only for taxes actually paid, whereas under the previous system credit was given at a standard rate, whether tax had been paid at the corporate level or not. This is discussed further below.

The corporate tax rate is now 52 percent, but the payment of dividends creates liability for payment by the corporation of an advance corporation tax, or ACT, equal to 33/67 of the amount of the distribution. This tax can, however, be offset against the firm's corporate income tax, up to 33 percent of taxable income.[9] For a corporation with only taxable income the ACT serves merely as a withholding tax against the ultimate corporate income tax liability. For firms with income not fully subject to the corporate tax the ACT serves a more important purpose, as described below.

The British shareholder is allowed to take credit against his personal tax liability for 33/67 of any dividend he receives, though he must, of course, include the amount of this credit in his income for tax purpose by "grossing up" his cash dividend to 100/67 of the amount received. On fully taxed distributed corporate-source income this gross-up and credit, which corresponds to the French avoir fiscal, exactly equals the ACT, or 45.5 percent ($33/67 \times 48/52$) of the corporate income tax previously paid. As in the French system, the benefits of gross-up and credit are not available to nonresidents, except as provided by treaty. Charitable and educational institutions, however, are allowed to benefit from the gross-up and credit.

As in France, there is no intention to provide relief from double taxation of dividends in instances in which income has not been fully taxed at the corporate level. The real purpose of the ACT is to help restrict the gross-up and credit to those instances in which tax has been paid at the corporate level; that is, the ACT serves much the same purpose as the précompte in the French system. Recall that the ACT is collected on all dividends and that shareholders receive tax credits equal to the amount of the ACT. The limitation on the offset of the ACT against the regular corporate tax to 33 percent of *taxable* income assures that the corporation with income that has not been subject to tax at the full corporate rate cannot use ACT to offset tax on retained earnings, and that all distributed corporate-source income has paid a tax of at least 33 percent, the rate at which the shareholder credit is given. Thus, when distributed, corporate-source preference income is subject to the marginal tax rates of shareholders, as in the French system.[10]

9. The "surplus ACT," though, can be carried back two years and, if not absorbed there, can be carried forward indefinitely.
10. See also note 4, which is equally applicable here.

The United Kingdom provides somewhat more liberal treatment of intercompany dividends than France. Such distributions, including the ACT credits pertaining to them, are exempt in the hands of the recipient corporation, regardless of the extent of ownership in the paying corporation. Moreover, in the case in which corporation A pays dividends to corporation B, which in turn pays dividends to corporation C, corporation B need pay the ACT only to the extent that its payments to corporation C exceed those from corporation A.

West Germany (Present System)

On January 1, 1977, the Federal Republic of Germany became the first member of the European Community to eliminate the double taxation of dividends. It did so by adopting a hybrid system involving elements of both the imputation and split-rate systems. The basic corporation income tax is levied at a rate of 56 percent, but that rate is reduced to 36 percent when income is distributed.[11] The shareholder then includes in his income 36/64 more than the amount of cash dividends actually received and takes credit for the amount by which he has grossed up his dividends (36/64 percent of dividends).[12] As in the United Kingdom and France, refunds are paid to individual shareholders whose credits for corporate tax exceed total tax liability. As in France, tax-exempt organizations are not accorded the benefits of dividend relief.[13]

Like the French and British, the West Germans wanted to allow relief from double taxation only when a double tax would otherwise be paid. The West German firm establishes three "available net equity" accounts in which it enters amounts of retained earnings (in-

11. This rate is applied to the distributed earnings before tax. Under the previous split-rate system the 15.45 percent rate was applied to the cash distribution, so that income subject to the 52.53 percent tax on undistributed profits had to be used to discharge the tax liability, bringing the real rate of tax on distributed earnings to 24.6 percent. (All these rates include a 3 percent supplementary levy.)

12. A withholding tax of 25 percent is also applied to dividends, but this does not alter the basic mechanics of the system of dividend relief.

13. One reason for retaining the split-rate feature in which part of the relief from double taxation is provided at the corporate level was, however, the desire to cushion the impact of full imputation on tax-exempt organizations. Whereas income distributed to such organizations under the old split-rate system was subject to a tax of only 24.6 percent, the tax would have been 56 percent if a straight imputation system had been adopted. The 36 percent rate seems to have been a compromise—but one equally motivated by political and international considerations.

cluding those earned in the current period) available for distribution. These accounts contain (1) amounts that have borne the full 56 percent corporate tax, (2) amounts that have been taxed at a rate of 36 percent, and (3) amounts that have borne no tax.[14] Since a given firm might have income taxed at effective rates other than these three rates, a given amount of income taxed at an effective rate of x, between 36 and 56 percent, would be allocated between the first two accounts so that the weighted average rate of tax would be x. Similarly, in the case of income taxed at an effective rate of y, between 0 and 36 percent, the allocation would be such as to produce the weighted average rate of y.

Dividends are presumed to have been made first from the available net equity account bearing the highest tax rate.[15] That is, dividends would be assumed to come from the account taxed at 56 percent (and would carry credit to the corporation of 20 percent) until that account is exhausted; then they would be assumed to come from the 36 percent account (but would carry no corporate credit). If the 36 percent account were also exhausted, the tax-exempt account would be assumed to be tapped. Since the shareholder takes a gross-up and credit for 36/64 of all dividends, the corporation must pay an equal amount to the treasury on any distributions made from the tax-exempt account.[16] Thus it can be seen that the supplemental payments contingent upon distribution from the zero-tax account are equivalent in purpose (and almost in form) to the French précompte and the British advance corporation tax. Finally, the ordering rules just described assure both that tax preferences (and the foreign tax credit or exemption) are effective only to the extent that earnings

14. This last account is further subdivided into foreign income, other increases in net worth not covered by the two following categories, equity carried from the previous system, and capital contributions made under the new system. (These subdivisions are discussed below.)

15. Note that this system, which Hugh Ault has labeled HIFO (highest in, first out), applies without regard to when after January 1, 1977, the earnings were accumulated—in marked contrast to the French system, which collects précompte if earnings are distributed more than five years after accumulation.

16. Dividends paid from income earned before initiation of the new system are, as noted above, assumed to come from the zero-tax account, so that précompte is collected for them. But in the presumptive order of distribution they are assumed to follow all income taxed at 56 or 36 percent and all tax-exempt current income. Thus only firms paying out more than current earnings would find this a problem, and even then would do so only if all earnings retained since 1976 had been exhausted.

are retained and that all preferences (and the foreign tax credit or exemption) are stacked first against retained earnings.[17]

Since the advantage of tax preferences is lost if dividends exceed fully taxed earnings, "this provision makes it extremely important for German companies in the future to have the right 'mix' of tax-free foreign income and fully taxed domestic income in order to avoid an increase in tax on distributions of foreign source income." The same reasoning is equally applicable to tax-preferred domestic income. This fact could have important implications for industrial structure.[18]

Under the previous West German system intercorporate dividends were a source of particular complexity. The complexity has been eliminated for distributions from one West German firm to another, since under the new system no special rules are needed. As noted earlier, the West German subsidiary pays a rate of 36 percent on all income distributed. If the West German parent company retains the income received from the subsidiary, the 56 percent rate applies, as it does to all ordinary income, but the parent takes the 36 percent credit attached to the distribution, so that the subsidiary's tax is exactly offset. If the parent distributes the income it receives from the subsidiary, its corporate rate is reduced to 36 percent (thus offsetting the subsidiary's tax) and the individual shareholder receives credit for the 36 percent tax. In short, the 56 percent rate applies to fully taxed income retained within the corporate sector, but the indi-

17. In the terminology of chapter 4, preference income is "stacked last" (assumed to be distributed after taxable income), but preferences are "washed out" (nullified) to the extent they are distributed.

18. The quotation is from Ault, "Germany," p. 271. There is an important difference in the availability of tax preferences in the United States and West Germany. By law, book income and income for tax purposes must be virtually identical in West Germany; moreover, any time a West German corporation distributes more than its book income the excess is deemed to be a distribution of capital subject to the 36 percent corporate tax. Thus to the extent that there are tax preferences they are sanctioned by accounting practices, and the problems created by tax preferences may appear not to exist. But the validation of tax preferences by accounting standards does not force the definition of income for tax purposes into conformity with an economic definition such as the Haig-Simons one. (The Haig-Simons definition is discussed in Richard Goode, "The Economic Definition of Income," in Joseph A. Pechman, ed., *Comprehensive Income Taxation* [Brookings Institution, 1977], pp. 7–30.) Tax preferences are stacked against retained earnings even in a system requiring conformity of book and taxable income, so long as both deviate from the Haig-Simons definition.

vidual taxpayer's marginal rate rules on income distributed from that sector.[19]

Table 3-1 is intended to illustrate the workings of the West German system and pave the way for the comparison of the French, British, and West German systems that follows. Column 1 illustrates the situation in which there are no tax preferences and no foreign-source income. Line 4 shows that 100 units of corporate-source income draws a tentative corporate tax liability of 56 units, so that fully taxed available net equity initially increases by the remaining 44 units (line 5). Dividends of 40 units reduce available net equity —but by only 27.5 units, since the dividend-paid credit necessary to reduce the effective corporate tax rate on distributed earnings to 36 percent makes up the other 12.5 units.[20] On balance, the effective tax rate at the corporate level in this example is 43.5 percent, composed of 56 percent on the 37.5 percent of income giving rise to retentions and 36 percent on the 62.5 percent of income leading to distributions.[21]

The remaining columns, though more complicated, follow the same pattern as column 1. In column 2 it is assumed that the 37.5 units of income giving rise to retentions is preference income (or foreign-source income exempt from West German tax).[22] In this case the tentative corporate tax is only 35 percent (56 percent of the 62.5 percent of income that is taxable). In order to produce a weighted average tax rate of 35 percent it is necessary to assign the 37.5 units of preference income to the tax-free available net equity account and the remaining after-tax income—27.5 units—to the fully taxed account.[23] Payment of 40 units of dividends produces

19. Note, however, that when dividends paid out of tax-exempt income of the subsidiary are retained by the parent firm the rate of tax rises from 0 to 56 percent. A less extreme result occurs when the parent retains income paid from the subsidiary's 36 percent available-net-equity account.

20. Taxation at the shareholder level is not considered in detail. The shareholder simply includes 25/16 of his cash dividends in income for tax purposes and takes 9/25 of the included amount as a credit for corporate tax paid on his behalf. Nor is the 25 percent withholding tax on dividends considered here, as it is of no immediate relevance for issues at hand.

21. Note that 40 (cash dividends) \div 0.64 = 62.5, and 16.5 (retentions) \div 0.44 = 37.5.

22. If the foreign-source income is taxed in the country of origin the table would need to be adapted to allow for the foreign tax.

23. If the 35 percent were the effective rate applied to a given income flow, income would be assigned to the tax-free and 36-percent accounts in the proper pro-

Table 3-1. Tax Calculations for the West German System of Dividend Relief, without and with Preference Income[a]
Monetary units

| | | *Preference or foreign-source income* | | | |
| | | | | *Exceeds retained earnings* | |
Item[b]	*None*[c] (1)	*Equals retained earnings*[d] (2)	*Equals 20 units*[d] (3)	*And equals 37.5 units*[e] (4)	*And equals total net income*[e] (5)
1. Corporate-source income	100	100	100	100	100
2. Preference or foreign-source income	0	37.5	20	37.5	100
3. Taxable income [1 − 2]	100	62.5	80	62.5	0
4. Tentative corporate income tax [56% of 3]	56	35	44.8	35	0
5. Net income [1 − 4] = increase in available net equity	44	65	55.2	65	100
a. Tax-free [from 2]	0	37.5	20	37.5	100
b. Fully taxed [5 − 5a]	44	27.5	35.2	27.5	0
6. Dividends paid	40	40	40	64	64
a. From fully taxed available net equity [44/64 of 6, but ≤5b]	27.5	27.5	27.5	27.5	0
b. By tax reduction [20/44 of 6a]	12.5	12.5	12.5	12.5	0
c. From tax-free available net equity [6 − 6a − 6b]	0	0	0	24	64
7. Change in corporate tax [7a + 7b]	−12.5	−12.5	−12.5	1	36
a. Tax reduction (induced by distribution from fully taxed available net equity) [from 6b]	−12.5	−12.5	−12.5	−12.5	0
b. Tax increase (induced by distribution from tax-free available net equity) [36/64 of 6c]	0	0	0	13.5	36
8. Net corporate tax [4 + 7]	43.5	22.5	32.3	36	36
9. Retained earnings [1 − 6 − 8]	16.5	37.5	27.7	0	0
10. Final available net equity [10a + 10b]	16.5	37.5	27.7	0	0
a. Fully taxed [5b − 6a]	16.5	0	7.7	0	0
b. Tax free [5a − 6c − 7b]	0	37.5	20	0	0

a. Terms relating to integration systems are explained in the glossary. In this table the 25 percent withholding tax on all dividends is ignored.
b. Except for percentages and fractions, the numbers in brackets refer to the lines of this table.
c. See also table 3-2.
d. See also table 3-3.
e. Assumes maximum distribution of income. See also table 3-4.

exactly the same effects on the available net equity accounts as in column 1. But the final available net equity account (line 10) is greater in column 2; because the tax preference is stacked against retained earnings, it is left intact. That this is true is emphasized by noting that total corporate taxes paid are less in column 2 than in column 1 (and retained earnings are greater) by 21 units, exactly the amount of preference income (37.5) multiplied by the 56 percent corporate tax rate applied to income generating retentions.

In columns 4 and 5, I assume not that 40 units of income is distributed, as in columns 1 through 3, but that dividends are the maximum possible, which is 64 units.[24] Since the bottom line results are the same in both columns, I focus on column 4, and note differences later. Through line 6b (except for line 6) the entries in column 4 are identical to those in column 2. But line 6c shows that once the fully taxed available net equity account is exhausted, 24 units of dividends must be paid from the tax-free available net equity account. This is the maximum amount that can be distributed from this account, since the remaining 13.5 units are required for the payment of tax needed to bring the total tax on the 37.5 units of tax-preferred corporate-source income up to 36 percent upon distribution. This tax payment is indicated in line 7b. The result of these entries is, of course, an effective corporate tax rate of 36 percent, no final available net equity, and no retained earnings. The important economic implication of the entries, however, is that tax preferences have a value determined by the tax rate the corporation pays on retentions so long as retentions are no less than preference income, but become worthless to the extent that they exceed retentions. Column 5 illustrates the same result for the extreme case in which the firm has only preference income. It shows that even if *all* income were tax-preferred, the preferences would be washed out (and a corporate rate of 36 percent applied) to the extent that income was distributed. In the examples of columns 4 and 5 the 36 percent rate would be creditable

portions to produce the 35 percent effective rate. But in the present example it is assumed for convenience that there are two distinct income flows, one tax exempt and the other fully taxable.

24. Column 3, in which there are 20 units of preference income, is used primarily to compare the French, British, and West German systems, and is of no great relevance at this point. Note, however, that the value of the tax preference in terms of reduced tax (11.2 units) is again equal to the product of the 20 units of preference income and the 56 percent corporate tax rate.

Table 3-2. Mechanics of French, British, and West German[a] Methods of Dividend Relief, Assuming Fully Taxed Income

Rates in percent; other data in monetary units

Item[b]	French method (1)		British method (2)		West German method (3)	
1. Corporate-source income	100		100		100	
2. Dividends paid	40		40		40	
3. Tentative corporate income tax[c]	50		50		56	
4. Advance corporation tax [50% of 2]	...		20		...	
5. Mainstream corporate tax liability [3 − 4]	...		30		...	
6. Dividend-paid credit [20/64 of 2]		12.5	
7. Total net tax liability[d]	50		50		43.5	
8. Retained earnings [1 − 2 − 7]	10		10		16.5	
9. Gross-up and credit[e]	20		20		22.5	
10. Taxable gross dividends [2 + 9]	60		60		62.5	
11. Alternative marginal personal tax rates	20	60	20[f]	60	20	60
12. Gross personal tax [10 × 11]	12	36	12	36	12.5	37.5
13. Shareholder credit [from 9]	20	20	20	20	22.5	22.5
14. Net personal tax [12 − 13]	−8	16	−8	16	−10	15
15. Total taxes [7 + 14]	42	66	42	66	33.5	58.5

... Not applicable to this country.

a. The West German system is described in greater detail in table 3-1 and in the textual discussion thereof.

b. Except for percentages and fractions, the numbers in brackets refer to the lines of this table. Terms relating to integration systems are explained in the glossary.

c. Calculated at 50, 50, and 56 percent, respectively, of line 1 for the three countries.

d. French [from 3]; British [4 + 5]; West German [3 − 6].

e. Calculated at ½, ½, and 9/16, respectively, of line 2 for the three countries.

f. The advance corporation tax and the shareholder credit in the British system actually equal the lowest personal marginal rate.

at the shareholder level, making the total tax paid depend on the shareholder's marginal personal rate—but not the preference.

Comparison of the French, British, and West German Systems

Tables 3-2 through 3-5 should help to make understandable the results of the French, British, and present West German systems, if not the details of administration. To facilitate comparisons of the French and British systems I use the French corporate tax rate of 50 percent (the actual British rate is 52 percent) and an advance corporation tax and gross-up and credit of one-half of cash dividends (up to a limit of 33⅓ percent of taxable income) instead of 33/67 (up to 33 percent).

In table 3-2 it is assumed that all corporate-source income is fully taxable and that 40 units of every 100 units of before-tax income is

paid out as dividends.[25] In the British system the 40-unit dividend carries with it liability for ACT of 20 units, something not found in the other systems. When the ACT is offset against the corporate income tax of 50 units, the net liability (called the mainstream corporate tax) is only 30 units. The French system shows no such reduction, since there is no ACT. The West German system shows a reduction in corporate tax liability, but not because of an advance corporation tax. Rather, the corporate tax is reduced by a dividend-paid credit equal to 5/16 of cash dividends, to reduce the corporate tax applied to distributed income to 36 percent, the figure at which the shareholders are allowed credit. Since dividends are 40 units, the credit at the corporate level is 12.5 units (which repeats table 3-1, column 1), so that the aggregate corporate tax is only 43.5 percent, despite its nominal rate of 56 percent.

It can be seen that in the case under examination the French and British systems of dividend relief produce identical results.[26] On the other hand, retained earnings are markedly higher in the West German case because, given the assumption that dividends are equal in the three cases, they reflect the lower average tax rate applied to West German profits. Yet another way to see the same influences at work is to examine the final line of the table, which presents the total tax burdens at two points in the marginal personal rate structure in the three countries.

Table 3-3 is designed to illustrate the treatment of tax preferences in the three countries. Dividends are assumed to be the same as in the example of table 3-2. Retained earnings are assumed in columns 1, 3, and 6 to equal preference income. In the other three columns retentions are essentially a residual determined by the interplay of dividends and the assumption made about preference income; in the French and British cases it is assumed that preference income exceeds

25. The amounts assumed to be paid out are chosen to simplify calculation of tax burdens, gross-up and credits, and so on, as well as comparisons across countries. The amounts paid out as dividends are held constant across the primary examples of tables 3-2 and 3-3, so that differences in taxation manifest themselves entirely in differences in retained earnings.

26. In actuality retained earnings would be about 2 units lower in the British system because the corporate tax is 52 percent instead of 50 and the shareholder credit would be slightly smaller than indicated because it is only 33/67 instead of 1/2 of dividends. Throughout I ignore the fact that in the United Kingdom no personal rate is lower than the rate of shareholder credit.

retentions, but in the West German case retentions exceed preferences.

This choice of cases is intended to show the difference between the French and the British treatment of preferences. And it also shows that for comparable amounts of dividends and preference income the West German, British, and French systems produce different results because of the difference in partial and complete dividend relief. On the other hand, all three systems can produce comparable results in the sense that they involve (at least some) washing out of tax preferences to the extent that preference income is distributed.

In column 1 retained earnings equal preference income in the French system, so that no précompte is necessary to ensure that dividends are from fully taxed income. In column 2, on the other hand, tax preferences exceed retentions and a précompte of 4.4 units is necessary.[27]

Column 6 for West Germany is analogous to column 1 for France in that retained earnings equal preference income. But unlike the French system, in which a précompte may be required to increase the corporate tax paid on income attributed to distributions, a dividend-received credit is necessary to bring the effective rate of 35 percent *down* to 22.5 percent (the weighted average of zero applied to the 37.5 units retained and 36 percent on the 62.5 units of income giving rise to distribution; see table 3-1 and the separate discussion of the West German system). As is shown subsequently, to the extent that retentions are less than preference income, as in column 2, the West German dividend-paid credit would be less and the advantage of the preference would be washed out, as it is (in part) in the French case. In the example of column 5, in which dividends equal those in column 1, retentions are more than enough to absorb all preference income.

The results can be markedly different in the British system in the case in which preference income exceeds retentions. In column 3, in which retentions equal preferences, the result is identical to that in the French system (column 1). Moreover, in all three systems the value of preferences is the amount of the preference income multiplied by the marginal tax rate (applied to retained earnings in the

27. Regular corporate tax is 31.25 units. Dividends from taxable income are an equal amount, given the 50 percent corporate rate. Thus 8.75 units of dividends are from preference income. This amount results in a précompte of 4.38 units. If, alternatively, dividends were only 31.25 units, no précompte would be required.

Table 3-3. French, British, and West German Methods of Dividend Relief When Retained Earnings Are Equal to, Less Than, or More Than Preference Income[a]

Monetary units

Item[b]	French method		British method		West German method	
	Preference income equals retained earnings (1)	Preference income exceeds retained earnings (2)	Preference income equals retained earnings (3)	Preference income exceeds retained earnings (4)	Retained earnings exceed preference income (5)	Preference income equals retained earnings (6)
1. Corporate-source income	100	100	100	100	100	100
2. Dividends paid	40	40	40	40	40	40
3. Advance corporation tax [50% of 2]	...	37.5	20	20
4. Preference income	20	37.5	20	37.5	20	37.5
5. Taxable income [1 − 4]	80	62.5	80	62.5	80	62.5
6. Tentative corporate income tax[c]	40	31.25	40	31.25	44.8	35
7. Précompte [(2 − 6) × tax rate[d]; (36/64 of 2) − 6, but ≥ 0]	0	4.38	0	0
8. Dividend-paid credit[e] [20/64 of 2]	12.5	12.5
9. Credit for advance corporation tax[f] [from 3]	20	20
10. Total corporate tax [6 + 3 + 7 − 8 − 9]	40	35.63	40	31.25	32.3	22.5
11. Retained earnings [1 − 2 − 10]	20	24.37	20	28.75	27.7	37.5
12. Value of preferences[g]	10	14.37	10	18.75	11.2	21

... Not applicable to this country.

a. Terms relating to integration systems are explained in the glossary.

b. Except for fractions and percentages, the numbers in brackets refer to the lines of this table.

c. Calculated at 50, 50, and 56 percent, respectively, of line 5 for the three countries.

d. The French tax rate is 50 percent.

e. Dividend-paid credit is given only for distributions from fully taxed income. See also table 3-4.

f. Limited to 33⅓ percent of taxable income.

g. Excess of retained earnings over comparable figure in table 3-2. Ignores tax and credit at shareholder level, because these are as in table 3-2.

West German system). But column 4 shows a substantial difference from the result in the comparable column for the French system (column 2). Because of the difference in the advance corporation tax mechanism and the précompte mechanism (or its West German counterpart), the preferences in excess of retentions are not necessarily washed out under the British system; rather, they continue to have a marginal value equal to the marginal corporate tax rate. The crucial difference is that the ACT is fully creditable against the tentative corporate tax so long as it does not exceed a given percentage (33⅓ in this example; 34 percent, in fact) of taxable income. Thus preferences are washed out only to the extent that they exceed that percentage of taxable income. In the example of column 4 the entire ACT is creditable. As noted below, the maximum distribution from totally exempt income is 66⅔ percent, given an ACT of 1/2 of cash dividends (67 percent with an ACT of 33/67 of dividends). This result is the same as in the French system for comparable tax rates and degrees of dividend relief.

Table 3-4 carries the logic of table 3-3 to its conclusion; in it all income is distributed, despite the disadvantage of losing preferences on distributed income. In the West German system the précompte increases the corporate tax to the point that the tax preferences are entirely washed out. In the French system the précompte equals the shareholder credit on distributed preference income rather than the corporate tax that would otherwise be paid. Thus only half the distributed preferences are washed out.[28] In the example of column 3 the advance corporation tax exceeds 33⅓ of taxable income, so it is not fully creditable against the corporate tax.[29] Therefore some of the tax preference is washed out, but not as much as in the French system.[30] Only if all income were preference income would the French

28. Only half of distributed preferences are washed out in the sense that the précompte is only half the amount of cash dividends paid from preference income. With a 50 percent corporate rate the précompte must equal the cash dividends paid from preference income to achieve complete washout. But recall that when taxation at the shareholder level is taken into account, the French system results in an aggregate rate of tax equal to the shareholder's marginal personal rate.

29. Note, however, that carry-back or carry-forward of excess ACT may result in full crediting.

30. A comparison of tables 3-3 and 3-4 shows that in the British system the increment in corporate-level tax is 2.2 units, relative to 17.8 units of added dividends paid from preferences (column 3, lines 2 and 10, in both tables), compared to 6.7 units of extra tax and 13.3 units of extra dividends in the French system (column 1).

Table 3-4. French, British, and West German Methods of Dividend Relief with Preference Income and 100 Percent Payout[a]

Monetary units

Item[b]	French method		British method		West German method	
	Preference income equals retained earnings in table 3-3 (1)	Preference income equals total income (2)	Preference income equals retained earnings in table 3-3 (3)	Preference income equals total income (4)	Preference income equals retained earnings in table 3-3 (5)	Preference income equals total income (6)
1. Corporate-source income	100	100	100	100	100	100
2. Dividends paid (maximum possible) [from 11]	53.3	66.7	57.8	66.7	64	64
3. Advance corporation tax [50% of 2]	28.9	33.3
4. Preference income[c]	20	100	20	100	37.5	100
5. Taxable income [1 − 4]	80	0	80	0	62.5	0
6. Tentative corporate income tax[d]	40	0	40	0	35	0
7. Précompte [(2 − 6) × tax rate[e]]; [(36/64 of 2) − 6, but ≥ 0]	6.7	33.3	1	36
8. Dividend-paid credit[f]	0	0
9. Credit for advance corporation tax [from 3, but ≤ 33⅓% of 5]	26.7	0
10. Total tax [6 + 3 + 7 − 8 − 9]	46.7	33.3	42.2	33.3	36	36
11. Available for distribution [1 − 10]	53.3	66.7	57.8	66.7	64	64
12. Increase in dividends due to preference income[g]	3.3	16.7	7.8	16.7	0	0

... Not applicable to this country.

a. Terms relating to integration systems are explained in the glossary.

b. Except for percentages and fractions, the numbers in brackets refer to the lines of this table.

c. From line 4 of table 3-3, columns 1, 3, and 6, respectively.

d. Calculated at 50, 50, and 56 percent, respectively, of line 5, for the three countries.

e. The French tax rate is 50 percent.

f. There is no dividend-paid credit because dividends are paid from taxable income. See also table 3-3.

g. Excess of dividends over dividends if all income were taxable. Allowance is made for personal tax in table 3-5.

and British systems produce the same result in the case at hand. As shown in columns 2 and 4 the maximum distribution is 66⅔ units in either system.

Table 3-5 presents the comparison of the French and British systems from yet another angle. The aggregate taxes paid at the corporate and personal levels on the income streams described in table 3-4 are calculated and compared with the equivalent figures in situations in which there are no preferences.[31]

Line 9 of columns 3, 4, 7, and 8 shows that total payout results in the shareholder's marginal rate being collected on preference income. Under partial dividend relief the aggregate rates collected in the absence of preferences exceed these marginal rates (line 10). Thus preferences are washed out in one sense (producing taxation at the shareholder's marginal rate), but not another (replicating taxation in the absence of preferences). To produce washout in the second sense the précompte or its equivalent would have to equal the forgone corporate tax rather than just the shareholder credit.

In the less extreme case in which preferences fall short of total income, the results in the two countries differ. In the French example the value of the preference at any income level is simply proportionate to the fraction preferences are of total income. But in the United Kingdom preferences are 47 percent as valuable in columns 5 and 6 as in columns 7 and 8, even though they are only 20 percent as large. This results, of course, from the fact that only part of the ACT is not creditable in the example.

A comparison of tables 3-3, 3-4, and 3-5 suggests some powerful, and not especially desirable, incentive effects. Suppose that preferences are 20 units in the French system, so that column 1 is the relevant one in each table.[32] In such a case it is necessary to give up 20 units of retentions to obtain 13.3 additional units of dividends. Given that dividends are taxed at personal tax rates but retentions may result in little tax liability (in present-value terms), it may be necessary for the shareholder in the 60 percent marginal rate bracket to give up 20 units of retentions to obtain a mere 8 units of net divi-

31. There is no need to consider the German case; in it the washout of preferences is complete, so the preference income is subject to the shareholder's marginal tax rate in the aggregate.

32. In each case we choose as a point of reference the situation in which preferences equal retentions, so that paying additional dividends creates liability for précompte or its functional equivalent.

Table 3-5. Value of Preference Income under French and British Methods of Dividend Relief, Assuming 100 Percent Payout[a]
Rates in percent; other data in monetary units

| Item[b] | French method | | | | British method | | | |
| | Preference income equals retained earnings in table 3-4 | | Preference income equals total income | | Preference income equals retained earnings in table 3-4 | | Preference income equals total income | |
	(1)	(2)	(3)	(4)	(5)	(6)	(7)	(8)
1. Marginal personal tax rate	20	60	20	60	20	60	20	60
2. Dividends (from table 3-4)	53.3	53.3	66.7	66.7	57.8	57.8	66.7	66.7
3. Gross-up and credit [50% of 2]	26.7	26.7	33.3	33.3	28.9	28.9	33.3	33.3
4. Taxable dividends [2 + 3]	80	80	100	100	86.7	86.7	100	100
5. Gross personal tax [1 × 4]	16	48	20	60	17.3	52	20	60
6. Shareholder credit [from 3]	26.7	26.7	33.3	33.3	28.9	28.9	33.3	33.3
7. Net personal tax [5 − 6]	−10.7	21.3	−13.3	26.7	−11.6	23.1	−13.3	26.7
8. Corporate-level taxes (from table 3-4)	46.7	46.7	33.3	33.3	42.2	42.2	33.3	33.3
9. Total tax [7 + 8]	36	68	20	60	30.6	65.3	20	60
10. Tax with no preference income[c]	40	70	40	70	40	70	40	70
11. Value of preferences [10 − 9]	4	2	20	10	9.4	4.7	20	10

a. Terms relating to integration systems are explained in the glossary.
b. Except for percentages, the numbers in brackets refer to the lines of this table.
c. 25 + (line 1 × 75).

dends.[33] Likewise, in the West German example (column 6 in table 3-3 and column 5 in table 3-4) it is necessary to give up 37.5 units of retentions for 24 units of cash dividends (and 15 net units for the shareholder in the 60 percent bracket).[34] Clearly there can be strong incentives to retain at least an amount equal to preference income. Or, seen from the other end, if firms are committed to paying a certain level of dividends (say 40 units in the French example), tax preferences can have little or no stimulative impact beyond a certain point (where preferences equal retentions).

In the British case the result is somewhat different. Here, under comparable assumptions, retentions are traded for gross dividends on a roughly one-for-one basis—even considering the least advantageous case in which the constraint on the creditability of the advance corporation tax is binding. Even so, there is a substantial disincentive for the payment of dividends out of preference income.[35] This is especially true once the constraint on the full crediting of the ACT against the corporate tax becomes binding.

Canada

Though the Canadian system of dividend relief (which is similar to the Belgian one) resembles the French, British, and West German systems, it differs in one crucial respect.[36] Whereas the latter three systems have quite detailed provisions intended to prevent relief from corporate income tax not actually paid, the Canadian system provides gross-up and credit equal to approximately one-third of dividends received (one-half from January 1, 1978), without regard to whether any corporate income tax has been paid. Canada probably

33. The increase in dividends of 13.3 units carries with it a gross-up credit of 6.7 units, so that taxable income increases by 20, producing an increase in gross personal tax liability of 12 units and a net increase of 5.3, so that the net increase in cash received is 8 units.

34. Taxable income increases by 37.5 units, gross personal tax by 22.5 units, net tax by 9 units, and net dividends by 15 units.

35. A comparison of column 3 in tables 3-3 and 3-4 shows that 20 units of retentions are exchanged for 17.8 units of gross dividends, which are grossed up to 26.7 units. For the shareholder in the 60 percent marginal rate bracket the added gross liability is 16 units. The increase in the shareholder credit is 8.9 units, so the increase in net dividends is 10.7 units.

36. There are also important exceptions to the general rule that Canadian corporations are able to exclude dividends received from other Canadian corporations. See Hammer, "Taxation of Income," p. 325.

Table 3-6. Analysis of Canadian System of Dividend Relief with Alternative Dividend Distributions, Preference Incomes, and Retained Earnings[a]
Monetary units

Item[b]	Dividend distribution of 40			Maximum dividend distribution		
	No preference income (1)	Preference income and retained earnings each equal 20 (2)	Preference income exceeds retained earnings (3)	No preference income (4)	Preference income equals 20 (5)	Preference income equals 100 (6)
1. Corporate-source income	100	100	100	100	100	100
2. Preference income	0	20	37.5	0	20	100
3. Taxable income [1 − 2]	100	80	62.5	100	80	0
4. Corporate tax [50% of 3]	50	40	31.3	50	40	0
5. Available for distribution [1 − 4]	50	60	68.7	50	60	100
6. Dividends	40	40	40	50	60	100
7. Gross-up and credit [50% of 6]	20	20	20	25	30	50
8. Taxable dividends [6 + 7]	60	60	60	75	90	150
9. Gross personal tax [60% of 8]	36	36	36	45	54	90
10. Shareholder credit [from 7]	20	20	20	25	30	50
11. Net personal tax [9 − 10]	16	16	16	20	24	40
12. Total tax [4 + 11]	66	56	47.3	70	64	40
13. Net dividends [6 − 11]	24	24	24	30	36	60
14. Retained earnings [5 − 6]	10	20	28.7	0	0	0
15. Value of preferences[c]	6	30
16. Net dividends gained by loss of retentions of 10[d]	18.7	6	6	...

... Not applicable.
a. Terms relating to integration systems are explained in the glossary.
b. Except for percentages, the numbers in brackets refer to the lines of this table.
c. Columns 2 and 3 of line 14 are compared to column 1 of that line; columns 5 and 6 of line 13 are compared to column 4 of that line.
d. Columns 4 and 5 of line 16 are calculated by comparing column 1 with column 4 and column 2 with column 5 in lines 13 and 14. The same comparison based on columns 3 and 6 is not possible, because different amounts of preference income are involved in the two columns.

made this choice because it adopted dividend relief more as a stimulus to investment than as relief from double taxation of dividends per se. (A similar provision in the pre-1965 British law was roundly criticized and replaced by the advance corporate tax system when the United Kingdom returned to use of the gross-up and credit in 1973.) Furthermore, this benefit extends to certain institutions that are not themselves subject to tax, as in the United Kingdom.

Table 3-6 can be used to illustrate the difference in treatment of preferences under the European and Canadian approaches. Columns 1 through 3 replicate the results in the analogous cases for a shareholder in the 60 percent marginal rate bracket under the British system described in tables 3-2 and 3-3. But whereas the French system contains the précompte, and the value of preferences can be lost under the British system if a firm has substantial preference income and a high dividend payout rate, the Canadian system has no such feature. Comparison of columns 5 and 6 of table 3-6 with columns 2 and 6, and 4 and 8, of table 3-5 reveals that the total tax is below that paid in France or the United Kingdom in comparable circumstances. As shown in greater detail in chapter 4, the amount by which this is true is greater the lower the marginal tax rate of the shareholder. Thus the use of the statutory rate to calculate gross-up and credit, with no précompte, does not neatly result in the washing out of preferences.

Canada's rejection of full integration in favor of a form of dividend relief that allows tax preferences to benefit shareholders in a rather haphazard and inequitable way is usually viewed with disappointment by public finance experts. Yet a more charitable interpretation is possible if one considers the policy objectives that influenced the choice, and the setting in which the choice was made. First, it is hardly fair to chastise the Canadians for not taking the lead down the road to full integration; had the Royal Commission on Taxation not recommended integration no one would have expected Canada to adopt it, and no other country has yet dared to follow the commission's recommendations. Second, it is true that the imputation scheme actually adopted in Canada is rather crude when compared with the ideal of full integration proposed by the Royal Commission, or even with imputation schemes that would neatly pass through or wash out tax preferences. But though the Canadian approach is imperfect, it is clearly a substantial step forward from the earlier system that

allowed a 20 percent credit for dividends received, but without gross-up.[37]

West Germany (Old System)

The system of dividend relief in effect in West Germany from 1953 to 1977 is of interest because it is one of the best known and well-developed approaches based on the split-rate system, and therefore one that helps to highlight the problems that arise from that approach. Under this system a resident company was taxed at a rate of 24.6 percent on income used to pay dividends, but at a rate of 52.53 percent on the income it retained.[38] Being provided in this way, the relief from roughly half of the double taxation of dividends extended to nontaxable organizations and to nonresidents as well as to resident individuals.

Dividends received by corporations holding portfolio investments in the shares of other West German corporations were subject to tax. But firms holding as much as 25 percent of the shares of another firm were allowed the Schachtelprivileg (holding privilege), under which dividends were exempt in the hands of the parent firm. It was intended that this "affiliate privilege" would be available only to the extent that earnings received from the subsidiary were redistributed by the parent. Otherwise earnings that would be subject to a rate of 51 percent when retained by the subsidiary would be taxed at a rate of only 15 percent when distributed to the parent. However, a Nachsteuer (back tax) of 36 percent was collected from the parent on any earnings exempted under the Schactelprivileg but not distributed within the year. (The Nachsteuer was refunded upon subsequent distribution).

The Proposal of the Commission of the European Communities

On August 1, 1975, the Commission of the European Communities submitted to the Council of the European Communities a pro-

37. For the faults of such an approach, see Charles E. McLure, Jr., "Integration of the Personal and Corporate Income Taxes: The Missing Element in Recent Tax Reform Proposals," *Harvard Law Review,* vol. 88 (January 1975), pp. 553–54.

38. As mentioned in note 11, the tax rate on *dividends* was only 15 percent, but the "shadow effect" (resulting from the need to pay the 51 percent tax on the amount used to pay the tax on dividends), together with the 3 percent supplementary levy on the corporate tax liability, brought the total tax on the *income* from which dividends were paid to 24.6 percent.

posal for a directive on the harmonization of corporate taxation and of withholding taxes on dividends.[39] The bulk of the provisions of this draft directive are discussed under the international aspects of integration, but it is appropriate here to outline the proposed system.

First, the draft directive suggested that all member countries should adopt corporate income taxes at rates ranging from 45 percent to 55 percent and that they should use the imputation method to eliminate from 45 to 55 percent of the burden of the corporate tax on dividends.[40] Thus the French system lies exactly in the middle of the range for both the corporate tax rate and the degree of dividend relief. The draft directive also provided for the payment of refunds when credits exceeded tax liabilities and for the extension of the benefits of imputation to institutions that were in the "public interest."[41]

The draft directive followed common European practice in providing for a compensatory tax (such as the French précompte) to be levied whenever dividends are paid from income that has not borne the full tax at the corporate level, but acknowledged that a system such as the British advance corporation tax could serve the same purpose. The rules for the order in which funds were assumed to be used to pay dividends resembled the French system (except that income falling in a given category was deemed to be derived on a proportionate basis from income earned in any member nation).[42] This practice was intended to provide the maximum advantage to firms—especially those with substantial foreign income—consistent with not allowing relief for taxes not paid, since income not subject to domestic tax (in any nation of the European Community) was assumed to be distributed last.

Finally, intercorporate dividends would be treated so as to provide the advantage of imputation if the funds were ultimately distributed

39. Commission of the European Communities, "Proposal for a Council Directive Concerning the Harmonization of Systems of Company Taxation and of Withholding Taxes on Dividends," *Bulletin of the European Communities,* Supplement 10/75: *Harmonization of Systems of Company Taxation* (Luxembourg: Office for Official Publications of the European Communities, 1975). This proposal failed to be approved in December 1977 by the European Parliament. *Intertax* (January 1978), p. 1.

40. Commission of the European Communities, "Proposal for a Council Directive," articles 1, 3, 8.

41. Ibid., articles 4, 5.

42. Ibid., articles 9, 12.

Table 3-7. Key Features of Income Tax Systems in Selected Countries[a]

Feature	United States	Netherlands	France	United Kingdom
Basic structure	Separate entity	Separate entity	Dividend credit	Dividend credit
Tax rates[b]				
Corporation tax	46 percent	46 percent	50 percent	52 percent
Withholding of personal income tax on dividends	None	25 percent	None	None
Dividend credit				
On net dividends	50 percent	49.3 percent
On grossed-up dividends	33⅓ percent	33 percent
Intercorporate dividends				
General treatment	Generally, 85 percent exemption	Participation exemption (5 percent ownership)	Participation exemption (10 percent ownership)	Generally, exemption
Nachsteuer on retention
Measures for uniform dividend credit	Précompte, levied on certain dividends, not deducted from corporation tax	Advance corporation tax levied on all dividends, deducted from corporation tax

Sources: Mitsuo Sato and Richard M. Bird, "International Aspects of the Taxation of Corporations and Shareholders," International Monetary Fund, *Staff Papers*, vol. 22 (July 1975), p. 451; Hugh J. Ault, "Germany: The New Corporation Tax System," *Intertax: European Tax Review* (August 1976), pp. 262–75; Richard M. Hammer, "The Taxation of Income from Corporate Shareholders: Review of Present Systems in Canada, France, Germany, Japan and the U.K.," *National Tax Journal*, vol. 28 (September 1975), pp. 315–34; Commission of the European Communities, "Proposal for a Council Directive Concerning the Harmonization of Systems of Company Taxation and of Withholding Taxes on Dividends," *Bulletin of the European Communities*, Supplement 10/75: *Harmonization of Systems of Company Taxa-*

Table 3-7 (*continued*)

Federal Republic of Germany		Canada	Proposed directive for the European Community	Japan
Pre-1977	Post-1976			
Split rate	Hybrid system	Dividend credit	Dividend credit	Mixed
Retained, 51 percent; distributed, 15 percent	Retained, 56 percent; distributed, 36 percent	50 percent	45–55 percent	Retained, 40 percent; distributed, 30 percent
25 percent	25 percent	None	25 percent (optional)	15 percent
...	56.3 percent	50 percent	45–55 percent	10 percent (or 5 percent)^c
...	36 percent	33⅓ percent	31–35.5 percent	...
Participation exemption (25 percent ownership)	No special rules needed	Generally, exemption	Shareholder credit offset against advance corporation tax or précompte of parent	Generally, exemption
36 percent (51 percent minus 15 percent)	One-fourth of dividends retained taxed at 40 percent
...	Credit or précompte if dividends not from income taxed at 36 percent	None: allowed regardless of effective corporate rate	Précompte or advance corporation tax	None

tion (Luxembourg: Office for Official Publications of the European Communities, 1975); unpublished material for updating (see note a).

a. Except as updated to include the post-1976 German system and the change in the tax rates in the United States and the United Kingdom, the information in this table reflects tax treatment as of the mid-1970s. Terms relating to integration systems are explained in the glossary.

b. Basic or representative rates, not including local taxes or temporary surtaxes.

c. The credit is 5 percent if the total taxable income of dividend recipients exceeds 10 million yen.

to shareholders, but not if the funds were retained. This would be achieved by setting off the credit attached to the dividends against the précompte or the advance corporation tax on the dividends paid by the parent firm.[43]

Survey of Domestic Issues

Key features of the systems of dividend relief found in France, West Germany, Canada, and the United Kingdom, the system proposed in the directive of the Commission of the European Communities, the classical systems of the United States and the Netherlands, and the mixed Japanese system are summarized in table 3-7. This brief review of foreign practice shows that a number of questions must be answered by any country that decides to provide relief from double taxation of dividends, even if full integration and international problems are not considered.[44]

What should be the relation between the basic corporate income tax rate and the top bracket rate under the personal income tax?

What portion of that basic corporate tax should be offset by the scheme for dividend relief adopted?

Should the split-rate approach, the imputation method, the dividend-paid deduction, or some combination of two of these be used?

How can intercorporate dividends be treated so that the problems that necessitated the Nachsteuer under the old German system are avoided?

Should tax preferences be passed through or washed out on distributed income? And what are to be the presumptive ordering rules? Should tax preferences be stacked first (against dividends) or last (against retained earnings)? Or should preferences be attributed proportionately to distributed and retained earnings? What technique should be used to achieve the desired tax treatment of tax prefer-

43. Ibid., article 10.

44. The way these questions are listed does not necessarily imply that there is any order of priority or sequence in which they should be answered, or even that they can be answered independently of one another. Additional important issues not covered in this review include such questions as (1) how to treat net operating losses, audit adjustments, and amended returns; (2) whether or not a distinction should be drawn between dividends and return of capital; (3) the tax implications of corporate reorganizations, liquidations, and so on; (4) transition rules and technical difficulties arising in the transition from a classical system to dividend relief. Questions 1 and 2 are addressed in chapters 4 and 5; questions 3 and 4 are beyond the scope of the book.

ences? Should there be a time limit within which income must be distributed if it is not to be considered preference income subject to corporate taxation (précompte) again, as in the French system?

If the imputation method is chosen, several additional problems must be addressed:

Should excess credits be refunded to both individual and corporate portfolio shareholders?

Should credits be allowed tax-exempt organizations, or would the answer depend on the nature of various organizations? (An analogous question in the case of the split-rate and dividend-paid deduction methods is whether integration should be joined with a tax on the dividends or investment income of such organizations.)

International Aspects

Though the provisions outlined in the first part of this chapter may seem complex to the reader accustomed to a classical system like that of the United States, dividend relief, using either the split-rate (or dividend-paid deduction) or the imputation method, would be relatively simple if there were no international capital flows.[45] The existence of foreign investment and the need to mesh the tax treatment accorded income from such investment (dividends paid to foreign shareholders or received from foreign firms) in various countries adds materially to the complexity of any proposal for dividend relief.

France

French shareholders can take advantage of the credit for the avoir fiscal only if French tax has in fact been paid at the corporate level. (The tax may be the ordinary corporate tax, the précompte, or the avoir fiscal or précompte passed through from a subsidiary.) Thus French portfolio investors in foreign corporations must pay the full French corporate or personal tax on foreign-source dividends, with no avoir fiscal credit.[46] Redistributions by corporate portfolio shareholders do, of course, carry the avoir fiscal.

45. The other principal problem in designing a system for dividend relief is in the treatment of tax preferences. That issue is discussed further in chapter 4; international aspects of integration and dividend relief are treated in chapter 6.

46. Under the basic French law shareholders are not allowed credit for foreign withholding taxes on dividends; thus the shareholder can take only a deduction for the withholding taxes paid to nontreaty countries. However, most tax treaties do provide for credit for withholding taxes.

As noted in the first section, France generally employs the territorial principle for corporations and therefore does not tax income earned abroad by corporations through either branches or foreign subsidiaries. Thus foreign-source income retained by the French firm is not subject to French tax. On the other hand, précompte is collected on foreign-source income that is distributed (or redistributed, in the case of a French parent of a foreign subsidary). Subsequent use of the imputation technique implies that net dividends paid from foreign-source income are taxed at marginal rates appropriate to the shareholder. But taken together, the foreign tax and the domestic tax usually exceed what would be paid on purely domestic income. In short, the foreign corporate tax is not integrated into the French personal income tax, because the latter is ignored in the imputation process. This is true whether dividends paid from foreign-source income are received directly from a foreign firm or are received indirectly through the subsidiary- (or branch-) parent route.

Dividends paid by French firms to foreign shareholders do not carry the benefit of the avoir fiscal, even if précompte has been paid, except as provided by treaty. France has, however, been quite willing to provide such benefits through bilateral treaties to certain residents of countries whose fiscal authorities are willing to affirm to the French administration that the dividends have been subject to tax in the country of residence of the shareholder.[47] Corporate portfolio in-

47. Organisation for Economic Co-operation and Development, *Company Tax Systems*, pp. 100–01, distinguishes three cases. First, if there is no treaty, shareholders receive dividends net of a 25 percent withholding tax collected on the dividends inclusive of the avoir fiscal. (Précompte is due on the dividends if they have not borne the full French tax, for example, because they are from foreign sources.) Thus 100 francs of earnings result in 25 francs of net dividends. Second, in countries having a treaty with France, but no protocol extending the avoir fiscal to their residents, the avoir fiscal credit cannot be claimed, but the withholding tax is reduced and sometimes waived and France refunds the précompte to the shareholder. Third, in the case of most countries having treaties that provide the French avoir fiscal credit to their residents, the shareholder receives from the French treasury an amount equal to the avoir fiscal minus a withholding tax of 15 percent. But the withholding tax is charged on the dividend grossed up by the amount of the avoir fiscal, so that it is 22.5 percent in the case of a shareholder residing in the United States. On balance, then, the shareholder who receives a cash dividend of 100 francs obtains a refund from the French treasury of 27.50 francs and credits the withholding tax of 22.50 francs against his personal tax liability in his country of residence. Though the mechanics of the treaty with West Germany differ somewhat from those described above, which are contained in most of the French treaties, the result is the same. Ibid., pp. 52–54.

vestors and individual investors are treated in the same way, but the avoir fiscal is not extended to foreign parents of French firms.[48]

Branches of foreign firms operating in France are treated substantially less generously. They are taxed on their income at the 50 percent rate, without benefit of avoir fiscal, and a 25 percent branch profits tax (a withholding tax) is levied on income after deduction of the corporate tax. The latter tax, equivalent to a withholding tax on dividends, is often reduced by treaty (for example, to 10 percent in the case of the United States), and it is refunded (at least in part) if it can be shown that income remitted abroad was less than the amount earned. The French taxes can, of course, be credited against domestic tax in the country of residence of the home office if that country provides such credits.

United Kingdom

The U.K. approach to the taxation of international flows of capital income is similar to the French. But unlike France, the United Kingdom employs a worldwide definition of income. Thus corporate shareholders in foreign affiliates, as well as individual and corporate portfolio investors, are taxable on dividends from abroad. British portfolio investors cannot take advantage of shareholder credits on foreign-source dividends, since no ACT has been paid on the dividends. Nor is the indirect foreign tax credit (for foreign corporate taxes) available to such investors, though the direct credit (for withholding taxes) is.[49]

British firms are taxed on the income of foreign branches and the dividends of foreign subsidiaries, but can take credit for certain foreign taxes paid. Credit can be taken for foreign withholding taxes and (in the case of parents of foreign subsidiaries) for foreign corporate income taxes.[50] But the foreign tax credit can be used only to offset the "mainstream" corporate income tax; that is, it cannot be used to offset the ACT. As a result, foreign tax credits are not passed through

48. Recall that a French parent firm would not pay tax on dividends in the analogous situation. See ibid., p. 101.

49. However, the ACT levied on redistributions by British firms cannot be reduced by credit for the foreign withholding tax.

50. In the British system the indirect credit for corporate tax goes down through as many tiers of corporate ownership as are linked by a 10 percent voting interest, so that in many cases the foreign tax credit substantially offsets liability for U.K. tax. See Hammer, "Taxation of Income," p. 333.

to shareholders, and thus are of benefit only in reducing the tax on retained earnings.

The advance corporation tax must be paid on all dividends of British firms, whether paid to domestic shareholders, foreign portfolio investors, or foreign parents of British firms. Though the last two groups are not automatically allowed shareholder credit for the ACT, they are no longer liable for any withholding tax on the dividends they receive. Moreover, in the draft double taxation treaty with the United States, the United Kingdom has agreed to essentially the same relief for foreign portfolio investors as the French treaties provide (credit for ACT minus 15 percent withholding tax on the dividends grossed up by the amount of the ACT credit). Finally, in the same treaty, the United Kingdom would grant that dividends paid by British subsidiaries to American parents would carry credit for one-half the ACT minus a 5 percent withholding tax on the grossed-up dividend. No other country has offered to extend the benefits of the imputation method to foreign direct investors.[51] As in France, branches of foreign firms operating in the United Kingdom are subject to the ordinary income tax, with no allowance for ACT credits.

Table 3-8 should help to clarify the tax treatment of foreign-source income in the United Kingdom.[52] Column 1 shows that if all net income is retained the corporation receives full benefit from the foreign tax credit; this is true regardless of the proportion of income represented by foreign income. A similar result occurs if, as in columns 2 and 3, foreign-source income, and hence foreign tax, is relatively small, even if, as in column 3 the dividend payout rate is high. But the British firm may be unable to take full advantage of foreign

51. See Harry G. Gourevitch, *Integration of Corporate and Shareholder Taxes on Income: The European Experience* (Library of Congress, Congressional Research Service, 1977), p. 85.

52. In the United Kingdom foreign-source income is included in the taxable income of a corporation, but a foreign tax credit is allowed, subject to limits described above. In France, on the other hand, foreign-source income is normally exempt from corporate tax. In West Germany the treatment of foreign-source income is mixed; such income can, as in France, be exempt (but usually only by treaty), or it can be taxed but carry a foreign tax credit, as in the United Kingdom. West Germany does not generally have treaties with other developed countries which allow exemption in both West Germany and the country of origin of income. But this is a useful device for providing tax-sparing for developing countries. If foreign-source income is exempt in France and West Germany, and carries no tax in the country of origin either, it really is preference income (judged relative to a norm based on taxation of worldwide income). In such a case the discussion of tables 3-3 and 3-4 is relevant.

Table 3-8. Tax Treatment of Foreign-Source Income under British System of Dividend Relief[a]

Monetary units

Item[b]	Low payout		100 percent payout	
	High foreign-source income (1)	*Low foreign-source income* (2)	*Low foreign-source income* (3)	*High foreign-source income* (4)
1. Corporate-source income	100	100	100	100
2. Foreign-source income	100	20	20	100
3. Foreign tax [50% of 2]	50	10	10	50
4. Dividends	0	40	50	33.3
5. Advance corporation tax [50% of 4]	0	20	25	16.7
6. Taxable corporate income [from 1]	100	100	100	100
7. Tentative corporate income tax [50% of 6]	50	50	50	50
8. Advance corporation tax [from 5]	0	20	25	16.7
9. Net mainstream tax [7 − 8]	50	30	25	33.3
10. Foreign tax credit [lesser of 3 and 9]	50	10	10	33.3
11. Net corporate tax liability [9 − 10]	0	20	15	0
12. Total domestic tax [5 + 11]	0	40	40	16.7
13. Total taxes [3 + 12]	50	50	50	66.7
14. Available for distribution [1 − 13]	50	50	50	33.3
15. Retained earnings [14 − 4]	50	10	0	0

a. Terms relating to integration systems are explained in the glossary. For convenience, a British corporate tax rate of 50 percent and a shareholder credit and advance corporation tax of 50 percent of dividends are employed, as in tables 3-3 through 3-5.

b. Except for percentages, the numbers in brackets refer to the lines of this table.

tax credits if it has substantial foreign-source income and distributes a high proportion of its income. Column 4 shows the extreme case in which income is entirely from foreign sources and the maximum dividends are paid. In such a case the credit for foreign taxes paid is limited to the amount of the mainstream tax (33.3 units or percent of pretax income in the present case, as in the case of complete distribution of preference income), so that the aggregate (domestic and foreign) tax burden substantially exceeds the domestic tax rate. Thus it is in the interest of the British firm with substantial foreign-source income and a high payout rate to have adequate domestic income to

assure that the foreign tax can be fully credited (as in column 2 or 3). As a result, the British tax treatment of foreign-source income encourages mergers and concentration of economic activity.[53]

West Germany (Present System)

Like France, West Germany sometimes exempts income earned abroad, but it does not extend the exemption to dividends on portfolio investment in foreign firms. Thus such dividends enter the tax base of both individuals and corporations making portfolio investments outside West Germany (but without gross-up). Individuals pay tax on the dividends, taking direct credit for withholding tax but not indirect credit for foreign corporate tax. In the case of corporate portfolio investors, the dividends, if retained, are taxed at the full rate of 56 percent. If they are redistributed the corporate rate is reduced to 36 percent and the shareholder takes credit for the corporate tax; thus, as in France, the shareholder's marginal tax rate applies to such dividends paid out of income net of foreign tax.

As noted earlier in the chapter, profits of foreign branches and dividends received by a West German parent from its foreign subsidiary are either tax exempt under a treaty or taxable and eligible for foreign tax credit against the West German tax. West Germany does not, however, recognize the foreign tax for purpose of assigning income to the various available net equity accounts; all foreign-source income is simply attributed to the account on which no German tax has been paid. Thus, if distributions are presumed to be made from this account, the 36 percent précompte must be paid. As in the French and British systems, foreign tax credits are useful only to the extent that earnings are not distributed (by the parent firm, in the case of affiliated companies). Therefore, to the extent that dividends are paid from foreign income (other than portfolio dividends), "integration" is incomplete.

And also as in the French and British systems, the dividend-received credit is automatically available only to domestic shareholders; thus the 36 percent tax collected on distributed earnings is a final tax so far as those dividends are paid to foreigners.[54] It seems

53. This raises the specter of "trafficking in excess ACT," similar to the problem of trafficking in losses. Of course, much the same problem exists under present law in the United States because of the existence of excess foreign tax credits and limitations on the investment tax credit.

54. In addition, net dividends are subject to a 25 percent withholding tax.

likely, however, that credit for the corporate tax will eventually be granted portfolio investors in countries that extend credit for their tax to West German portfolio investors (France being the only extant example), and if the British case is exemplary, the credit may even be made available to direct investors.

Canada

Canadian shareholders include dividends from foreign corporations in their taxable income. Individuals can take foreign tax credit for withholding taxes, up to a maximum of 15 percent, with any excess being deductible. The same treatment is accorded corporate shareholders, except that dividends from a controlled (more than 50 percent ownership) subsidiary resident in a country with which Canada has a treaty are exempt to the parent corporation. Even though income from foreign sources may not bear the full Canadian tax because of exemptions or foreign tax credits, Canada does not require any supplemental payment of tax, such as the précompte or advance corporation tax, when such income is distributed. Canada does, then, in a rough way, provide for the integration of its own personal income tax on dividends with foreign corporate taxes.

Dividends paid by Canadian corporations to foreign shareholders do not qualify for the shareholder credit. Although there seems to be no inclination in Canada to extend the credit to nonresidents, Canada is under tremendous pressure from the United States to extend the credit to U.S. investors and may be no more successful in resisting than France and the United Kingdom have been. Moreover, both dividends and branch profits of foreign firms are subject to a withholding tax of 25 percent unless the rate is reduced by treaty. Branch profits are also subject to the regular corporate tax before application of the branch profits tax.

As mentioned earlier, an important reason for providing dividend relief in Canada was to stimulate investment. Therefore, it may be more reasonable to appraise the Canadian system, with its anomalous treatment of tax preferences, on the basis of its contribution to investment than to judge it an inferior approach to integration. Seen in this light, the Canadian treatment of dividends paid to nonresidents also takes on a new complexion. Canada could afford even less than many countries the revenue loss that extending dividend relief to nonresidents would have entailed. But more to the point, given the purpose

of dividend relief in Canada, may be the question of whether it is desirable to encourage *all* investment in Canada or only investment by Canadians.

West Germany (Old System)

The split-rate system, providing relief from double taxation of dividends at the firm level, does not lend itself to the mitigation of double taxation on dividends received from abroad. Under the old West German system dividends on foreign portfolio investments were therefore taxed to the West German shareholder, whether corporate or individual, with direct credit for foreign withholding tax but no relief from the foreign corporate tax. Redistributed foreign-source income would, of course, qualify for the reduced rate of 15 percent.

West Germany did not extend the Schachtelprivileg to foreign-source dividends, except as provided by treaty. Dividends from foreign subsidiaries were therefore fully taxed as part of the income of the parent firm subject to the two-rate system, though the double tax burden would be reduced by foreign tax credit.

Dividends paid by West German firms were subject to only the reduced rate of corporate tax, whether paid to West German shareholders or to foreigners. In this sense, the benefits of dividend relief were extended automatically to foreign shareholders in West German firms. Dividends paid to foreign shareholders were, however, subject to withholding tax. This tax was levied at a rate of 15 percent on portfolio dividends. On dividends paid by West German subsidiaries to foreign parents the withholding rate was increased to 25 percent under some tax treaties (for example, the Franco-German treaty), provided the West German tax rate applied to retained earnings exceeded that applied to dividends by at least 20 percentage points. Under the treaty with the United States the tax rate would be raised to 25 percent if a U.S. parent corporation reinvested more than 7.5 percent of the dividend in the West German subsidiary. West German branches of foreign firms were subject to a 49 percent tax, whether profits were distributed or retained.

The Proposal of the Commission of the European Communities

It should be readily apparent from an examination of the tax systems of France, West Germany, and the United Kingdom that there are significant areas in which the various tax systems will not be

mutually consistent in their treatment of flows of income from foreign investment. The problem is accentuated when one considers the still further differences in the way other member nations of the European Community treat such income flows, and especially when one realizes that some countries (for example, the Netherlands and Luxembourg) do not provide relief from the double taxation of dividends. Thus, if a unified European capital market is to be achieved, as was envisaged by the Treaty of Rome, the tax systems of member countries must be harmonized. The latest effort in that direction is the proposal for a directive released by the Commission of the European Communities on August 1, 1975. The most important features of the draft directive that pertain to the international side of integration are reviewed here briefly.

Perhaps the key proposition of the draft directive is that dividend-received credits would be allowed the residents of any member state that received dividends from a corporation residing in any member state, provided the (grossed-up) dividends were included in the taxable income of the shareholder in his country of residence.[55] The credits would be based on (that is, would be 45 to 55 percent of) the tax prevailing in the country of residence of the corporation (which would be levied at a rate of 45 to 55 percent), and that country would bear the budgetary burden of the credits through a system of transfers to the countries of residence of shareholders.[56] Thus the current French practice of extending credits to nonresident shareholders would be made universal so far as international dividend flows within the member countries were concerned. The upshot would be that the country of residence of the corporation would retain roughly half of the corporate tax paid on income resulting in dividends. The other half of the tax on dividends would be credited to shareholders, who pay tax on partially grossed-up dividends on a residence basis, as part of their global income. Thus the country of residence of the corporation and the country of residence of the shareholder would split the tax proceeds attributable to such dividends. (The country of residence

55. Commission of the European Communities, "Proposal for a Council Directive," articles 4, 8. Article 6 provides for the optional extension of similar treatment to shareholders in nonmember countries.

56. Ibid., articles 8, 13. This approach differs from that of France in that article 5 provides that the shareholder would take the dividend credit on his tax return to his country of residence rather than deal with the fiscal authorities of the country of residence of the corporation, as in the present French system.

of the firm, if it were a member of the European Community, would rebate part of the tax it had collected on the dividends, including précompte, to the country of residence of the shareholder, to offset the credit given the shareholder.) On the other hand, income retained by the corporation would result in tax liability to the country of residence of the corporation.

The commission wanted the result to be the same whether an individual shareholder invested directly in a foreign corporation (the situation just described) or, indirectly, through an intermediary domestic corporation. If a domestic corporation received and redistributed dividends on portfolio investment in foreign firms, this result would occur naturally through the mechanism just described. In the case of direct investment made through a foreign subsidiary, article 10 of the draft directive formalized the arrangement. The parent corporation would include in income the dividend it received from the foreign subsidiary, grossed up by the amount of the dividend credit attached to the dividend. It would then take credit against its précompte arising from redistribution for the amount of the tax paid in the country of residence of the subsidiary.[57] As a result, the redistribution would carry the uniform credit attached to all dividends in the country of residence of the parent corporation. A similar approach would apply to branches; this would represent a break from present practice, which is to discriminate against branches.

To prevent evasion, a withholding tax of 25 percent would be collected on dividends, except those to parent firms and shareholders who were readily identifiable. This tax would be set off against the final liability of the shareholder, with transfers of funds between fiscal authorities similar to those for the dividend-received credits.[58]

Appraisal

The systems already existing in other countries provide the United States with patterns for possible ways to treat flows of capital income across national borders, especially under an imputation system. Moreover, though the proposed directive for the European Community has not been approved, it provides a starting point for discus-

57. There is, however, an exception to this rule. If the tax rate in the country of residence of the subsidiary exceeded that of the country of residence of the parent, the excess would not be refundable. Ibid., article 10.

58. Ibid., articles 14, 16, 17.

sion in future negotiations of tax treaties if the United States should opt for an imputation system. And if the draft directive is eventually adopted in Europe, its provisions will condition any U.S. decisions made under—and, indeed, for—split-rate, dividend-paid deduction, or full integration systems. But because it would allow the elimination of only about half the double taxation of dividends, whereas West Germany currently provides complete dividend relief, the draft directive may not be quickly ratified.

Reasons for European Practices

In chapter 2 I gave the apparent reasons for European and Canadian decisions to provide dividend relief. Here I look into why certain forms of dividend relief have been chosen instead of others and why particular detailed provisions have been adopted. In many cases it can be seen that objectives in the taxation of international flows of capital income were paramount.

France

France originally wanted to deny the benefits of dividend relief to foreign investors, in order to forestall foreign takeover of French firms, hold down revenue costs, limit the benefits of those costs to Frenchmen, and prevent benefits from being enjoyed by Frenchmen who evaded French taxes through the use of foreign nominee accounts. This provided much of the motivation for adoption of the imputation method rather than the split-rate system.[59] It came to be felt, however, that the anticipated salutary effects on stock prices were disappointing, perhaps because the imputation system seemed

59. Additional reasons were concern that shareholders might not benefit from dividend relief, since dividends might not be increased in response to relief provided by the split rate, and the perceived administrative difficulty of applying the split rate to distributions out of previous years' earnings. See Organisation for Economic Co-operation and Development, *Company Tax Systems,* p. 47, and Gourevitch, *Integration of Corporate and Shareholder Taxes,* p. 55. The generally accepted problem that occurs when dividends exceed current income arises because it is not enough merely to apply the lower rate to dividends. Since dividends are being paid from income that has already been subject to the higher rate on retentions, it would be necessary to allow credit for the tax that had previously been paid at the time of retention.

to discriminate against foreign investors.[60] In 1969, therefore, France began to extend dividend relief to foreign investors through bilateral treaties, provided only that it had certification of payment of tax on the grossed-up dividend in the shareholder's country of residence.

West Germany

In West Germany several characteristics of the split-rate system resulted in its being replaced in part by the imputation system. These largely involve the taxation of flows of income crossing borders, since except for tax-exempt organizations and foreign shareholders, the choice between a split-rate and an imputation system is of little consequence. First, under certain conditions the earnings of a foreign-owned subsidiary that were reinvested in West Germany could be taxed more favorably than income earned and retained by a West German firm or group of firms. This Auslaendereffekt occurs because the earnings of the foreign-owned subsidiary, net of the 23.4 percent tax on distributed earnings, would be subject to only a 25 percent withholding tax rather than the 36 percent Nachsteuer paid on retentions by West German parent firms. Thus the total West German tax on the earnings of the foreign-owned firm that were reinvested in West Germany would be only 42.6 percent, as compared to the 51 percent tax collected on retained earnings from the West German firm or group of firms.[61] This problem is easily avoided under the imputation method since all retentions are subject to the same tax.

Second, even apart from the problem just described, the split-rate

60. The performance of the French stock market is reviewed in Organisation for Economic Co-operation and Development, *Company Tax Systems,* pp. 48–49, and that of markets in both France and the United Kingdom is examined in Jacobus T. Severiens, "The Imputation Tax System: A Re-appraisal," *Bulletin for International Fiscal Documentation,* vol. 30 (April 1976), pp. 143–49. The effect of dividend relief cannot be measured, because other things were changing and some of the benefits of dividend relief may have been discounted before it was enacted. Note, for example, that the French system came in just as taxes on fixed-interest securities were being reduced and that the British system was implemented only months before the Arab oil embargo and the imposition of limitations on dividend policy.

61. See Dieter Biehl and Karl-Heinz Jüttemeier, "German Experience with an Integrated Corporate Shareholder Tax System," prepared for the U.S. Department of the Treasury, Office of Tax Analysis (Kiel: January 1976), p. 9. The 23.4 percent tax rate includes the "shadow effect" mentioned in note 38, but not the 3 percent supplementary rate. Moreover, the 25 percent withholding tax is applied to the 76.6 percent of retentions that remains after the 23.4 percent tax on retentions, whereas, of course, the 36 percent Nachsteuer is added to the 15 percent tax. See also chapter 5.

system extends what may be considered an undesirable degree of benefit to foreign investors in shares of West German firms. This occurs because a uniform tax rate is applied to all dividends, whether received by residents or nonresidents. In theory, so far as concerns foreign investors, it would be possible to offset the relief inherent in the lower rate on dividends by raising the withholding tax applied to dividends paid abroad. But the United States has generally been unwilling to countenance such a practice in its tax treaty negotiations. Instead, it has traditionally demanded mirror-image reciprocity in the withholding taxation of dividends, regardless of whether it is dealing with a country using the classical system, the imputation method of dividend relief, or the split-rate system.[62]

United Kingdom

When the United Kingdom decided to return from the classical system used from 1965 to 1973 to a system of dividend relief, it had three basic alternatives: the pre-1965 system in which gross-up and credit were based on the statutory tax rate, regardless of the effective tax rate actually paid; the imputation system actually adopted, in which gross-up and credit is given only for British taxes actually paid; and the split-rate system. Many business groups favored the pre-1965 approach, which did not require the payment of the advance corporation tax, because it would be more favorable to foreign invest-

62. A clear statement of this policy is contained in Stanley S. Surrey, "The United States Tax System and International Tax Relationships," *Canadian Tax Journal,* vol. 12 (November–December 1964), p. 463:

The United States has found itself in the position of being asked to agree to a treaty provision under which our withholding rate on dividends to a particular country would be less than the rate levied by that country on dividends moving to the United States. We have in these cases—in order to protect our investors from an increased level of foreign taxation and to protect the United States from revenue loss under the foreign tax credit— taken the firm position that international withholding rates should be reciprocal and hence we cannot agree to an upward adjustment by other countries to accommodate to their internal tax policies.

This statement, also quoted in Gourevitch, *Integration of Corporate and Shareholder Taxes,* p. 66n, was made while Surrey was assistant secretary of the treasury. More recently, in negotiations with less-developed countries, the United States has relaxed its demands for reciprocity.

Although the United States did consent to an increase in the West German withholding rate to 25 percent in those instances in which at least 7.5 percent of dividends are immediately reinvested, the more common provision of West German treaties has been to allow a 25 percent withholding rate if there is at least a 20 percent difference in the rates applied to dividends and retentions. This helps to explain the retention of the split rate in the present imputation system.

ment and would be less likely to encourage merger than the system actually adopted.[63] This approach was opposed by the Inland Revenue because it would subsidize foreign operations, it could result in loss of national income, and it would involve credit for taxes not paid to the British treasury. When this position prevailed, the Inland Revenue then favored the split-rate system, arguing that it was less subject to erosion than the imputation method, since it retained a firm demarcation between the firm and the shareholder.[64] Nonetheless, the imputation method was adopted, in large part so that the United Kingdom would be in a better position to renegotiate its double tax treaty with the United States. Specific reference was made to the West German inability to negotiate a treaty with the United States that recognized the basic difference in the corporate tax in a classical system and in a system that provides dividend relief.[65]

Appraisal

There seems to be general agreement that the dividend-paid deduction or split-rate system would be somewhat easier to implement than, and therefore preferable to, the imputation system if only domestic considerations were taken into account. And even international capital flows need not necessarily reverse that choice, provided that all countries took a fairly flexible position on withholding rates in tax treaties between countries using various (classical, imputation, and split-rate or dividend-paid deduction) systems of company taxation. But given the historical U.S. unwillingness to allow foreign withholding rates to be higher than those levied in the United States—even if the foreign country used the split-rate system—any country considering dividend relief may have effectively been forced to adopt the imputation method. Now, since the leading European countries have done so, the United States may find its choice in this

63. This discussion is based on Sato and Bird, "International Aspects," pp. 432–36. As explained in greater detail earlier, the present system can encourage mergers because of the need to have fully taxed domestic income from which to pay dividends if a substantial amount of income is from foreign sources and therefore subject to nonrefundable ACT if distributed. The same point is made in discussion of the new West German system in Ault, "Germany," p. 271.

64. The feared erosion was in the ACT; it was feared that the tax would be changed so that ACT would not always be collected on dividends paid from foreign income (or would be offset by credit for foreign taxes paid).

65. See Gourevitch, *Integration of Corporate and Shareholder Taxes,* pp. 56–61, and Sato and Bird, "International Aspects," pp. 434–35.

area effectively foreclosed.[66] Unless it is willing to adopt the dividend-paid deduction (or split rate) and face a fairly likely turning of the tables of reciprocity, there may be little alternative but to scratch from the agenda the dividend-paid deduction (and the split rate).

A final aspect of the European choice that is worth noting because it may be relevant for U.S. policy is the public reaction to dividend relief provided under the imputation method. In a 1970 television debate it was noted that in 1968 a married French worker with two children receiving an annual income of 50,000 francs would pay taxes of almost 5,000 francs, whereas the same amount received entirely as dividends would entitle the taxpayer to a refund of individual income tax of almost 2,600 francs, because of the avoir fiscal credit. Moreover, in 1971 a French newspaper showed that Jacques Chaban-Delmas, then prime minister, had paid no income tax (and in fact had received a small refund) in 1967 when he was president of the National Assembly, in part because of the avoir fiscal credit on dividend income. Of course, in the case of both the hypothetical shareholder and Chaban-Delmas a refund rather than a net liability occurs because, under the imputation method, tax on dividends received is deemed to have been withheld at the corporate level. But the intellectual power of the conduit view and other arguments for integration notwithstanding, the public may find it unfair that there should appear to be little or no (or even negative) personal tax liability on dividends received. That West German politicians found the Chaban-Delmas affair instructive has been alleged to be one of the reasons for the retention of the split rate under the new German system; with part of the dividend relief occurring at the corporate level it is less likely that dividend relief would result in high-income shareholders paying no taxes or receiving refunds.[67] Of course, under the extreme version of this reasoning, the traditional split rate or dividend-paid deduction would be the vehicle of dividend relief. Though the issue would then be joined at the corporate level, the appearance might be politically less unfavorable to dividend relief.

66. This presumption would have been even stronger had the directive proposed by the Commission of the European Communities on harmonization of company taxes been adopted.

67. The above discussion is taken from Gourevitch, *Integration of Corporate and Shareholder Taxes*, pp. 86–90. The analogous problem in the context of the proposal of the Canadian Royal Commission on Taxation is discussed by Gourevitch in ibid., pp. 45–46.

Treatment of Tax Preferences

WHEN Secretary of the Treasury William E. Simon proposed in July 1975 that the United States introduce a system for the complete relief from double taxation of dividends, an outcry was raised against what some took to be the inequity of the approach proposed. Besides objecting that dividend relief, rather than full integration, had been suggested, critics of the Simon proposal found fault with its use of the statutory corporate rate in calculating the amount of dividend relief. The proposal would, in the words of Gerard Brannon, produce "a bonanza for the wealthy stockholder."[1] Since tax preferences create strong emotions in a classical system and are perhaps even more controversial in a world of integration or dividend relief, their treatment must be examined at length.[2]

1. Gerard M. Brannon, "Dividend Relief and Tax Reform," *Tax Notes,* vol. 3 (August 11, 1975), p. 4. (The Simon proposal is cited in chap. 1, n. 1.)

2. For an excellent discussion of the issues and administrative difficulties in the area of tax preferences, see Alvin C. Warren, Jr., "Integration of the Individual and Corporate Income Taxes," paper presented to an American Law Institute–American Bar Association Conference on Federal Income Tax Simplification, Warrenton, Virginia, January 1978 (forthcoming in proceedings volume to be published by ALI), and comments on that paper by Richard S. Koffey. Little other literature exists on this subject in the United States, but see also chapter 3 and references cited there.

A Working Definition of Preferences

Though tax preferences must be defined explicitly and in detail if any adjustment is to be made for them in a scheme for integration or dividend relief, a relatively simple and crude conceptual definition will suffice here. In a classical system, a tax preference is any provision that reduces the corporate tax to below what it would be if the standard tax rate were applied to economic income; thus preferences can be (1) provisions that reduce taxable income by exclusions from taxable income or deductions in excess of what is required to define economic income; (2) preferential rates applied to certain forms or amounts of income; and (3) credits that reduce tax liability even when standard rates are applied to economic income. Some preferences reverse over time and hence involve just postponement of tax liability rather than outright reduction of liability;[3] the initial excess and subsequent shortfall of actual depreciation allowances over economic depreciation that occurs under accelerated depreciation is the prime example of such a reversible preference.

Examples of the first type of preference, which is hereafter called a *deductible preference,* are the exclusion of interest on state and local securities from taxable income and the excess of percentage depletion over cost depletion. The 28 percent alternative rate on long-term capital gains and the exemption of the first $100,000 of income from the corporate surcharge rate are the best examples of the second category of preference. The investment tax credit is the prime example of the last type—the *creditable preference.* (Another example is the employment credit. The foreign tax credit is excluded from consideration until chapter 6.)

The first and third types of tax preference can be defined analogously under an integrated system.[4] The first would reduce the corporate *income* attributed to shareholders and the third would re-

3. From an economic point of view postponement and exemption can be equivalent. But they may be handled in different ways administratively.

4. The statements in the rest of this paragraph are most easily interpreted in the context of full integration. If integration is less than complete, either because it does not apply to retained earnings or because it is applied to less than 100 percent of total earnings, the statements in the text pertain only to the "integrated" part of corporate earnings. So far as the taxes are unintegrated, preferences are defined as in a classical system.

duce the *tax* paid by the shareholder on a given amount of taxable corporate-source income. The second type of preference has no ready counterpart in an integrated system, since it pertains inherently to a classical system. This issue is considered further below; for now the application of the 28 percent maximum rate to corporate long-term capital gains is treated as equivalent to an exclusion of $(18/46=)$ 39.1 percent of such gains from income for tax purposes.

Having thus defined tax preferences, I can now define two more concepts. A tax preference is *passed through* to shareholders in a full integration scheme when it reduces tax liability at the personal level as much as if the shareholders had invested directly in the activity benefiting from the tax preference; for example, through a partnership or proprietorship. On the other hand, the corporate tax preference is *washed out* when the income from an activity that would be tax-preferred in the noncorporate sector is taxed as ordinary income to the shareholders, without benefit of preference. Under dividend relief the corporate income tax retains its separate existence so far as retained earnings are concerned; thus the analogous definitions in a world of dividend relief are more complicated than under integration.

Pass-through and washout are easily illustrated by a numerical example.[5] Suppose that three taxpayers who receive noncorporate income of 100 have marginal tax rates of 0, 20 percent, and 60 percent, as indicated in table 4-1. *Deductible preferences* of 20 would reduce the tax liabilities of the three by 0, 4, and 12, respectively, but a *creditable preference* of 4 would produce a tax reduction of 4 for each taxpayer, independently of his marginal tax bracket.[6] Thus the total tax saving from combining the two preferences would be 4, 8, and 16 for the three taxpayers, and total income tax collected on 100 of economic income benefiting from these two preferences would be minus 4, 12, and 44, rather than 0, 20, and 60. An integrated system that reproduced this pattern of tax rates could be said to involve pass-

5. Much of the discussion in the rest of the chapter is adapted from, and builds upon, Charles E. McLure, Jr., "Integration of the Income Taxes: Why and How," *Journal of Corporate Taxation,* vol. 2 (Winter 1976), pp. 445–47 and 458–62.

6. These examples are based on the assumption that credits result in refunds if the taxpayer owes too little tax to absorb the full credit. Complications created by limitations on admissible credits are ignored in the interest of simplicity. Such complications could not, however, be ignored if preferences and limitations were retained.

Table 4-1. Treatment of Tax Preferences in Computing Tax Liability in the Noncorporate Sector, by Selected Marginal Personal Tax Rates[a]

Monetary units

Item[b]	Marginal personal tax rate (*percent*)		
	0	*20*	*60*
1. Economic income	100	100	100
2. Deductible preference income	20	20	20
3. Taxable income [1 − 2]	80	80	80
4. Gross tax liability [marginal personal tax rate × 3]	0	16	48
5. Creditable preferences	4	4	4
6. Net personal tax liability [4 − 5]	−4	12	44
7. Total value of tax preferences [(marginal personal tax rate × 1) − 6]	4	8	16
Due to deductible preferences [marginal personal tax rate × 2]	0	4	12
Due to creditable preferences [from 5]	4	4	4

a. Deductible and creditable preferences are explained in the text.
b. The numbers in brackets refer to the lines of this table.

through of preferences. On the other hand, the preferences would be washed out in a fully integrated system if the shareholder paid his full statutory marginal rate on corporate-source economic income.

Full Integration

A tendency exists to believe that pass-through of preferences would be achieved if one simply allowed gross-up and credit by using the statutory corporate tax rate.[7] This is not true, however— use of the statutory rate can involve going well beyond pass-through rather than just reducing taxation to the level shown in table 4-1.

An example may help to clarify this. Suppose that for each 100 of economic income the corporation has the tax preferences assumed in table 4-1. Thus, if the statutory corporate rate is 50 percent, the

7. Break and Pechman, in referring to the tax preference problem under the imputation method, state: "If the undertaxation of certain corporate profits is viewed as an incentive measure whose effects should be passed through to the stockholders, a full tax credit at the nominal corporate tax rate is the appropriate solution." George F. Break and Joseph A. Pechman, *Federal Tax Reform: The Impossible Dream?* (Brookings Institution, 1975), p. 99. Use of the statutory rate does not exactly pass preferences through under either full integration or dividend relief.

Table 4-2. Illustration of Full Integration, Using Statutory Tax Rate in Presence of Tax Preferences[a]

Monetary units

Item[b]	Marginal personal tax rate of shareholder (percent)		
	0	*20*	*60*
1. Corporate-source economic income	100	100	100
2. Deductible preference income[c]	20	20	20
3. Taxable income [1 − 2]	80	80	80
4. Gross corporate income tax [50% of 3]	40	40	40
5. Creditable preferences[c]	4	4	4
6. Net corporate income tax [4 − 5]	36	36	36
7. After-tax income [1 − 6]	64	64	64
8. Gross-up and credit [from 7]	64	64	64
9. Grossed-up corporate-source income [7 + 8]	128	128	128
10. Gross personal income tax [marginal personal tax rate × 9]	0	25.6	76.8
11. Credit [from 8]	64	64	64
12. Total taxes [6 + 10 − 11]	−28	−2.4	48.8
13. Value of tax preferences [(marginal personal tax rate × 1) − 12]	28	22.4	11.2
14. Value of noncorporate tax preferences (from table 4-1)	4	8	16

a. Terms relating to integration systems are explained in the glossary.
b. Except for percentages, the numbers in brackets refer to the lines of this table.
c. Preferences assumed are those in table 4-1.

firm's tax liability is 36 and its after-tax income is 64 (per 100 of gross income). Using the 50 percent statutory tax rate to gross up the 64 of corporate earnings would produce personal tax liabilities after credit that, when compared to the effective rates reported in table 4-1, are too low at the bottom of the income scale and too high at the top, as shown in table 4-2.

Complete Pass-Through of Preferences

How, then, can exact pass-through be achieved? Table 4-3, which is based on the same assumptions about preferences as tables 4-1 and 4-2, helps to answer that question. The gross-up must include the corporate income tax actually paid, as if there were no tax preferences. But deductible preferences must be subtracted from the amount of the tax in computing the gross-up if they are to pass through in exact amount to shareholders. Thus in the example in

Table 4-3. Illustration of Complete Pass-Through of Tax Preferences under Full Integration[a]

Monetary units

	Marginal personal tax rate of shareholder (*percent*)		
Item[b]	*0*	*20*	*60*
1. Corporate-source economic income	100	100	100
2. Deductible preference income[c]	20	20	20
3. Taxable income [1 − 2]	80	80	80
4. Gross corporate income tax [50% of 3]	40	40	40
5. Creditable preferences[c]	4	4	4
6. Net corporate income tax [4 − 5]	36	36	36
7. Net corporate income [1 − 6]	64	64	64
8. Gross-up [6 − 2]	16	16	16
9. Grossed-up corporate-source income [7 + 8]	80	80	80
10. Gross personal tax liability [marginal personal tax rate × 9]	0	16	48
11. Shareholder credit [6 + 5]	40	40	40
12. Net personal tax liability [10 − 11]	−40	−24	8
13. Total taxes [6 + 12]	−4	12	44
14. Value of tax preferences [(marginal personal tax rate × 1) − 13]	4	8	16

a. Terms relating to integration systems are explained in the glossary.
b. Except for percentages, the numbers in brackets refer to the lines of this table.
c. Preferences assumed are those in table 4-1.

table 4-3, the gross-up is only 16 (36−20), and grossed-up income is 80. If this figure is taxed as income to the shareholder, the gross tax liabilities shown in line 10 of table 4-3 result. Now the shareholder takes credit for the sum of the corporate income tax (36) and the creditable preferences (4), or for 40. Since this credit reduces the total amount of tax paid at the corporate and shareholder levels to exactly the figures in line 6 of table 4-1, exact pass-through of preferences is achieved.

One of the reasons Europeans favor the précompte or the advance corporation tax is that it allows the shareholder to use a standard gross-up rate. (In France, for example, the gross-up and credit equals 50 percent of cash dividends received.) This might be called the *uniform gross-up approach.* In the absence of the précompte or ACT the shareholder would sometimes be required to apply a *variable gross-up* if the same end result were to be achieved; that is, the firm would report to the shareholder both cash dividends and a frac-

tion to use in calculating the gross-up and credit.[8] Alternatively, the firm could make the requisite calculations of the appropriate amounts for shareholders to use in grossing up dividends and report that to the shareholder, much as employers report income tax withheld on wages.

It should be apparent from table 4-3 that the uniform gross-up cannot be applied directly to total net corporate income if tax preferences are to be passed through to shareholders, because (1) the amount by which income must be grossed up (for a given effective rate at the corporate level) depends on the split between deductible and creditable preferences, and (2) the same amount is not generally used in grossing up income and taking the credit at the shareholder level.[9] Thus, if pass-through is desired, there is no alternative to having the firm make the necessary calculations and provide information to shareholders.

But in a system of full integration this requirement would cause few problems beyond those discussed in chapter 5. Inherent to integration is the notion that various kinds of income flows should retain their identities in the hands of shareholders. This being the case, the corporation described in table 4-3 would report to shareholders gross taxable income of 80, exempt income (or deductions from gross income) of 20, and credits of 4, over and above any withholding tax collected at the corporate level (36 in this example). Thus the shareholder would automatically enter taxable income of 80 and tax

8. Note that the use of either variable gross-up rates or a précompte system could create new requirements for financial disclosure.

9. The reader may find it instructive to compare the case in tables 4-1 and 4-3 with alternatives in which the same effective corporate rate (36 percent) is produced through (1) a deduction of 28 (and no credits), or (2) a credit of 14 (and no deductions). The implications of pass-through are, of course, quite different. In table 4-3, the gross-up is 16 (the corporate tax minus the deductible preferences), while the shareholder credit is 40 (the sum of the corporate income tax and the creditable preferences). In the first alternative case the gross-up would be 8, but the credit would be 36, while in the second case the gross-up would be 36 and the credit 50. More generally, the appropriate amount of gross-up to assure pass-through can be expressed as $G = T - D$, where G is the amount of gross-up, T is the net corporate tax liability, and D is the deductible preferences. Similarly, the proper shareholder credit, or credits, is $S = T + C$, where C is creditable preferences. The gross-up equals the shareholder credit (that is, $G = S$) if and only if (1) there are no preferences, or (2) one component of the preferences is negative, but equal in magnitude to the other (so that $D + C = 0$). Though the second possibility is of some theoretical interest, its practical relevance is limited.

credits of 40 on his tax return and the desired result would be achieved.[10]

An implication of the above analysis is that more attention would need to be paid to the structure of preferences under an integrated system than under the classical system. Under the latter, if one ignores the relatively small number of preference items appearing on returns for unincorporated businesses and subchapter S corporations, preferences structured as deductions have largely the same effects as those structured as credits; that is, if the statutory rate of 46 percent applies, a deduction of $100 is essentially equivalent to a credit of $46.[11] But under full integration tax deductions that were passed through would carry a value (in terms of taxes avoided) that depended on the marginal tax rates of shareholders, whereas credits are equally valuable to all shareholders.[12]

Washout of Preferences

The easiest way to wash out preferences in a fully integrated system is, of course, not to allow them to the corporate sector in the first place. If there were no deductible preferences in the calculation of corporate income, economic income would be attributed to shareholders and included in their taxable income. Then, if there were no creditable preferences, no further adjustments would be needed at the shareholder level to assure that the preferences were not available

10. For an elegant explanation of how this technique can be used so that both creditable and deductible preferences can be passed through under a system of dividend relief, see Frederic W. Hickman's testimony in *The President's 1978 Tax Reduction and Reform Proposals,* Hearings before the House Committee on Ways and Means, 95 Cong. 2 sess. (Government Printing Office, 1978), pt. 6, pp. 3465–3503. Carl Shoup in a personal communication suggested a similar approach.

11. The existence of the exemption from the corporate surtax rate does not greatly affect this conclusion, which involves the equivalence of credits and deductions for a given corporation rather than uniformity of rates across firms. Of course, though credits are equally valuable to all firms, deductions are worth most to firms subject to the 46 percent marginal rate. Finally, as a practical matter, credits and deductions differ in the extent to which they are limited in both amount and carryover privileges; this complication is ignored for now.

12. One might therefore expect a tendency for corporations with substantial deductible preferences to be owned largely by high-income shareholders and those with primarily creditable preferences to be particularly attractive to low-income shareholders and tax-exempt ones (provided, in the last case, that tax-exempt shareholders were allowed the benefits of integration, including pass-through of preferences).

Table 4-4. Illustration of Use of Effective Tax Rate for Gross-up and Credit to Wash Out Tax Preferences under Full Integration[a]

Monetary units

Item[b]	Marginal personal tax rate of shareholder (percent)		
	0	20	60
1. Corporate-source economic income	100	100	100
2. Deductible preference income[c]	20	20	20
3. Taxable income [1 − 2]	80	80	80
4. Gross corporate income tax [50% of 3]	40	40	40
5. Creditable preferences[c]	4	4	4
6. Net corporate income tax [4 − 5]	36	36	36
7. Net corporate income [1 − 6]	64	64	64
8. Gross-up [from 6]	36	36	36
9. Grossed-up corporate-source income [7 + 8]	100	100	100
10. Gross personal tax liability [marginal personal tax rate × 9]	0	20	60
11. Credit [from 8]	36	36	36
12. Net personal tax liability [10 − 11]	−36	−16	24
13. Total taxes [6 + 12]	0	20	60
14. Value of tax preferences [(marginal personal tax rate × 1) − 13]	0	0	0

a. Terms relating to integration systems are explained in the glossary.
b. Except for percentages, the numbers in brackets refer to the lines of this table.
c. Preferences assumed are those in table 4-1.

to the shareholder. Though this is clear enough if integration is complete, it becomes less clear if integration is either incomplete or limited to dividends, or if preferences are to be passed through on retained earnings but not on dividends. It will therefore be convenient for purposes of discussion to have an alternative, if somewhat artificial, means of washing out corporate tax preferences under full integration. Table 4-4 provides such an alternative: it uses the effective corporate rate, rather than the statutory rate, to gross up corporate-source income. In each marginal tax bracket, grossed-up corporate-source income is taxed at the marginal tax rate of shareholders, despite the existence of preferences at the corporate level.[13]

13. An alternative and even more artificial approach would be, of course, to use a précompte procedure similar to that in the French system. Thus in the example of table 4-4 the précompte would be 14, bringing up both the total tax paid at the corporate level and the shareholder gross-up and credit to the statutory rate of 50 percent. In either event, the grossed-up corporate-source income would be 100 and the credit would offset the corporate tax.

Partial Pass-Through of Preferences

It might be decided, for any number of reasons (revenue considerations being the most obvious), that pass-through should be allowed but should not be complete. Conceptually this is easily accomplished if one calculates the gross-up by using the corporate tax liability minus only some fraction of deductible preferences or calculates the shareholder credit by adding only some fraction of creditable preferences to corporate tax liability.[14] Table 4-5 illustrates *partial pass-through* for the shareholder in the 60 percent marginal tax bracket under full and under 50 percent integration. It is readily seen that 50 percent pass-through produces a result midway between that for zero pass-through (washing out preferences) and that for complete pass-through, regardless of the extent of integration.[15]

Though it is easy enough to understand the concept of partial pass-through of preferences, it is difficult to see how such a concept fits into the overall scheme of integration based on the conduit view of the corporation. If, for example, interest on state and local securities is tax exempt to individuals (as a constitutional datum, in the opinion of some), what sense does it make to allow only a partial exemption for such interest when it is received through a corporation? Similar comments can be made about the investment tax credit, accelerated

14. In the terminology of note 9, one has $G = T - dD$ and $S = T + cC$, in which d and c, the pass-through ratios for deductions and credits, respectively, are fractions between zero and one. The complete washout of preferences is, of course, the special case in which c and d are both zero. (There is no theoretical reason why the pass-through ratios should be bounded on either the top or the bottom. But the extension to "negative" and "over" pass-through is obvious and beyond the scope of this book.)

15. In the formulas in note 14, T would be replaced by iT ($0 \leqq i \leqq 1$) to allow for partial integration. It may be instructive to note that 50 percent integration produces an aggregate tax burden in the zero pass-through case (67.2 percent) that lies halfway between the tax burden on dividends in the classical case (74.4 percent) and that in the 100 percent integration, zero pass-through case (60 percent). From these benchmarks of 60 and 67.2 percent, various degrees of pass-through reduce the aggregate tax burdens by some percentage of 16 (in the present case). Another set of columns could be added for zero integration (defined implicitly in the appendix to chapter 1 as allocation of retentions without shareholder gross-up and credit). In such a case the tax preferences would have the same values as in line 15 for given degrees of pass-through. Under an alternative definition, the right-hand side of the formulas in the previous footnote would be multiplied by j, the degree of integration. In such a case the last three entries in line 15 would be 0, 4, and 8, and preferences would be valueless in the zero integration case.

Table 4-5. Calculations for Alternative Degrees of Integration and of Pass-Through of Tax Preferences for Taxpayer in 60 Percent Marginal Personal Tax Bracket[a]

Degrees of pass-through in percent; other data in monetary units

Item[b]	Total integration			50 percent integration[c]		
1. Degree of pass-through[d]	0	50	100	0	50	100
2. Corporate-source economic income	100	100	100	100	100	100
3. Deductible preference income[e]	20	20	20	20	20	20
4. Taxable income [2 − 3]	80	80	80	80	80	80
5. Gross corporate income tax [50% of 4]	40	40	40	40	40	40
6. Creditable preferences[e]	4	4	4	4	4	4
7. Net corporate income tax [5 − 6]	36	36	36	36	36	36
8. Net corporate income [2 − 7]	64	64	64	64	64	64
9. Gross-up[f]	36	26	16	18	8	−2
10. Grossed-up corporate-source income [8 + 9]	100	90	80	82	72	62
11. Gross personal tax liability [60% of 10]	60	54	48	49.2	43.2	37.2
12. Credit[g]	36	38	40	18	20	22
13. Net personal tax liability [11 − 12]	24	16	8	31.2	23.2	15.2
14. Total taxes [7 + 13]	60	52	44	67.2	59.2	51.2
15. Value of tax preferences[h]	0	8	16	0	8	16

a. Terms relating to integration systems are explained in the glossary.

b. Except for percentages, the numbers in brackets refer to the lines of this table.

c. See the appendix to chapter 1 for a discussion of partial integration and note 14 for a discussion of degrees of integration and pass-through.

d. Assumes that the pass-through ratio for deductions equals the pass-through ratio for credits.

e. Preferences assumed are those in table 4-1.

f. Calculated from $(iT - dD)$, where $i = 1.0$ for total integration and 0.5 for 50 percent integration, T is net corporate income tax, D is deductible preferences, and d is percentage pass-through of deductions (see text notes 14 and 15).

g. Calculated from $(iT + cC)$, where C is creditable preferences, c is percentage pass-through of credits, and other symbols are as in note f.

h. Total tax in absence of preferences minus line 14. Total tax is 60 percent for full integration and 67.2 percent for 50 percent integration in the absence of preferences.

depreciation, and other preferences. Partial pass-through simply makes very little sense under full integration. If, however, only dividend relief is being considered, partial pass-through is somewhat more attractive (and the issue must be faced head-on, in any event).

A final complication under 100 percent integration would arise if, for whatever reason, it were desired that tax preferences be passed through only to the extent that corporate-source income was retained. It might be thought, for example, that excess depletion allowances and the investment tax credit should be passed through only on retained income and washed out on distributed income. Table 4-6 illus-

trates such a case.[16] For purposes of this table it is assumed that one-fourth of net corporate income is distributed and the other three-fourths is retained and that preferences are allocated between distributed and retained earnings in the same proportion.[17] Thus the gross-up applied to distributed earnings is 9, or 25 percent of the figure in table 4-4, where preferences are entirely washed out, and gross-up applied to retentions is 75 percent of that in table 4-3, which illustrates complete pass-through of preferences. The aggregate value of preferences in table 4-6 is only 75 percent of the figures in tables 4-1 and 4-3, as must happen if preferences are passed through on only the 75 percent of income that is retained. Of course, if the assumed distribution and retention rates had been reversed (or if it had been assumed that preferences should be available only for distributed earnings), the value of preferences would have been only 25 percent as great as in the benchmark case. The availability of pass-through only for retained (or for distributed) earnings would be expected to affect dividend payout rates.

Use of the précompte procedure and a uniform gross-up to wash out tax preferences on distributed corporate-source income is quite unworkable so long as preferences are to be passed through on retained earnings. In the example of table 4-6 it would be a simple matter to use a précompte of 3.5 on distributed earnings to bring the effective corporate rate on that part of income up to the statutory rate of 50 percent. But, as shown above, if tax preferences are to be passed through, the gross-up cannot equal the credit. Thus it is not possible to use the précompte procedure and a uniform gross-up for the retained part of the corporate earnings—and therefore not possible for the entire amount of corporate-source income. If the policy illustrated in table 4-6 is to be implemented, the variable gross-up

16. The distributed and retained columns in table 4-6 are included to assist the reader in seeing how the firm would calculate the amounts of gross-up and credit to report to shareholders; only the combined figures shown in the total column would actually be communicated to shareholders under the variable gross-up system.

17. The possibility of alternative rules for the allocation of preferences between distributions and retentions is discussed below. Once the purist view of integration were abandoned, as would be implicit in any differential treatment of preferences attributed to dividends and retentions, there would seem to be little reason not to use partial pass-through of preferences. Thus, for example, it might be argued that preferences attributed to retentions should be fully passed through but that only half of those attributed to dividends should be passed through.

Table 4-6. Illustration of Pass-Through of Tax Preferences for Retained Earnings and Washout for Dividends under Full Integration, Assuming 75 Percent Retention and Proportionate Allocation of Preferences to Dividends and Retained Earnings[a]

Monetary units

	Marginal personal tax rate of shareholder (percent)								
	0			20			60		
	Net income			Net income			Net income		
Item[b]	Dis-tributed	Retained	Total	Dis-tributed	Retained	Total	Dis-tributed	Retained	Total
	(1)	(2)	(3)	(4)	(5)	(6)	(7)	(8)	(9)
1. Corporate-source economic income	25	75	100	25	75	100	25	75	100
2. Deductible preference income[c]	5	15	20	5	15	20	5	15	20
3. Taxable income [1 − 2]	20	60	80	20	60	80	20	60	80
4. Gross corporate income tax [50% of 3]	10	30	40	10	30	40	10	30	40
5. Creditable preferences[c]	1	3	4	1	3	4	1	3	4
6. Net corporate income tax [4 − 5]	9	27	36	9	27	36	9	27	36
7. Net corporate income [1 − 6]	16	48	64	16	48	64	16	48	64
8. Gross-up [6]; [6 − 2][d]	9	12	21	9	12	21	9	12	21
9. Grossed-up corporate-source income [7 + 8]	25	60	85	25	60	85	25	60	85
10. Gross personal tax liability [marginal personal tax rate × 9]	0	0	0	5	12	17	15	36	51
11. Credit [6]; [6 + 5][d]	9	30	39	9	30	39	9	30	39
12. Net personal tax liability [10 − 11]	−9	−30	−39	−4	−18	−22	6	6	12
13. Total taxes [6 + 12]	0	−3	−3	5	9	14	15	33	48
14. Value of tax preferences[e]	0	3	3	0	6	6	0	12	12
15. Value of noncorporate tax preferences (from table 4-1)	4	8	16

... Not relevant.
a. Terms relating to integration systems are explained in the glossary.
b. Except for percentages, the numbers in brackets refer to the lines of this table.
c. Preferences assumed are those in table 4-1.
d. The formulas relate to columns 1, 4, and 7, and columns 2, 5, and 8, respectively; columns 3, 6, and 9 = sum of the two preceding columns in each instance.
e. (Marginal personal tax rate × line 1) − line 13.

procedure is essential. Though this could be achieved if the shareholder were told to multiply the sum of dividends received and retained earnings allocated to him by 85/64 to calculate his gross-up and by 39/64 to derive his shareholder credit, it would appear to be far simpler to have these calculations made by the corporation and reported to the shareholder along with the allocation of retained earnings.

In table 4-6 it is assumed that preferences would be allocated on a pro rata basis to retained and distributed income. But there are other alternatives. For example, it might be assumed that dividends are paid first from fully taxable income (or from tax-exempt income) and only after that is exhausted are distributions assumed to come from preference income (or from taxable income). Stacking preferences last (or first) in this way maximizes (or minimizes) their value in a system in which preferences are washed out only if distributed. Given the assumptions on which table 4-6 is based, no preferences would be washed out if they were stacked last. (Complications arising from the need for stacking rules are discussed at greater length in the following section.)

Dividend Relief by the Imputation Method

At the end of the preceding section I raised the possibility that under full integration preferences might be allowed for retained corporate income but washed out on corporate distributions. I turn now to the equivalent problem under dividend relief. First I discuss the basic issues in a simplified example; then I consider the administrative problems that arise in a more realistic situation.

Table 4-7 presents six prototypes for the treatment of tax preferences under 100 percent dividend relief. Tax preferences can either be passed through to shareholders receiving dividends (first column) or be washed out on dividends (second column).[18] But it is not enough to have just such general statements; it is also necessary to have rules for the "stacking" of tax preferences. Thus in the first line it is assumed that preferences are stacked first, so that they constitute the

18. In most of what follows cases are considered in which both deductible and creditable preferences are either passed through or washed out. But there is no reason why, in principle, one of them could not be passed through and the other washed out.

Table 4-7. Alternative Treatment of Tax Preferences with 100 Percent Dividend Relief

	Tax preferences on dividends	
Stacking rule	Passed through	Washed out
	Case identification	
1. Preferences stacked first (against dividends)	1a	1b
2. Preferences prorated between distributed and retained income	2a	2b
3. Preferences stacked last (against retentions)	3a	3b

first element of any dividend paid. In the third line the assumption is just the opposite; preferences are stacked last, so that dividends are assumed to be paid first from fully taxed income, as is common in the European systems. In the second line it is assumed that dividends are paid in proportional amounts from fully taxed and tax-preferred income, as in table 4-6. Stated differently, tax preferences are pro-rated across distributed and retained income. Thus six different cases can be created by choosing one line and one column from table 4-7. In case 1a, for example, it is assumed that tax preferences are stacked to come out first and are passed through to shareholders. In case 1b, on the other hand, preferences are stacked to come out first, but are washed out in the hands of shareholders.

Complete Stacking of Preferences

To give a better understanding of the implications of these six cases, I present, in tables 4-9 through 4-13, illustrations of the tax treatment of 100 of corporate-source economic income subject to 20 of deductible preferences and 4 of creditable preferences under each of the six tax regimes. To simplify the analysis, I assume (1) that the examples pertain to the corporation's first year of existence, and (2) that dividends or retentions are sufficient to absorb all of tax preferences if they are stacked to come out first or last, respectively. The reason for these assumptions will become clear when they are later relaxed. In addition, I make the simplifying assumption that the fractions of gross corporate-source income eventually giving rise to dividends and retentions can be determined before the application of deductible preferences, corporate tax, and creditable preferences.[19]

19. This is done only to assure the comparability of the results shown in the various tables. There is no presumption that dividend payout rates would not be affected by the way tax preferences are treated. Nor are various preferences traced to specific parts of the income stream.

Table 4-8. Benchmark for Analysis of Tax Preferences under Imputation Method (Case 0)[a]

Rates in percent; other data in monetary units

	Earnings		
Item[b]	*Undistributed*	*Distributed*	
1. Marginal personal tax rate of shareholder	[c]	0 · 20 · 60	
2. Corporate-source economic income	50	50 · 50 · 50	
3. Deductible preference income	0	0 · 0 · 0	
4. Taxable corporate income [2 − 3]	50	50 · 50 · 50	
5. Gross corporate income tax [50% of 4]	25	25 · 25 · 25	
6. Creditable preferences	0	0 · 0 · 0	
7. Net corporate income tax [5 − 6]	25	25 · 25 · 25	
8. Net corporate income [2 − 7]	25	25 · 25 · 25	
9. Gross-up [7 − 3]	...	25 · 25 · 25	
10. Grossed-up corporate-source income [8 + 9]	...	50 · 50 · 50	
11. Gross personal tax liability [1 × 10]	...	0 · 10 · 30	
12. Shareholder credit [7 + 6]	...	25 · 25 · 25	
13. Net personal tax liability [11 − 12]	...	−25 · −15 · 5	
14. Total tax in column [7 + 13]	25	0 · 10 · 30	
15. Total tax liability[d]	[e]	25 · 35 · 55	

... Not applicable to undistributed earnings.

a. In case 0 there are no tax preferences. Terms relating to integration systems are explained in the glossary.

b. Except for percentages, the numbers in brackets refer to the lines of this table.

c. For undistributed earnings, the marginal personal tax rate of the shareholder is immaterial.

d. Columns for distributed earnings are figures in line 14 plus the 25 tax on undistributed earnings.

e. Included in the other three columns.

Thus in tables 4-9 through 4-13 I assume that the 100 of corporate-source income can be split into 50 that will eventually give rise to dividends and 50 that will lead to retention of earnings. To gauge the value of tax preferences in each of the six cases, I present table 4-8 as a benchmark in which there are no tax preferences. For purposes of reference I label this case 0. Finally, I ignore any personal tax that may be due on capital gains resulting from retained earnings.

In case 0, the corporate tax of 50 percent halves the corporate-source economic income, whether the latter is retained or distributed. But for the distributed part the corporate tax is a withholding tax that is imputed to the shareholder. It increases his personal taxable income by forming the basis of the gross-up, but is also creditable against tax liability. Thus gross distributed corporate-source income bears tax at exactly the shareholder's personal marginal tax rate (line 11). On the other hand, the corporate tax levied on income giving

Table 4-9. Illustration of Pass-Through under Imputation Method, with Preferences Stacked First (against Dividends) and Passed Through (Case 1a)[a]

Rates in percent; other data in monetary units

Item[b]	Earnings		
	Undistributed	Distributed	
1. Marginal personal tax rate of shareholder	[c]	0 20	60
2. Corporate-source economic income	50	50 50	50
3. Deductible preference income[d]	0	20 20	20
4. Taxable corporate income [2 − 3]	50	30 30	30
5. Gross corporate income tax [50% of 4]	25	15 15	15
6. Creditable preferences[d]	0	4 4	4
7. Net corporate income tax [5 − 6]	25	11 11	11
8. Net corporate income [2 − 7]	25	39 39	39
9. Gross-up [7 − 3]	...	−9 −9	−9
10. Grossed-up corporate-source income [8 + 9]	...	30 30	30
11. Gross personal tax liability [1 × 10]	...	0 6	18
12. Shareholder credit [7 + 6]	...	15 15	15
13. Net personal tax liability [11 − 12]	...	−15 −9	3
14. Total tax in column [7 + 13]	25	−4 2	14
15. Total tax liability[e]	[f]	21 27	39
16. Taxes in absence of preferences (from table 4-8)	[f]	25 35	55
17. Total value of tax preferences [16 − 15]	[f]	4 8	16
Due to retained earnings	[f]	0 0	0
Due to distributed earnings, creditable preferences [from 6]	...	4 4	4
Due to distributed earnings, deductible preferences [1 × 3]	...	0 4	12

... Not applicable to undistributed earnings.
a. Terms relating to integration systems are explained in the glossary.
b. Except for percentages, the numbers in brackets refer to the lines of this table.
c. For undistributed earnings, the marginal personal tax rate of the shareholder is immaterial.
d. Preferences assumed are those in table 4-1.
e. Columns for distributed earnings are figures in line 14 plus the 25 tax on undistributed earnings.
f. Included in the other three columns.

rise to retentions is a final tax. In sum, the two taxes produce the aggregate tax burdens shown in line 15 of table 4-8.

In case 1a, illustrated in table 4-9, preferences are stacked first and passed through to shareholders. Thus they have the same value as they would have in the noncorporate sector. (Compare line 17 of table 4-9 with line 7 of table 4-1.) For this result to be achieved, it is necessary that the dividends of 39 carry a gross-up of *minus* 9, reflecting the fact that the deductible preferences to be passed through

exceed the net tax paid at the corporate level on income resulting in dividends.[20]

It might seem that the task of reporting and explaining this negative gross-up would strain corporate abilities.[21] But it would, in fact, be relatively simple (except for problems to be noted later) to achieve the desired result. In a way comparable to that in the case of full integration discussed earlier, the firm would report 30 of taxable income and 20 of exempt income and a combined credit for withheld taxes and the investment tax credit of 15. Given those amounts, the figures in lines 11, 14, and 15 of table 4-9 follow directly.[22]

Case 3b is, in a sense, the direct opposite of case 1a. In 3b preferences are washed out to the extent that dividends are paid but are stacked last. Because of my assumption that retained income is large enough to absorb all preferences, aggregate taxes at all levels of income are reduced by 14, the value of the corporate income tax applied to the 20 of deductible preferences plus the 4 of creditable preferences[23] (see table 4-11, line 17). Moreover, the same result occurs in case 3a: since it is assumed that preferences are stacked entirely against retained earnings, it is immaterial whether preferences are passed through or washed out on distributed corporate income. More generally, the results could be quite different. In the extreme case of a firm paying out 100 percent of earnings, the preferences would be washed out in case 3b but passed through in case 3a. And in case 3a, if the corporate tax rate differed from the average of the marginal personal tax rates paid by shareholders, once enough

20. Recall from the discussion earlier in the chapter that the gross-up required to assure pass-through is equal to the net corporate tax liability (on distributed income in the present case) minus deductible preferences. The shareholder credit, on the other hand, is the net corporate tax plus creditable preferences.

21. The firm would know dividends (39), retained earnings (25), and taxes imputed to retained earnings (25). Thus the tax attributed to dividends must be the residual (11). Subtraction of deductible preferences (20) from this figure produces the negative gross-up mentioned above.

22. See also Hickman's testimony in *President's 1978 Tax Reduction and Reform Proposals.*

23. This tends to be the result in Europe, though it is achieved through the use of a précompte rather than of a variable rate for computing gross-up and credit (see chapter 3). Because preferences attributable to dividends are washed out, there is a reluctance to pay dividends out of preference income. Note that in the present U.S. system, so long as preference income is retained, the result is as described in the text. If all earnings are paid out as dividends, the preference is washed out, as in case 3b.

Table 4-10. Illustration of Pass-Through under Imputation Method, with Preferences Prorated and Passed Through on Dividends (Case 2a)[a]

Rates in percent; other data in monetary units

Item[b]	Earnings			
	Undistributed	Distributed		
1. Marginal personal tax rate of shareholder	[c]	0	20	60
2. Corporate-source economic income	50	50	50	50
3. Deductible preference income[d]	10	10	10	10
4. Taxable corporate income [2 − 3]	40	40	40	40
5. Gross corporate income tax [50% of 4]	20	20	20	20
6. Creditable preferences[d]	2	2	2	2
7. Net corporate income tax [5 − 6]	18	18	18	18
8. Net corporate income [2 − 7]	32	32	32	32
9. Gross-up [7 − 3]	...	8	8	8
10. Grossed-up corporate-source income [8 + 9]	...	40	40	40
11. Gross personal tax liability [1 × 10]	...	0	8	24
12. Shareholder credit [7 + 6]	...	20	20	20
13. Net personal tax liability [11 − 12]	...	−20	−12	4
14. Total tax in column [7 + 13]	18	−2	6	22
15. Total tax liability[e]	[f]	16	24	40
16. Taxes in absence of preferences (from table 4-8)	[f]	25	35	55
17. Total value of tax preferences [16 − 15]	[f]	9	11	15
Due to retained earnings[g]	[f]	7	7	7
Due to distributed earnings, creditable preferences [from 6]	...	2	2	2
Due to distributed earnings, deductible preferences [1 × 3]	...	0	2	6

... Not applicable to undistributed earnings.

a. Terms relating to integration systems are explained in the glossary.

b. Except for percentages, the numbers in brackets refer to the lines of this table.

c. For undistributed earnings, the marginal personal tax rate of the shareholder is immaterial.

d. Preferences assumed are those in table 4-1.

e. Columns for distributed earnings are figures in line 14 plus the 18 tax on undistributed earnings.

f. Included in the other three columns.

g. Creditable preferences attributable to retentions plus 50 percent of deductible preferences attributed to retentions.

dividends had been paid to exhaust fully taxed income the cost of dividends in terms of retentions would change.

Case 1b is another extreme contrast to case 1a: preferences are stacked first (against dividends) but are then washed out. Thus they become worthless to the extent dividends are paid, as shown in line 17 of table 4-12. Finally, the results in cases 2a and 2b, involving the prorating of preferences between distributed and retained income, fall midway between those for cases 1a and 3a and for cases 1b and

Table 4-11. Illustration of Pass-Through under Imputation Method, with Preferences Stacked Last (against Retentions) (Cases 3a and 3b)[a]

Rates in percent; other data in monetary units

	Earnings		
Item[b]	*Undistributed*	*Distributed*	
1. Marginal personal tax rate of shareholder	[c]	*0* *20*	*60*
2. Corporate-source economic income	50	50 50	50
3. Deductible preference income[d]	20	0 0	0
4. Taxable corporate income [2 − 3]	30	50 50	50
5. Gross corporate income tax [50% of 4]	15	25 25	25
6. Creditable preferences[d]	4	0 0	0
7. Net corporate income tax [5 − 6]	11	25 25	25
8. Net corporate income [2 − 7]	39	25 25	25
9. Gross-up [7 − 3]	...	25 25	25
10. Grossed-up corporate-source income [8 + 9]	...	50 50	50
11. Gross personal tax liability [1 × 10]	...	0 10	30
12. Shareholder credit [7 + 6]	...	25 25	25
13. Net personal tax liability [11 − 12]	...	−25 −15	5
14. Total tax in column [7 + 13]	11	0 10	30
15. Total tax liability[e]	[f]	11 21	41
16. Taxes in absence of preferences (from table 4-8)	[f]	25 35	55
17. Total value of tax preferences [16 − 15]	[f]	14 14	14
Due to retained earnings[g]	[f]	14 14	14
Due to distributed earnings	...	0 0	0

... Not applicable to undistributed earnings.

a. Terms relating to integration systems are explained in the glossary. Retentions are assumed to absorb all preferences in both cases. Thus cases 3a and 3b are equivalent.

b. Except for percentages, the numbers in brackets refer to the lines of this table.

c. For undistributed earnings, the marginal personal tax rate of the shareholder is immaterial.

d. Preferences assumed are those in table 4-1.

e. Columns for distributed earnings figures in line 14 plus the 11 tax on undistributed earnings.

f. Included in the other three columns.

g. Creditable preferences attributable to retentions plus 50 percent of deductible preferences attributed to retentions.

3b, respectively. (See tables 4-10 and 4-13.) In each case half the advantage of attributing preferences entirely to retained earnings (7) is realized. In case 2b there is no further advantage, since the preferences prorated to dividends are washed out. But in case 2a half the advantages in case 1a are also realized because the preferences imputed to dividends are passed through to shareholders.

Incomplete Stacking of Preferences

The assumption was made above that any stacking of preferences against either dividends or retentions could be complete; for exam-

Table 4-12. Illustration of Pass-Through under Imputation Method, with Preferences Stacked First (against Dividends) and Washed Out (Case 1b)[a]

Rates in percent; other data in monetary units

	Earnings			
Item[b]	Undistributed	Distributed		
1. Marginal personal tax rate of shareholder	[c]	0	20	60
2. Corporate-source economic income	50	50	50	50
3. Deductible preference income[d]	0	20	20	20
4. Taxable corporate income [2 − 3]	50	30	30	30
5. Gross corporate income tax [50% of 4]	25	15	15	15
6. Creditable preferences[d]	0	4	4	4
7. Net corporate income tax [5 − 6]	25	11	11	11
8. Net corporate income [2 − 7]	25	39	39	39
9. Gross-up [from 7]	...	11	11	11
10. Grossed-up corporate-source income [8 + 9]	...	50	50	50
11. Gross personal tax liability [1 × 10]	...	0	10	30
12. Shareholder credit [from 7]	...	11	11	11
13. Net personal tax liability [11 − 12]	...	−11	−1	19
14. Total tax in column [7 + 13]	25	0	10	30
15. Total tax liability[e]	[f]	25	35	55
16. Taxes in absence of preferences (from table 4-8)	[f]	25	35	55
17. Value of tax preferences [16 − 15][g]	0	0	0	0

... Not applicable to undistributed earnings.

a. Terms relating to integration systems are explained in the glossary.

b. Except for percentages, the numbers in brackets refer to the lines of this table.

c. For undistributed earnings, the marginal personal tax rate of the shareholder is immaterial.

d. Preferences assumed are those in table 4-1.

e. Columns for distributed earnings are figures in line 14 plus the 25 tax on undistributed earnings.

f. Included in the other three columns.

g. Preferences have no value in the first column because they are attributed entirely to dividends; in the last three columns because they are washed out.

ple, if preferences were stacked first (against dividends), it would not be necessary to consider the problem that arises when dividends are small relative to preferences and some residual must be stacked against retentions. That assumption is now relaxed. Primary attention is devoted to case 3b because it most closely describes common European practice; but the principles involved carry-over to other cases, as is shown by the consideration later of case 3a.

Note first that incomplete stacking of preferences can have at least two meanings. Under one definition, incomplete stacking against retained earnings would result only if deductible preferences exceeded retained earnings, so that the taxable corporate income figure

Table 4-13. Illustration of Pass-Through under Imputation Method, with Preferences Prorated and Washed Out on Dividends (Case 2b)[a]

Rates in percent; other data in monetary units

		Earnings		
Item[b]	*Undistributed*	*Distributed*		
1. Marginal personal tax rate of shareholder	[c]	0	20	60
2. Corporate-source economic income	50	50	50	50
3. Deductible preference income[d]	10	10	10	10
4. Taxable corporate income [2 − 3]	40	40	40	40
5. Gross corporate income tax [50% of 4]	20	20	20	20
6. Creditable preferences[d]	2	2	2	2
7. Net corporate income tax [5 − 6]	18	18	18	18
8. Net corporate income [2 − 7]	32	32	32	32
9. Gross-up [from 7]	...	18	18	18
10. Grossed-up corporate-source income [8 + 9]	...	50	50	50
11. Gross personal tax liability [1 × 10]	...	0	10	30
12. Shareholder credit [from 7]	...	18	18	18
13. Net personal tax liability [11 − 12]	...	−18	−8	12
14. Total tax in column [7 + 13]	18	0	10	30
15. Total tax liability[e]	[f]	18	28	48
16. Taxes in absence of preferences (from table 4-8)	[f]	25	35	55
17. Total value of tax preferences [16 − 15]	[f]	7	7	7
Due to retained earnings[g]	[f]	7	7	7
Due to distributed earnings[h]	...	0	0	0

... Not applicable to undistributed earnings.

a. Terms relating to integration systems are explained in the glossary.

b. Except for percentages, the numbers in brackets refer to the lines of this table.

c. For undistributed earnings the marginal personal tax rate of the shareholder is immaterial.

d. Preferences assumed are those in table 4-1.

e. Columns for distributed earnings are figures in line 14 plus the 18 tax on undistributed earnings.

f. Included in the other three columns.

g. Creditable preferences attributable to retentions plus 50 percent of deductible preferences attributed to retentions.

h. Preferences are washed out on distribution.

in the first column of table 4-11 would be negative. Under this definition, illustrated in the first pair of columns in table 4-14, any excess deductible preferences would be attributed to dividends and washed out, but creditable preferences would continue to be attributed to retained income. Under an alternative definition, preferences would be considered to be excessive if creditable and deductible preferences together produced a negative net corporate income tax figure in the first column of table 4-11. As can be seen in the second and third pair of columns in table 4-14, whether the creditable preferences or the

Table 4-14. Alternative Definitions of Excess Preferences Stacked against Retentions and Washed Out (Case 3b)[a]

Monetary units

Item[b]	Only deductible preferences potentially attributable to dividends[c]		Deductible and creditable preferences potentially attributable to dividends[d]			
			Deductible preferences attributed first to dividends		Creditable preferences attributed first to dividends	
	Undistributed earnings (1)	Distributed earnings (2)	Undistributed earnings (3)	Distributed earnings (4)	Undistributed earnings (5)	Distributed earnings (6)
1. Corporate-source economic income	10	90	10	90	10	90
2. Deductible preference income[e]	10	10	2	18	10	10
3. Taxable corporate income [1 − 2]	0	80	8	72	0	80
4. Gross corporate income tax [50% of 3]	0	40	4	36	0	40
5. Creditable preferences[e]	4	0	4	0	0	4
6. Net corporate income tax [4 − 5]	−4	40	0	36	0	36
7. Net corporate income [1 − 6]	14	50	10	54	10	54
8. Gross-up [from 6]	...	40	...	36	...	36
9. Grossed-up corporate-source income [7 + 8]	...	90	...	90	...	90
10. Gross personal tax liability [60% of 9]	...	54	...	54	...	54
11. Shareholder credit [from 8]	...	40	...	36	...	36
12. Net personal tax liability [10 − 11]	...	14	...	18	...	18
13. Total tax in column [6 + 12]	−4	54	0	54	0	54
14. Taxes in absence of preferences [50% of undistributed in 1; 60% of distributed in 1]	5	54	5	54	5	54
15. Value of tax preferences[f] [14 − 13]	9	0	5	0	5	0

... Not applicable.

a. Assumes that the marginal personal tax rate of the shareholder is 60 percent. Terms relating to integration systems are explained in the glossary.

b. Except for percentages, the numbers in brackets refer to the lines of this table.

c. Deductible preferences are attributed in part to dividends if net income attributed to retentions would otherwise be negative.

d. Preferences are attributed in part to dividends if net corporate tax attributed to retentions would otherwise be negative.

e. Preferences assumed are those in table 4-1.

f. Creditable preferences attributable to retentions plus 50 percent of deductible preferences attributable to retentions.

deductible preferences are attributed to distributed income is immaterial here; the results are the same in either event, since there is no corporate tax on retentions and all preferences are washed out.

The taxpayer would, of course, prefer the first definition, since it allows the benefits of the investment tax credit to be retained at the corporate level, regardless of the amount of dividends paid, rather than to be attributed to dividends and washed out.[24] Moreover, this preference does not depend on the marginal tax rate of the shareholder.[25]

The results in case 3a, which also stacks preferences last, but allows pass-through of preferences allocated to dividends, are quite different.[26] In this case preferences are equally valuable in the first and last pairs of columns (1, 2, 5, 6) of table 4-15 (creditable preferences disregarded in applying stacking rules and creditable preferences applied first to dividends when they are not disregarded) regardless of the tax bracket of the shareholder. In either event, the credit is worth 4, the 10 of deductible preferences attributable to retentions is worth 5, and the 10 of deductible preferences passed through to shareholders has a value that depends on the marginal tax rate of the shareholder. On the other hand, the value of preferences in columns 3 and 4 (creditable preferences not disregarded, but applied last to dividends) depends on the marginal tax rate of the shareholder and is equal to that in the other columns if and only if the shareholder and the corporation are in the same tax bracket. In the example of table 4-15, in which the taxpayer is in a higher tax rate than the corporation, the deduction of 8 is worth more to him than a credit of 4. Thus not only is it important to have stacking rules for the determination of whether dividends are being paid out of fully

24. This is somewhat of an overstatement, since it must be assumed that the credit would not be available for retention by the corporation if it distributed all its cash flow. In a sense the approach of the first pair of columns of table 4-14 and of table 4-15 creates a third "stack" for creditable preferences, to be reached after taxable income and deductible preferences are exhausted.

25. Note that in the example of table 4-14 the benefits of preferences, occurring entirely at the corporate level on retained earnings, are the same for all shareholders. Of course, all the tables in this section ignore the taxation of capital gains resulting from retentions.

26. There is, of course, no reason that deductible and creditable preferences must be treated identically; both stacking rules and the decision whether to wash out or pass through could be different. In the extreme case, credits might be stacked first and passed through while deductions were stacked last and washed out.

Table 4-15. Alternative Definitions of Excess Preferences Stacked against Retentions and Passed Through (Case 3a)[a]

Monetary units

| Item[b] | Only deductible preferences potentially attributable to dividends[c] | | Deductible and creditable preferences potentially attributable to dividends[d] | | | |
| | | | Deductible preferences attributed first to dividends | | Creditable preferences attributed first to dividends | |
	Undistributed earnings (1)	Distributed earnings (2)	Undistributed earnings (3)	Distributed earnings (4)	Undistributed earnings (5)	Distributed earnings (6)
1. Corporate-source economic income	10	90	10	90	10	90
2. Deductible preference income[e]	10	10	2	18	10	10
3. Taxable corporate income [1 − 2]	0	80	8	72	0	80
4. Gross corporate income tax [50% of 3]	0	40	4	36	0	40
5. Creditable preferences[e]	4	0	4	0	0	4
6. Net corporate income tax [4 − 5]	−4	40	0	36	0	36
7. Net corporate income [1 − 6]	14	50	10	54	10	54
8. Gross-up [6 − 2]	...	30	...	18	...	26

Line				
9. Grossed-up corporate-source income [7 + 8]	80	80	72	80
10. Gross personal tax liability [60% of 9]	48	48	43.2	48
11. Shareholder credit [6 + 5]	40	40	36	40
12. Net personal tax liability [10 − 11]	8	8	7.2	8
13. Total tax in column [6 + 12]	−4	0	43.2	44
14. Taxes in absence of preferences [50% of undistributed in 1; 60% of distributed in 1]	5	5	54	54
15. Total value of tax preferences	···	···	···	···
Due to retained earnings[f] [14 − 13]	9	5	···	···
Due to distributed earnings, creditable preferences [from 5]	···	0	0	5
Due to distributed earnings, deductible preferences [60% of 2]	6	6	10.8	6

··· Not applicable to this column.

a. Assumes that the marginal personal tax rate of the shareholder is 60 percent. Terms relating to integration systems are explained in the glossary.

b. Except for percentages, the numbers in brackets refer to the lines of this table.

c. Deductible preferences are attributed in part to dividends if net income attributed to retentions would otherwise be negative.

d. Preferences are attributed in part to dividends if net corporate tax attributed to retentions would otherwise be negative.

e. Preferences assumed are those in table 4-1.

f. Creditable preferences attributable to retentions plus 50 percent of deductible preferences attributable to retentions.

taxed or tax-preferred income; but those rules may need to specify whether creditable preferences are to be disregarded in making that determination. Moreover, if preferences are stacked last, explicit rules may be needed for the order in which creditable and deductible preferences are assumed to be paid out in dividends.

Though the discussion up to now has dealt with case 3, in which preferences are stacked last (against retained earnings), it should be clear that analogous problems arise in case 1, in which preferences are stacked first (against dividends). Are deductible preferences assumed to be the first source of dividends, or are creditable preferences? Or are creditable preferences assumed never to constitute the basis for dividends? In a system with progressive personal rates these decisions will generally be relevant.

Effects on Dividend Policy

It may be useful to digress here to note a rather interesting incentive effect created by the combination of stacking rules and washout of preferences on distributed corporate-source income. In table 4-16 I present an example in which preferences are assumed to be stacked last and washed out (case 3b) and there are alternative assumptions about dividend payout rates: that all after-tax income is retained; that income is retained only to the extent of deductible preferences; and that all after-tax income is distributed. For the last two cases I also consider the aggregate tax burden on corporate-source income attributable to shareholders in the 20 percent and 60 percent marginal tax brackets. In all cases the statutory corporate tax rate is 50 percent and there are 20 units of deductible preferences for every 100 units of economic income but no creditable preferences; thus the effective corporate rate is 40 percent.

Line 12 shows that the aggregate tax burden on the corporate-source income of the 60 percent taxpayer rises monotonically from 40 to 60 percent as the dividend payout rate rises from 0 to 100 percent. But the rise is not steady; given the figures in this example, the aggregate tax rate rises by only 8 percentage points as the payout rate rises from 0 to 80 percent,[27] but rises an additional 12 percentage points as the dividend payout rate goes from 80 to 100 percent. Thus

27. Note that these rates are calculated on the basis of *gross* (before-tax) income from which dividends are paid and income is retained. As a percentage of after-tax income, dividends rise to 66⅔ percent.

Table 4-16. Aggregate Tax Burden with Deductible Preferences Stacked Last and Washed Out (Case 3b) for Alternative Dividend Payout Rates and Personal Marginal Tax Rates[a]

Rates in percent; other data in monetary units

		Dividend payout rate			
		20 percent retained; 80 percent distributed			
Item[b]	*All retained*	*Retained*	*Distributed*	*All distributed*	
1. Corporate-source economic income	100	20	80	100	
2. Deductible preference income	20	20	0	20	
3. Taxable corporate income [1 − 2]	80	0	80	80	
4. Gross corporate income tax [50% of 3]	40	0	40	40	
5. Net corporate income [1 − 4]	60	20	40	60	
6. Gross-up [from 4]	40	40	
7. Grossed-up corporate-source income [5 + 6]	80	100	
8. Marginal personal tax rate of shareholder	c	c	20 60	20 60	
9. Gross personal tax liability [7 × 8]	16 48	20 60	
10. Shareholder credit [from 6]	40 40	40 40	
11. Net personal tax liability [9 − 10]	−24 8	−20 20	
12. Total tax liability [4 + 11]	40	0	16 48	20 60	
13. Taxes in absence of preferences [50% of retained in 1; 8 × distributed in 1]	50	10	16 48	20 60	
14. Value of tax preferences [13 − 12]	10	10	0 0	0 0	

... Not applicable to retained earnings.

a. Terms relating to integration systems are explained in the glossary.

b. Except for percentages, the numbers in brackets refer to the lines of this table.

c. For retained earnings, the marginal personal tax rate of the shareholder is immaterial.

dividends are extremely expensive once they begin to encroach on tax preference income, which, by assumption, can be used only to offset the retained part of corporate-source income.[28]

The situation is even more anomalous when a shareholder is in a marginal personal tax bracket below the corporate tax rate. In this case the aggregate tax applied to 100 of corporate-source income first falls as the dividend payout rate rises and then goes up as the

28. See also the discussion of this phenomenon in chapter 3.

payout rate continues to rise toward 100 percent. In particular, for the taxpayer in the 20 percent marginal rate bracket the aggregate rate falls from 40 percent to 16 percent as the dividend payout rises from zero to the point (80 percent in the example) at which only tax-preferred income is being retained. Then it rises to 20 percent as the dividend payout rate rises to 100 percent. Thus tax considerations would cause taxpayers at various points in the personal rate scale to prefer different payout performance. Those with personal rates above the corporate rate can be expected to prefer retentions over dividends, especially once the point is reached at which further dividends cause the advantages of tax preferences to be nullified.[29] On the other hand, shareholders with rates below the corporate rate would greatly prefer that the firm retain little more than enough to absorb preferences, but wouldn't care if they retained less than that amount. (The top panel of figure 4-1 expresses in diagrammatic form how the aggregate tax burdens at various points in the marginal rate scale depend on the payout choice of the firm.) All things considered, it seems likely that payout rates would settle down near the point where retentions exactly absorb preferences. This conclusion would be strengthened if capital gains were taxed as ordinary income.

Results analogous to those just presented, but opposite in direction, occur in case 1b, in which preferences are stacked first (against dividends) but are washed out. That is, the aggregate tax rate paid on corporate-source income attributable to shareholders subject to marginal personal rates below the corporate rate reaches a maximum at the point at which net dividends equal preference income. This is easily understood: if all income is retained, the deductible preference serves to reduce corporate tax by 10, but if the full amount of the preference is distributed, tax must be paid on it at the marginal rate of the shareholder, thereby increasing the aggregate burden. But as the payout rate rises further, the aggregate tax burden falls until, when all earnings are distributed, it is exactly the shareholder's rate (which in the case under discussion is lower than the corporate rate). In the case of the shareholder subject to a tax rate above the corporate rate, the rise in the aggregate rate is monotonic with the increase in the payout rate, though again not steady. In both cases the preferences become worthless once the point is reached at which all of

29. This is, of course, little different from the situation under present law.

Figure 4-1. Illustration of Aggregate Tax Burden with Alternative Dividend Payout Rates[a]

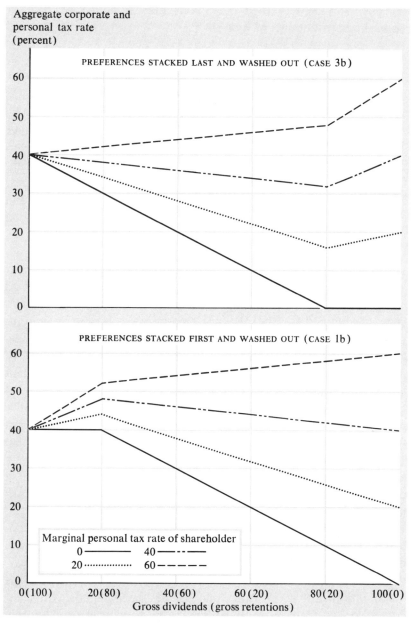

Aggregate corporate and
personal tax rate
(percent)

PREFERENCES STACKED LAST AND WASHED OUT (CASE 3b)

PREFERENCES STACKED FIRST AND WASHED OUT (CASE 1b)

Marginal personal tax rate of shareholder
0 ———— 40 —·· —
20 ·············· 60 — — — —

Gross dividends (gross retentions)

a. Assumes that deductible preferences are 20 percent of economic income and that the corporate tax rate is 50 percent.

them are assumed to be paid out as dividends and therefore washed out. The aggregate tax rates imposed at various points in the personal rate structure, depending on the payout ratio, are illustrated for case 1b in the bottom panel of figure 4-1.

Multiyear Situation

Despite the complexity of the methods needed to separate preferences attributable to dividends from those attributable to retentions, the calculation would be relatively simple if it only needed to be applied to income for one year, as in tables 4-14 and 4-15. A further complication—though one that may, in practice, simplify matters—exists: corporations are continuing concerns that generally accumulate earnings over a number of years. Suppose that a given corporation operating under the tax law implicit in case 3b (stack last and wash out) had the income, preferences, and dividends described in tables 4-11 and 4-14 in sequential years. The tax liabilities of the firm and its shareholders in the first year would be as already described, but the determination of tax liability in the second year would not be as described earlier in the discussion of table 4-14. This result is easily seen if the income and preference figures for the two years are lumped together. Retained corporate-source economic income (60) is more than enough to absorb all preference income, regardless of whether creditable preferences are potentially attributable to dividends. (The 8 of creditable preferences are equivalent to 16 of deductions, so that 56 of gross retained earnings are needed to absorb them and the 40 of deductible preferences.) To simplify the discussion, I am assuming that creditable preferences are ignored in applying the stacking rules, as in columns 3 and 4 of table 4-14. (Thus 40 of gross retentions in the two years would be adequate to absorb the deductible preferences.) If the 10 of gross undistributed corporate-source income for the second year is added to the accumulated taxable income of 30 carried over from the first year, the entire 20 of deductible preferences in the second year can easily be absorbed (with a carry-over of the excess 20 to the third year) without any preferences being attributed to dividends. Thus, though preferences attributable to dividends are washed out, as in Europe, the combination of stacking rules and use of accumulated taxable income accounts tends to result in all preferences being stacked entirely against retentions and, therefore, preserved.

With this background it is easier to understand the West German

Table 4-17. Alternative Interpretations of Stacking Rules

Alter-native	Case[a]	Preference income			Taxable income			Capital
		Current	Previously accumu-lated	Total	Current	Previously accumu-lated	Total	
		Presumptive order in which dividends are paid						
A	1	1	2	...	3	4	...	5
B	1	1	2	3
C	1	1	3	...	2	4	...	5
D[b]	2	1P	2P	...	1P	2P	...	3
E[b]	2	1P	1P	2
F	3	3	4	...	1	2	...	5
G	3	2	1	3
H	3	2	4	...	1	3	...	5

... Not relevant for this alternative.
a. Case numbers refer to table 4-7.
b. P in the ordering indicates that the dividends are prorated across two accounts as indicated.

system of "available net equity" accounts. In much the same way as in the example just described, the use of these accounts facilitates the stacking of preferences against retentions and the washing out of preferences attributed to distributed earnings. If the continued use of the split rate (which is of no relevance for the issue at hand) is ignored, there would be two accounts: one on which tax had been paid at the full rate and one on which tax had not been paid. Distributions from the former would be (and are) assumed to precede those from the latter and would carry full gross-up and credit. Distributions from the latter, on the other hand, carry the précompte (or would carry gross-up and credit equal only to corporate taxes paid), so that the preferences would be washed out on dividends.

It should be noted, though, that this is only one way that the rule of stacking preferences last in a multiyear situation might be interpreted. It is indicated in table 4-17 by alternative F or alternative G (which are equivalent). An alternative would be to assume that dividends are paid first out of current taxable income, then out of current preference income, and then out of previously accumulated taxable income and previously accumulated preference income, in that order, as in line H of table 4-17.[30] Compared with actual West German prac-

30. The variations on this theme are almost endless. As noted in chapter 3, the French assume that dividends come first from currently taxed income, then from retained earnings of the previous four years, in inverse order, and finally from preference income, with earnings accumulated more than four years previously reverting to the tax preference pot.

tice, this second approach (for case 3b) would involve keeping both current and accumulated accounts for taxable and preference income and washing out more tax preferences. Analogous comments can be made about the interpretation of case 1, which involves stacking preferences first (against dividends).

When one turns to systems involving pro rata attribution of preferences to dividends and retentions, things become somewhat more complicated. In case 2, alternative D, dividends are assumed to come in proportionate amounts from current preference and taxable income. If dividends exceed current net income, they are then assumed to come in proportionate amounts from previously accumulated preference and taxable income. But if current net income exceeds dividends, the excess must be attributed on a pro rata basis to the accumulated income accounts. Thus in this system both current and accumulated accounts must be maintained. By comparison, in case 2, alternative E, current preference and taxable income are added to the accumulated accounts before the prorating occurs (from the total accumulated accounts). This last system is simpler than the one involving both current and accumulated accounts, but its results may not be what is desired.[31]

Implicit in the above discussion is the necessity of calculating economic income as well as taxable income. Though economic income, from which tax preferences are subtracted to reach taxable income, is more or less equivalent to earnings and profits under present law, it is not exactly so. Moreover, whereas under present law firms need to calculate earnings and profits primarily to determine whether a given distribution is a dividend paid from earnings or a return of capital, under some of the approaches discussed the calculation of economic income would be quite common. This is especially true in cases 1 and 2, which do not involve stacking preferences last (against retentions). In those cases it would be necessary for virtually all firms to calculate economic income (or what is equivalent, given taxable income: preference income) to determine the allocation of

31. As noted above and discussed more fully later in the chapter, the choice of case 3b (preferences stacked last and washed out) and alternative G may be made as much on administrative grounds as on economic ones. The choice of approach E for case 2 would seem, on the other hand, to involve a certain internal inconsistency in that dividends would be assumed to come pro rata from *accumulated* taxable and *accumulated* preference income.

dividends between taxable and preference income. In case 3, however, the need to make this calculation would be rare, and under some schemes it would be avoided entirely. This point is discussed further in this chapter in the section on the role of earnings and profits.

Dividend-Paid Deduction

Washing out tax preferences is relatively simple under the dividend-paid deduction approach. Passing through preferences, on the other hand, is impossible under that approach, as ordinarily understood. But the basic approach can easily be modified to allow pass-through if gross-up and credit are grafted onto it.

Washout

For tax preferences to be washed out on dividends there must be no corporate income tax on the economic income giving rise to dividends; thus the only tax collected will be that levied at the personal level and that will be at the rate appropriate to assure washout. This implies that the deduction for dividends paid must be not the amount of dividends actually paid, but that amount reduced by the amount of deductible preferences attributable to dividends. (If, for example, there are 50 of gross corporate-source economic income giving rise to dividends and 20 of deductible preferences attributable to such dividends, as in case 1b, table 4-12, the deduction for dividends paid must be 30 rather than 50.) Alternatively, preferences simply would not be allowed to reduce taxable income to the extent that income was distributed. If in addition there are creditable preferences, the dividend-paid deduction must be reduced further, so that the combination of deductible preferences, creditable preferences, and dividend-paid deduction just offsets any corporate tax liability that would otherwise occur on income generating distributions. (In the example of table 4-12, which is based on a 50 percent marginal tax rate, the deduction would be only 22, the 8 further reduction in the deduction being necessary to offset the 4 of creditable preference.)

The upshot of this discussion is, of course, that washout is achieved for preferences attributable to dividends if either (1) the corporate income tax is simply abolished on distributed earnings (or a split-

rate system employed), or (2) preferences are disallowed to the extent attributed to dividends. Once the issue is stated in this way it becomes immediately apparent that the only important question is that of the stacking rule to be used to allocate preferences between distributed and retained corporate income.

Pass-Through

Though washing out preferences on dividends is trivial (except for the stacking problems), passing preferences through to shareholders is impossible unless the dividend-paid deduction is modified by the addition of special provisions. This is easily seen in case 1a. Assume for the moment that there are no creditable preferences. Table 4-18 presents information on the constellation of dividend-paid deductions, corporate taxes, and personal taxes that is necessary to pass 20 of deductible preferences through to shareholders in three different marginal personal tax brackets. Three things are worth noting about this table: (1) the corporate income tax must be negative so long as the marginal personal tax rate is positive; (2) the dividend-paid deduction necessary to assure pass-through generally exceeds the amount of dividends; and (3) both the dividend-paid deduction and the corporate income tax depend on the marginal tax rate of the shareholder.[32] Though the first two of these results may be mildly

32. These results are easily shown. Let T be the corporate income tax, P be the personal income tax, Y be corporate-source economic income, m be the marginal tax rate of the shareholder, D be deductible preferences, and X be the deduction for dividends paid. With a corporate tax rate of 50 percent, three equations can be written:

(1) $$T + P = m\,(Y - D)$$
(2) $$P = m\,(Y - T) \text{ and}$$
(3) $$T = 0.5\,(Y - D - X).$$

Substitution from equation 1 into equation 2 produces the following solution for the corporate income tax:

(4) $$T = \frac{-m}{(1 - m)}\,D.$$

We see from this that T is negative if m and D are positive (and is zero if either m or D is zero). Moreover, given the value of D, the value of T that assures pass-through varies positively with m. Finally we can solve equations 3 and 4 for X to yield the appropriate dividend-paid deduction:

(5) $$X = Y + \left(\frac{2m}{1 - m} - 1\right)D.$$

This, too, depends on the value of m.

Table 4-18. Illustration of Impossibility of Pass-Through of Deductible Preferences under Ordinary Dividend-paid Deduction (Case 1a)[a]

Rates in percent; other data in monetary units

		Earnings		
Item[b]		*Undistributed*	*Distributed*	
1. Marginal personal tax rate of shareholder	[c]	0	20	60
2. Corporate-source economic income	50	50	50	50
3. Deductible preference income	0	20	20	20
4. Income net of preferences [2 − 3]	50	30	30	30
5. Deduction for dividends paid[d]	...	30	40	90
6. Taxable income [4 − 5]	50	0	−10	−60
7. Corporate income tax [50% of 6]	25	0	−5	−30
8. Net corporate income [2 − 7]	25	50	55	80
9. Personal income tax [1 × 8]	...	0	11	48
10. Total tax in column [7 + 9]	25	0	6	18
11. Total tax liability[e]	[f]	25	31	43
12. Taxes in absence of preferences (from table 4-8)	[f]	25	35	55
13. Value of tax preferences [12 − 11]	[f]	0	4	12

... Not applicable to undistributed earnings.

a. Terms relating to integration systems are explained in the glossary.

b. Except for percentages, the numbers in brackets refer to the lines of this table.

c. For undistributed earnings the marginal personal tax rate of the shareholder is immaterial.

d. Deduction needed to produce line 13.

e. Columns for distributed earnings are figures in line 10 plus the 25 tax on undistributed earnings from line 10.

f. Included in the other three columns.

disconcerting, the third is devastating to the feasibility of using the ordinary dividend-paid deduction to achieve pass-through. The problems encountered in passing through creditable preferences are similar to those just described.[33]

33. In this case equations 1 and 3 are replaced with:

(1′) $T + P = mY - C$ and

(3′) $T = 0.5 (Y - X) - C,$

where C is creditable preferences. Thus

(4′) $T = \dfrac{-C}{1 - m}$ and

(5′) $X = Y + \dfrac{2m}{1 - m} C.$

Deductions for distributed income attributable to the three shareholders must be 50, 52, and 62, respectively, if there are 4 of creditable preferences.

The two approaches just discussed can be combined to allow either deductible or creditable preferences to be passed through to shareholders or to be washed out. Under one such approach the corporate income tax is eliminated for distributed corporate-source income; if no more is done, preferences are automatically washed out, as noted above. In addition, however, provision could be made for deductible or creditable preferences to be flowed through directly to shareholders. The shareholder would receive a statement not only of his cash dividends but of any preferences attributable to those dividends. He would include his dividends in his taxable income, but he would be allowed a deduction (or exclusion) for any deductible preferences passed through to him. Moreover, he would be allowed a credit equal to his proportionate share in the firm's creditable preferences attributable to dividends and reported to him. Such a scheme would clearly produce exact pass-through of both types of preferences.[34] Besides the need for stacking rules, the primary problem, which also arises under the imputation approach, seems to be the inability to provide information on a timely basis. (See also the section below on further problems of tax preferences.)

The Role of Earnings and Profits

Up to now I have dealt with amounts of income flowing into dividends and retained earnings as though it were a simple matter to know the magnitude of those flows (or the division of a given flow of income between dividends and retentions). But this is not necessarily the case; some of the most complex provisions of the tax code

34. Under one variant of this approach, which was suggested at the conference, deductible preferences would be treated as return of capital by both the corporation and the shareholder. The deduction for dividends paid in line 5 of table 4-18 would be only 30, even though 50 would actually be distributed to shareholders. This would totally offset income net of preferences (line 4) and eliminate the corporate tax. Since the 20 of deductible preferences would be treated as exempt income or a return of capital, only the 30 deductible at the corporate level would be taxable to the shareholder. Application of the assumed marginal tax rates in line 1 would produce the proper tax totals (line 10) and therefore result in exact pass-through of preferences. Note, however, that this approach requires that basis in shares not be reduced by "return of capital" resulting from distribution of preference income. It therefore seems substantially easier either (1) to treat the preference as exempt income to the shareholder, or (2) to disallow corporate deductions and credits for preferences to be passed through and allow shareholders to take the deductions and credits.

are those devoted to the determination of the conditions under which a given distribution by a corporation is a dividend instead of a return of capital. In this section I present a few preliminary thoughts on the role of "earnings and profits," the key concept (under current tax law) for the demarcation between dividends and other distributions, in a scheme of integration or dividend relief. But this discussion is far from definitive in an area in which important questions must be addressed and answered if proposals for integration or dividend relief are to be technically complete.

Under current tax law distributions are treated as dividends, a treatment that implies that they are taxed as ordinary income, up to the amount of earnings and profits.[35] Beyond that, distributions reduce the shareholder's basis in corporate shares, but not to below zero. Distributions in excess of both earnings and profits and basis are ordinarily taxed as capital gains. Thus, though earnings and profits are unimportant for most corporations, potentially they play an important role.[36]

Accumulated earnings and profits are similar in concept to retained earnings; thus they are more inclusive than accumulated undistributed taxable income. Of particular relevance for present purposes, they include the interest on state and local securities, the excess of accelerated over straight-line depreciation, and the excess of percentage depletion over cost depletion.[37] (Certain items usually identified as preferences, including excess deductions of bad debts of financial institutions, are not included in earnings and profits.) Thus,

35. Actually, distributions are also treated as dividends up to the amount of earnings and profits in the current year, without regard for the level of accumulated earnings and profits. This complication is ignored in most of what follows.

36. Earnings and profits are directly important for the shareholder, not for the corporation, as they have no direct bearing on its tax liability. But, of course, since earnings and profits determine whether its dividends must be included in taxable income of shareholders, the concept is hardly irrelevant for the firm. Moreover, the corporation is responsible for reporting to shareholders whether or not a given distribution is from earnings and profits.

37. If, for example, a firm with $100 of income calculated using straight-line depreciation (and including interest on municipal bonds) had a deduction for $20 of accelerated depreciation in excess of straight-line depreciation (or a $20 exclusion for interest on municipals), its taxable income would be $80, its tax liability would be $40, and its. net income would be $60. This last figure, and not the $40 that would result from subtracting tax from taxable income, is earnings and profits. That is, a distribution in excess of $40, but less than $60, would be treated as dividends rather than as a tax-exempt return of capital.

though income from these sources is exempt or tax preferred at the corporate level, distributions from such tax-preferred income must be taxed as dividends to the shareholders. In a sense, then, preferences are washed out when distributed. The important question is the role of earnings and profits in an integrated system or a system incorporating dividend relief.

It is perhaps most useful to begin a discussion of that question by noting that two important papers, written two decades apart, question the usefulness of the concept of earnings and profits, even under the present classical system.[38] Given the strength of the case against the earnings-and-profits limitation, a strong case indeed would be necessary to justify its retention under integration or dividend relief. Since it would be difficult to argue that distributions by ongoing firms were not dividends, the burden of proof should probably be on the government to show that a given distribution not in liquidation was not a dividend.[39] Moreover, perhaps no more than the original

38. William D. Andrews, " 'Out of Its Earnings and Profits': Some Reflections on the Taxation of Dividends," *Harvard Law Review,* vol. 69 (June 1956), pp. 1403–39, and Walter J. Blum, "The Earnings and Profits Limitation on Dividend Income: A Reappraisal," *Taxes—The Tax Magazine,* vol. 53 (February 1975), pp. 68–87.

39. The present limitation on dividends—that they be no larger than the greater of accumulated or current earnings and profits—is usually interpreted as assuring that distributions are not artificially construed as a return of investment instead of as dividends. That is, the purpose is seen as preventing the treatment of "true" dividends as reduction of basis or as capital gains in the hands of shareholders. But under dividend relief the interpretation and result could be just the opposite. Consider the case of the low-income shareholder (or tax-exempt organization if the benefits of integration extend to such organizations). He can be expected to prefer that a distribution be construed as a dividend rather than as a return of capital, since in the former case he gets the valuable dividend-received credit, but in the latter he gets only a reduction of basis (of only problematical value), or is taxed on the inferred capital gain. Thus, for many taxpayers, the provisions relating to earnings and profits would be turned on their head: though positions—by both taxpayers and the Internal Revenue Service—have been developed under the presumption that taxpayers would want distributions *not* to be classified as dividends, many taxpayers might suddenly prefer a contrary interpretation. (Under partial dividend relief the result could go either way, depending on the shareholder's tax rate, the extent of dividend relief, and the expected holding period.) The result would be similar in the case of the dividend-paid deduction except that the firm would have a more direct interest in having distributions classified as deductible dividends. Whether taxpayers or the Internal Revenue Service would have the better of the battle to reverse their positions, by citing arguments previously made for the other side, is unclear. (It is of some interest that the present limitation based on current earnings, to be applied where there are no accumulated earnings, dates from the period in the 1930s when the United States *did* allow a dividend-paid deduction and

amount of capital should be subject to question, in any event.[40] This would seem much "cleaner" than the present situation. But one thing is clear: thus far not enough attention has been devoted to the role of earnings and profits—or other ways of distinguishing between dividends and other distributions—in published discussions of integration and dividend relief.

Policy Issues in Pass-Through

Thus far in the chapter I have focused on the technical questions of tax design involved in implementing certain policies toward tax preferences under integration or dividend relief, taking those policies as given for purposes of the exercise. It is now time to turn to the less technical but more controversial question of what policy toward tax preferences should be. The issues seem to be fairly straightforward under full integration, but somewhat less clear under dividend relief.

Since the purpose of full integration is to tax income originating in equity investment in the corporate sector like other income received by individuals, there seems to be no legitimate argument over whether tax preferences should be passed through to shareholders; if they are not passed through, integration is not complete, because investment in the noncorporate sector—where preferences are available—and in the corporate sector—where they would be eliminated—will not be equivalent. Thus the investment tax credit, the excess of accelerated over economic depreciation,[41] the excess of percentage over cost depletion, and so forth (to the extent that they are available

it was in the interest of firms to have this interpretation. See Andrews, " 'Out of Its Earnings,' " p. 81, and Blum, "Earnings and Profits," pp. 1403–05.)

40. The new West German system treats return of capital as a taxable event for the corporation and the shareholder. But under the West German stacking rules capital contributions are assumed to be the last source of distributions. Moreover, the 36 percent personal credit just offsets the corporate tax.

41. Since I defined tax preferences relative to economic income instead of using the definition in U.S. law, I define the tax preference involved in accelerated depreciation relative to economic depreciation rather than relative to straight-line depreciation, which can be either more or less rapid than economic depreciation. Moreover, as my basis for comparison I take income rather than consumption, despite the many advantages of the latter. Under a consumption-based direct tax anything less than immediate expensing of investment involves negative tax preferences. But under such a tax regime it does not make sense to discuss integration of the corporate and personal income taxes, since the former tax does not even exist in the usual sense! For an exception, see J. A. Kay and M. A. King, *The British Tax System* (Oxford: Oxford University Press, 1978), pp. 200–02.

to the noncorporate sector)[42] should, as a matter of principle, be passed through to shareholders.

The same reasoning applies to interest on state and local securities. It would be anomalous, as well as politically unlikely and perhaps unconstitutional, not to allow the pass-through of the exclusion in an integrated system. But the situation is somewhat different for the special rates applied to the income of small corporations and for capital gains realized by corporations. Though neither of these provisions makes much sense in a classical system, they have no place at all in an integrated system. The basic rationale of integration—that income should not bear special rates because of its (corporate or noncorporate) source—applies as much to income from small corporations as to that from large ones and is as applicable to capital gains of corporations as to operating income. At most, all that is required is that capital gains retain their identity in the hands of the shareholders, and even this requirement vanishes if the personal tax rates applied to capital gains and to ordinary income are unified.

The only remaining question, therefore, is whether it would be appropriate under full integration to treat tax preferences attributable to dividends differently from those attributable to allocated retained earnings. Though the issues are not identical, the answer to that question bears on the proper treatment of tax preferences in a system providing just dividend relief.

Some might argue that on equity grounds preferences should be washed out on distributed corporate-source income. This group, which would probably include many of those identified in chapter 2 as opponents of integration and dividend relief, presumably dislikes most tax preferences.[43] Thus they would see little advantage in adopting a system of integration or dividend relief that treated corporations

42. This is not the place to rehash standard debates over the pros and cons of various items of tax preference; suffice it to say that it is doubtful that all extant preferences make sense when judged on their individual merits; that many tax preferences may exist only because the tax burden on corporate-source income would otherwise be too great; that preferences may be reduced if integration or dividend relief is adopted; that the statement in the text holds if tax preferences are to be available in the noncorporate sector; and that if they are not, the contents of this chapter should be irrelevant. But at times it will be necessary to review arguments for particular tax preferences, to form a judgment as to how the preferences in question should be treated.

43. Since there is little literature on the treatment of tax preferences under full integration, one can only surmise how various groups would react.

and noncorporate businesses equivalently so far as tax preferences were concerned; given their dislike for the preferences, they would prefer to disallow some of the preferences in the corporate sector, by stacking them first and washing them out, even if they could not eliminate them.

This view has great appeal if one's goal is to bring the tax system into agreement with a predetermined definition of a good system that includes no tax preferences. But if one believes that tax preferences in the noncorporate sector make sense, this view is less attractive, for it is not clear why the preferences would not be just as appropriate in the corporate sector. Nor is it obvious why preferences should be available in the corporate sector only if income is retained.

Under another approach the rationale for various preferences would be examined to determine how best to treat the particular preferences. Since much the same reasoning can be applied to many kinds of corporate preferences, I will use this approach to examine primarily one kind—the investment tax credit.

The purpose of the investment tax credit is presumably to encourage investment.[44] Some may tend to conclude, therefore, that the investment tax credit should be available only to the extent that corporate-source income is retained, that is, becomes part of business saving.[45] But this conclusion is not necessarily correct, for it takes a view of the saving-investment process that may be wrong; namely, that corporate investment is determined primarily by cash flow, including particularly retained earnings.

This argument has several fallacies. First, if it is assumed that demand management is performed with some minimum facility, ex ante investment will equal ex ante saving, and it is not clear which will be adjusted to the other. But it is not unreasonable for the investment tax credit to be viewed as an instrument to encourage saving instead of investment. Seen in this light, it may be as effective if

44. The investment tax credit, and especially short-run variations in it, can also be seen as a way of controlling aggregate demand and therefore offsetting tendencies toward cyclical instability. The implications of this view, like the general question of economic stabilization in an integrated system, has barely begun to be discussed.

45. One is again forced to debate nonexistent opponents in this discussion, because so little has been written on the proper treatment of tax preferences in integrated systems and systems with dividend relief. Though no sources can be given for certain viewpoints, it seems unlikely that only straw men are involved.

passed through to shareholders as it is if available only on retained earnings. It raises the rate of return on corporate-source income in either case, and evidence cited in chapter 2 suggests that shareholders "pierce" the corporate veil by treating corporate retained earnings as very good substitutes for personal saving. Investment may be influenced almost as strongly by cash flow to the corporation-shareholder unit under dividend relief as it is by corporate cash flow under a classical system. All things considered, it seems appropriate that availability of the investment tax credit be the same for dividends and retentions; and there seems to be even less reason for the value of most other preferences to depend on whether income is retained or distributed.

Whereas the basic reasoning behind integration leads directly to the passing through of some preferences under full integration and the washing out of others, the implications for the treatment of preferences under dividend relief are not so clear. But the most reasonable interpretation of what dividend relief tries to accomplish suggests that, in principle, most preferences should be allocated between distributed and retained income on a pro rata basis.[46] Whether the preferences thus allocated to dividends should be passed through or washed out depends, it seems, on the same factors as whether preferences attributed to dividends and those attributed to retentions should be treated differently under full integration.[47]

46. That is, if 90 percent of gross earnings gave rise to dividends (after payment of corporate tax) and only 10 percent to retentions, 90 percent of preferences would be allocated to dividends, and only 10 percent to the unintegrated part of the corporate tax.

The statement in the text implies that dividend relief is a compromise made necessary by the administrative difficulties of full integration. If, however, one believes that dividend relief is intended merely to provide relief from "double taxation of dividends," preferences should clearly be washed out on dividends. But it is equally plausible that preferences should be stacked first or last. Of course, the results are quite different in the two cases. This entire line of reasoning seems faulty, however, since there are more direct, though inappropriate, ways to eliminate the "second tax" on dividends.

47. Note the horrendous problems that could arise if an attempt were made to pass the preferential treatment of long-term capital gains through on dividends. First, pass-through could be interpreted as involving either the exclusion of some income from personal tax or the reduction of tax by some given amount (for every dollar of dividends). The results would be quite different under the two interpretations. Furthermore, it might be decided that corporate capital gains—and losses—should retain their character in the hands of shareholders. This would involve serious problems (see chapter 5).

It seems likely that dividend payout rates would rise dramatically if the top personal rate were dropped to the level of the corporate rate or realized capital gains were taxed as ordinary income. But if this occurred there would be a tendency for the results to resemble those under integration and the system of pass-through argued above to be proper in that context.[48] It is unlikely, however, that all income would be distributed if a system that stacked preferences first and washed them out were adopted, as noted above.

Finally, in the interest of simplification only one, or very few, of the many possible approaches to the problem of tax preferences discussed above should be adopted. It would seem totally unmanageable, for example, to have some preferences stacked first, some stacked last, and yet others allocated on a pro rata basis, and to have some preferences attributed to dividends passed through and others washed out. The inherent problem would not be at the shareholder level, since he could be told two or three numbers to use in preparing his tax return. Rather, it would be at the corporate level, where the records of accounts would become incredibly complicated, especially when there were intercorporate dividends. Moreover, complications that cannot even be foreseen might be created by the interaction of the various provisions. Fortunately, this would place no major limitation on policy choices, since it would seem appropriate that virtually all preferences that should not be abolished in the move to dividend relief should, as a matter of principle, be treated identically.

Further Technical Problems of Tax Preferences

I have argued in the previous section that the most sensible way to treat most tax preferences under dividend relief (other than those that should simply be abolished) is to allocate them on a pro rata basis to dividends and retained earnings and pass them through to

48. The appeal of approximation to the results under full integration is more than aesthetic; it involves both equity and efficiency. That is to say, if full integration could be approximated through dividend relief, much of the present distortion of economic choices and distributional anomalies alleged to exist in the present classical system would be eliminated. It is worth noting in this regard that welfare losses from distortionary taxation tend to be roughly proportionate to the square of the differential in tax rates. Thus, reducing a differential by 50 percent reduces welfare costs by 75 percent.

Table 4-19. Alternative Treatment of Tax Preferences Using Variable and Fixed Gross-up and Credit

Stacking rule	Preferences passed through, variable credit	Preferences washed out	
		Variable credit	*Fixed credit*
	Case identification		
1. Preferences stacked first (against dividends)	1a	1bV	1bF
2. Preferences prorated between distributed and retained income	2a	2bV	2bF
3. Preferences stacked last (against retentions)	3a	3bV	3bF

shareholders. The least sensible treatment is to stack preferences first (against dividends) and wash them out. But from an administrative point of view the most complicated approaches are those that allow pass-through of preferences and do not stack preferences against retentions. Thus there may be a direct conflict between administrative simplicity and desirable tax policy.

It would appear that the complications encountered in the imputation approach to dividend relief are essentially of two types: those entailed with informing the shareholder of the proper gross-up and credit accompanying a dividend and those entailed with maintaining at the corporate level records of accounts, especially those necessary to identify a distribution as coming from taxable or preference income. As will be seen, the former problems are minimized if a fixed gross-up and credit is employed and the latter if tax preferences are stacked last (against retentions).

Table 4-19 helps one to understand better the administrative feasibility of alternative approaches to dividend relief. It differs from table 4-7 in that the last column of table 4-7 has been subdivided, with the entries in the second and third columns of table 4-19 (involving washout of preferences) depending on whether or not a précompte allows the use of a fixed gross-up and credit. Thus, in one important respect, the second column is more like the first than like the third; that is, like the first column it involves use of a variable gross-up and credit, while the third column involves a fixed gross-up and credit. (I return to this difference later.)

The stacking rule has clear implications for tax administration. If retained earnings were large relative to preference income for most companies, as seems likely for well-established and profitable firms,

a last-out stacking rule would imply that tax preferences were generally presumed to be absorbed by retentions rather than paid out in part as dividends. Likewise, the bulk of dividends would be assumed to constitute fully taxed income, and the question of whether to pass through preferences or wash them out would not be crucial.[49] By comparison, under a system that stacked preferences first or allocated preferences between dividends and retentions on a pro rata basis, every corporation would need to keep records of economic income (or preference income) as well as taxable income. Moreover, under a stack-last approach any adjustments to preferences resulting, say, from audit, would have little effect at the shareholder level; instead, they would generally be absorbed from retained earnings.

Of course, there are cases in which preference income exceeds retentions and therefore must be allocated in part to dividends, even when preferences are initially stacked against retentions. In addition, in lines 1 and 2 of table 4-19, even the first dollar of dividends is assumed to come at least in part from preference income. In these cases it is administratively far easier to use a fixed gross-up and credit than a variable one.

One advantage of using the précompte and fixed gross-up and credit is that it allows any calculations occasioned by tax preferences to be lodged at the corporate, rather than the shareholder, level. That is, the shareholder receives a gross-up and credit that bears a fixed relation to his dividends, regardless of the rate of tax paid at the corporate level. The difference in method may not seem to be important in simple cases. After all, the shareholder could be told to use an effective rate in calculating gross-up and credit; or even easier, the corporation could simply tell the shareholder the figure to use for the gross-up and credit. But in more complicated cases this difference can be crucial. Even more important, if preferences are stacked last and a précompte or similar arrangement is used to wash them out on distributions, it is not even necessary to calculate economic income—something that is necessary if preferences are stacked first or if a variable gross-up is used, but that is generally agreed to be infeasible.[50]

49. The stacking rule and treatment of preferences would, however, probably affect dividend payout rates. I continue to ignore this complication.

50. In principle it would be possible to duplicate the effect of a précompte by allowing gross-up and credit only for dividends from taxable income. But this approach requires knowledge of economic income and is therefore also infeasible.

In what follows I give instances in which the stacking rules and choice between fixed and variable gross-up and credits can be quite important for the administrative feasibility of dividend relief. Among the problems considered are those that arise from the need to inform shareholders on a timely basis of their gross-up and credit, from chains of corporate ownership, from net operating losses (NOLs), from audits and adjustments, and from the need to reverse preferences that involve only timing advantages.

Suppose that a corporation with a fiscal year ending in November made a distribution of dividends in December 1978. A calendar-year shareholder would be required to include such dividends in his 1978 income for tax purposes in the return filed in April 1979. Moreover, this dividend should be reported on a grossed-up basis. Yet in the four cases in bold face in table 4-19, the corporation could not calculate the appropriate gross-up and credit until after November 1979 if it had any tax preferences; and based on present experience, it would not be unreasonable to expect that the corporate return would be filed only some nine to ten months after the close of the fiscal year, or perhaps five or six months after the individual shareholder had filed his return for the year *following* that in which the dividend was originally paid.[51] Thus a literal interpretation of the four cases in the upper left part of table 4-19 would require that each shareholder of the corporation in question file an amended return once full information on the appropriate gross-up and credit became available. This requirement would, of course, be an unacceptable complication of the tax process.

The problem is similar for intercorporate dividends, and is greatly accentuated for chains of corporate ownership. Corporation A holding stock in corporation B could not be informed of its gross-up and credit until corporation B were notified of the same information by corporation C, and so forth.

Though there is some presumption that for many corporations retentions would be enough to absorb preferences, the same problem could be encountered in cases 3a and 3bV, both of which involve

51. In the example, the distribution might be deemed to have been out of fiscal 1978 earnings, so that the lag would be cut by a year. But the information needed by the shareholder still would not be available on a timely basis. Moreover, the logic of that decision, carried to its extreme, would suggest that any dividend paid any time during 1978 should be attributed to 1977 earnings. Though such an arbitrary ruling would be possible, it might not be optimal for other reasons.

variable gross-up and credit. Only in the cases involving fixed gross-up and credit is there assurance that the corporation would be able to inform the shareholder of the appropriate gross-up and credit at the time that information was needed.

The situation is quite different for the cases in the last column of table 4-19. So far as the shareholder is concerned, corporate tax equal to his net dividend will have been paid; he therefore takes a gross-up and credit for the corresponding amount. Indeed, if there are no tax preferences, corporate tax *has been* (or will be) paid on the income leading to dividends. But even if there are tax preferences, in case 3bF corporate tax is presumed to be paid on such dividends; to the extent that preferences exceeded retentions (and for case 1bF and part of dividends in case 2bF) précompte is due. The précompte, besides being only a preliminary liability to be offset against ultimate liability in the final reckoning between the corporation and the treasury, would be of absolutely no relevance to the shareholder; and any delay in calculating corporate income would have ramifications for retained earnings only at the corporate level. In the case in point, the shareholder receiving a dividend in late 1978 would simply include it and the appropriate fixed-rate gross-up in his 1979 income for tax purposes. Of course, this is equally true in the case of corporate shareholders.

The situation is similar for audit adjustments and amended returns. To the extent that preferences were allocated to dividends and not nullified by a précompte and fixed gross-up and credit, any audit adjustment or amended return affecting preferences would force shareholders to file amended returns. This result is clearly untenable and renders cases 1a, 2a, 1bV and 2bV unacceptable. On the other hand, under cases 1bF, 2bF, and 3bF, and often under cases 3a and 3bV, any adjustments would be absorbed from retained earnings and would not affect the shareholder. A similar result occurs in the case of tax preferences that involve only the timing of a deduction rather than its total amount, such as accelerated depreciation. So long as the positive and negative preference items could be absorbed in retained earnings, they would create no problems under case 3a or the two 3b cases; but under cases 1a, 1bV, 1bF, 2a, 2bV, and 2bF, they would necessitate the keeping of books so that the proper adjustments could be made in the précompte or the gross-up and credit allowed shareholders.

Net operating losses can result either because there are no tax preferences but "ordinary" (nonpreference) deductions exceed gross income ("clean" NOLs) or because ordinary and preference deductions together exceed gross income ("dirty" NOLs). If NOLs are simply carried forward to reduce taxable corporate income in future periods there is no problem so long as the NOL is entirely of the clean type. To the extent that preferences are stacked against dividends, problems can arise if the NOL is composed in part of deductible preferences, since simply carrying dirty NOLs forward blurs the identity of their components. If preferences are to be treated differently from ordinary deductions, as they must under stacking rules 1 and 2, it is necessary to identify them in special accounts when they give rise to NOLs. But if preferences are to be stacked last (against retentions), as in case 3a and the two 3b cases, there is no need for special accounts, so long as retentions are always sufficient to absorb the carryovers of NOLs. Note finally, that in 3a, 3bV, and 3bF it would be possible to allow carry-back of dirty NOLs so long as they did not exhaust previously retained earnings, since doing so would have no effect at the shareholder level. But allowing carry-back in any case involving pass-through of preferences when preferences are not stacked last would clearly cause problems because it would necessitate reopening individual returns for the carry-back years.

From the preceding discussion, several conclusions seem clear.

First, the four cases in the upper left of table 4-19 would be substantially more difficult to administer than the other cases.

Second, from an administrative point of view the second column seems to be dominated by the third column—that is, the use of the précompte and fixed gross-up and credit would be administratively preferable to the alternative means of achieving the same result through variable gross-ups and credits. Thus, for practical purposes, consideration can be limited to cases 1bF, 2bF, 3bF, and 3a unless one is willing to assume substantial administrative burdens.

Third, since a presumption exists that retentions would generally absorb all preferences, for the vast majority of corporations it might be substantially easier to comply with a tax modeled after case 3bF (or even 3a) than with one modeled after case 1bF or 2bF, both of which require all firms to calculate economic income.

Fourth, in many instances there would not be any important administrative difference in cases 3a and 3bF, since all preferences

could be absorbed by retentions; but in some there would be a substantial difference—a difference that might tilt the balance in favor of 3bF.

These conclusions are, of course, rather unsettling, given the ordering of alternatives based on economic and equity considerations described in the preceding section. Whereas the first column of table 4-7 is clearly preferable to the second column on economic grounds, the ordering is reversed when administrative aspects of the choice are considered. Thus, it may be that 3bF in table 4-19 is the best alternative, not so much because of its economic merits, but because of its administrative ones.

Preferences under Partial Dividend Relief[52]

Thus far the discussion of this chapter has been entirely in the context of a system of complete dividend relief. But, as noted in chapter 3, complete relief from the double taxation of dividends is, in fact, rare and, for various reasons, including loss of revenue and reduction of distributional progressivity, is not likely to be enacted in any country. Partial dividend relief, besides being more common, is the more likely alternative.

By itself, partial dividend relief is not hard to understand or achieve. If the corporate tax rate is 50 percent, half of its extra burden on dividends can be eliminated by allowing a shareholder credit of 50 percent of dividends received (net of the credit), by allowing the corporation a deduction of 50 percent of dividends paid, or by applying a rate of only 25 percent to income resulting in dividends. But when tax preferences exist, if dividend relief is not complete many of the problems examined in this chapter become more complex and more policy decisions are necessary.

It will be useful to illustrate the policy alternatives that exist in a world of tax preferences and partial dividend relief in the context of a system using the dividend-paid deduction. Suppose that under complete dividend relief, deduction is allowed only for dividends paid from fully taxed income, so that preferences are washed out when

52. The discussion of this section has benefited materially from a paper by George Mundstock, "Dividend Relief: A Mechanism to Take Account of the Relationship Between Individual and Corporation Income Taxes" (1978). Analogous problems would arise under partial integration.

distributed. There are at least two reasonable alternative interpretations of the analogous approach under partial dividend relief. Under one interpretation deduction would be allowed so long as *dividends* did not exceed fully taxable income. Under the alternative and more liberal interpretation only the *deduction* would need to be compared with fully taxable income. If only half of dividends are deductible, only half as much of fully taxable income is "used up" by a given amount of dividends under the second approach ("deduction set off against taxed income") as under the first ("dividends set off against taxed income"), and the extra unused fully taxed income can be used to absorb deductions based on dividends paid from tax-preferred income.

The first approach is, of course, more consistent with the idea of washing out preferences when dividends exceed taxable income and, in fact, is the one implicitly used in France and the United Kingdom (though in the context of an imputation system).[53]

A second policy issue involves the rate at which précompte is collected when preference income is presumed to be distributed. Suppose that the corporate tax rate is 50 percent but that shareholders get a credit for only 50 percent of dividends received. Précompte could be collected at a rate of 50 percent on distributed preference income or it could be collected at a rate of only 25 percent, as in France. The second approach has the advantage that the précompte is exactly equal to the rate of shareholder credit, so that distributed preference income is taxed at the shareholder's marginal tax rate, as it would be under a system of complete dividend relief. But such a result is rather anomalous in that similar treatment has, by assumption, been explicitly rejected for nonpreferred income under a system of partial dividend relief. The first approach, though it is not currently employed, might therefore be more consistent with partial dividend relief because taxable income and distributed preference income would receive similar treatment under it.[54] Which of the approaches involves the conceptually preferable approach to wash-

53. It is also a feature of the schemes proposed to the White House by the Treasury Department in September 1977 and by Congressman Al Ullman (as it would be when fully implemented) in early 1978 (see also the appendix to this chapter and chapter 7).

54. For a further discussion of this difference, including numerical examples, see the discussion of the French system in chapter 3.

ing out preferences is open to question, since there seems to be no easy answer to whether washout of preferences under partial dividend relief should be measured relative to the tax treatment accorded ordinary (noncorporate) income or to that accorded distributed corporate income that is fully taxed to the firm. Even the definition proposed above as the benchmark for measuring pass-through of preferences in a world of complete integration or dividend relief is ambiguous if dividend relief is only partial. Finally, which approach is preferable as a matter of public policy depends on the objectives of policy.

Summary

Most of the published discussion of integration and dividend relief has, unfortunately, been in the context of a system in which there are no tax preferences. Once tax preferences are admitted, integration and dividend relief become much more complex administratively, especially if the integration or dividend relief is only partial. It becomes necessary to have arbitrary rules to specify the extent to which dividends are presumed to be paid from preference income and taxed income. But the rules that are easiest to administer may not make the best sense from the standpoint of public policy and they may have unwelcome effects on corporate dividend policy. The proper treatment of tax preferences under integration or dividend relief is one of the three questions—the other two being the feasibility of full integration and the proper treatment of international capital flows—most in need of further study.

Appendix: The Ullman Proposal

In early 1978 Chairman Al Ullman of the House Committee on Ways and Means introduced a proposal for the partial relief of double taxation of dividends.[55] Initially a shareholder credit would be al-

55. *Congressional Record,* daily ed., February 2, 1978, pp. H 640-42, and March 22, 1978, pp. H 2337-38. This proposal is quite similar to that said to have been proposed to President Carter by the Treasury Department in September 1977. See "Tax Reform Option Papers Prepared by Treasury Department, September 2, 1977, for the White House," Bureau of National Affairs, *Daily Report for Executives* (Special Supplement), DER 196 (October 7, 1977). See also chap. 7.

lowed for 10 percent of net dividend income, but the credit would increase until by 1985 (1987 in the subsequent proposal) it equaled 20 percent of net dividends. Thus the fraction of the corporate tax effectively eliminated on dividends paid from fully taxed corporate income would first have been 10.83 percent (10 percent of 52, or 5.2 as a percent of 48) and then have risen to 21.67 percent.

To limit the amount of credit allowed shareholders to the amount of taxes actually paid by the corporation, the Ullman proposal would establish a "shareholder credit account" (SCA) at the corporate level (called a refundable income tax account, or RITA, in chapter 7). Additions to this account would be a given percentage of net corporate tax liability for each firm.[56] A firm's SCA would be reduced by the amount of any credits allowed shareholders, and no shareholder credits could be taken once the firm's SCA was exhausted. The effect would be, in principle, quite similar to that of the British system with its advance corporation tax, described in chapter 3. Though shareholders could not take credit for taxes not paid, the corporation could contribute more than the stipulated percentage of its tax liability to the SCA so that its shareholders could take the full credit. Such extra contributions would be added to the SCA on a dollar for dollar basis; they are analogous to the précompte in European systems, but would be optional, so that the forced dividend features of the précompte would be absent.

Implicit in the mechanics of the system is the assumption that dividends would be paid first from taxable income, that is, that preferences would be stacked last. Thus, though preferences would be washed out to the extent distributed, the presumptive stacking rules

56. As the shareholder credit increased from 10 to 20 percent of dividends this percentage would have risen under the original Ullman proposal from 10.83 to 21.67. With the 48 percent corporate tax rate, $100 of taxable corporate source income could produce as much as $52 in dividends. This amount of dividends would generate $5.20 in shareholder credits if the shareholder credit rate were 10 percent ($10.40 if it were 20 percent). To produce an equal amount in the SCA, it would be necessary to allow corporations to add 5.2/48 or 10.83 percent (21.67 percent if the credit rate is 20 percent) of their tax to the SCA. Of course, the percentage of tax added to the SCA that would result in exact washout of preferences depends mathematically upon the corporate tax rate and the shareholder credit rate. With a 50 percent corporate tax rate the percentage of tax added to the SCA would equal the shareholder credit rate. But in his March 22 proposal Ullman increased the percentage of tax that could be added to the SCA to 100 percent in 1979 and 30 percent at the end of a transition period in 1987.

would work to minimize the amount of preferences that would be in fact washed out. But it would not be necessary to define tax preferences explicitly under the Ullman proposal. If the full rate of corporate tax had not been paid on income presumed to be distributed, additional tax would be automatically collected when the tax-preferred income was distributed, either from the firm (as a "voluntary" tax) or from the shareholder. Finally, under the revised Ullman proposal contributions to the SCA, at 30 to 100 percent of taxes paid, would exceed the contributions needed to achieve exact washout of preferences; the effect would therefore be more liberal than exact washout. (See also the section on preferences under partial dividend relief in this chapter.)

Other noteworthy features of the Ullman proposal include:

1. The shareholder credit would be denied to tax-exempt organizations and foreigners.

2. The current provisions for the deduction of intercorporate dividends received would remain intact. The recipient corporation could not use the shareholder credits connected with intercorporate dividends to offset its own tax liabilities; it could only add the credits to its own SCA.

3. Any time a negative balance was created in the SCA by net losses, audit adjustments, or amended returns, the firm would be required to pay enough tax to eliminate the deficit.

Administrative Feasibility of Integration

IT HAS recently come to be realized that the treatment of tax preferences involves the most fundamental issues in the debate over integration and dividend relief, aside from the prior question of whether or not to have integration or dividend relief, and if so, which kind. And, as chapter 4 should amply document, the treatment of preferences gives rise to some of the most complicated technical and administrative problems. Yet there are other difficult questions of administrative feasibility so important that the very decisions of whether and how to provide integration or dividend relief may hinge upon their solution. Some of these problems are discussed in this chapter.[1]

1. I do not, however, consider such complications as the tax treatment of corporate mergers, divisions, reorganizations, liquidations, redemptions of stock, and stock dividends. Though an appreciation of the problems involved and their potential solutions should condition any decision on integration, these issues are extremely complex and a thorough discussion of them is well beyond the scope of the book.

It is only fair to note, however, that full integration would somewhat reduce administrative complexity by making it possible to eliminate the provisions for personal holding companies. Rules for subchapter S corporations would seem to be superfluous, but they might be retained to make integration easier for firms with

It is widely accepted by economists—though perhaps not acknowledged by businessmen and their spokesmen who fully understand it —that full integration is socially preferable to dividend relief on conceptual, allocational, and distributional grounds.[2] Therefore, I examine the feasibility of full integration before I consider the feasibility of divers approaches to providing dividend relief, including those in use in other countries and variants of them.

Policy Issues in Full Integration

In this section I discuss some policy decisions that would have to be made before full integration could be implemented. Though these are not technical administrative issues, they would greatly affect the way in which the taxation of corporate-source income would impinge on corporate decisions and on the functioning of the economy. I deal first with the implications of integration for the taxation of long-term capital gains and then with the dual problem of the relation between the corporate withholding tax rate and the top personal income tax rate and the effects of integration on corporate liquidity.

especially simple capital structures. Whether the concept of earnings and profits and rules for the division between dividends and capital gains would be needed would depend in part on decisions of tax policy and technical questions of tax design. Furthermore, integration or dividend relief, to the extent that it implied or led to full taxation of capital gains or the elimination of tax preferences, could greatly simplify administration. This is discussed in Alvin C. Warren, Jr., "Integration of the Individual and Corporate Income Taxes," paper presented to an American Law Institute-American Bar Association Conference on Federal Income Tax Simplification, Warrenton, Virginia, January 1978, pp. 314–15 (forthcoming in proceedings volume to be published by ALI).

Likewise, the transition problems of any move to integration or dividend relief are not discussed. These problems are very important, but they are also likely to be extremely complicated. Moreover, the transition rules would probably depend on the approach (and subvariant) to integration or dividend relief that is adopted, and even under one approach there might be several different reasonable ways to deal with certain problems. Consequently, an exhaustive discussion of transition rules is also well beyond the scope of this study. For preliminary comments on rules for transition to a system of full integration, see U.S. Department of the Treasury, *Blueprints for Basic Tax Reform* (Government Printing Office, 1977), pp. 194–200. Other than this, little has been written on the subject.

Finally, no effort has been made to determine how businesses that are treated in a unique manner under present law, such as insurance companies, should be taxed if integration or dividend relief were adopted.

2. See the discussion in chapter 2 on how "integration" means different things to different people.

Implications for Long-Term Capital Gains Tax

Full integration is tantamount to taxing long-term capital gains resulting from the retention of corporate earnings as ordinary income on an accrual basis. This system has important advantages from both equity and efficiency points of view,[3] but it also has implications that have only rarely been recognized.

When undistributed earnings are taxed to shareholders under full integration, the basis of stock must be written up by the amount of the taxed earnings, to prevent double taxation of any subsequent capital gains resulting from the retentions. Thus taxable capital gains on the sale of shares would be less frequent and smaller than under the present tax system, and capital losses would be more common and larger.[4] Several salutary results can be expected.

First, shareholders would become more militant in their demands that corporate management retain and invest funds only when there is no better use for them. Such militancy would occur because unwise investment policies could lead to the failure of stock prices to keep up with the increase in basis resulting from retentions and therefore could generate book losses on shares. Under the present tax system the shareholder could also adversely interpret failure of share prices to rise with retained earnings; but under full integration there would be the added signal coming from the adjustment in basis for allocated retentions. Moreover, whereas under the present system inefficient investment policies may be tolerated because they are sheltered by the preferential taxation of long-term capital gains (at least for the wealthy shareholders who determine most corporate decisions), once all corporate-source income were taxed as ordinary income, the

3. The advantage from an equity point of view is that income generating such capital gains would be taxed at the rate applied to ordinary income rather than at an aggregate rate equal to the corporate rate plus the present-value equivalent of the long-term capital gains rate. Thus with the present rate structure the taxation of this form of income would increase at the top of the income scale and fall at the bottom. From an efficiency point of view, the primary advantages are that the allocation of capital between the corporate and noncorporate sectors would not be distorted, that use of debt financing would not be artificially encouraged, and that more capital income would be subjected to the test of the marketplace instead of simply being retained by those firms that happen to earn it. (These and related arguments are presented in greater detail in chapter 2.)

4. These statements ignore any flow-through of corporate capital gains and losses under integration.

shelter would be removed, and the shareholder would be less tolerant of inefficiency.

Second, lock-in, one of the traditionally decried faults with taxing capital gains only when realized, would be substantially reduced.[5] Though the benefits from increased fluidity of investment funds could not easily be measured, they would undoubtedly exist.

Because full integration is equivalent to taxing as ordinary income long-term capital gains on shares that result from retained earnings, it would seem grossly unfair not to allow shareholders to deduct against ordinary income capital losses reflecting failure of share prices to rise by the amount of retained income that had previously been taxed. But acceptance of this line of reasoning raises several important issues.

To begin with, should the deduction for capital losses extend to *all* losses on shares, or should it be limited to little more than the amount of previous adjustments to basis that reflects retained earnings taxed to the shareholder? Though such a limitation would be administratively bothersome, it might be preferable to unlimited deduction, which would involve further drastic changes in the tax law and enormous potential for abuse through the "culling" of portfolios.

Moreover, if deduction were made available for all losses on corporate shares, regardless of whether they reflected adjustments in basis, to prevent abuse it would be necessary to tax all capital gains on shares as ordinary income. Even then, investors would probably cull their portfolios to take advantage of the deduction, while holding shares with unrealized gains. Thus one might be led almost inexorably to a system of periodic constructive realization.[6] But would one really want to tax all long-term capital gains as ordinary income without making allowance for inflation? And would one want to adjust the asset side of the balance sheet to eliminate inflationary gains without also adjusting the liability side to tax gains resulting from the reduction in the real value of outstanding debt?[7] Of course,

5. See, for example, Martin David, *Alternative Approaches to Capital Gains Taxation* (Brookings Institution, 1968), pp. 198–208.

6. It might, for example, be possible to provide for gains to be constructively realized, say every two or three years, with appropriate averaging to relieve bunching of income.

7. On the general question of adjusting income for inflation, see Henry J. Aaron, ed., *Inflation and the Income Tax* (Brookings Institution, 1976). For an attempt to

taxation of all capital gains as ordinary income, full allowance of capital losses, constructive realization, and inflation adjustments have much to recommend them at the conceptual level and are in themselves legitimate goals for tax reform. But what is not often realized is that they may be part and parcel of any proposal to integrate the income taxes on retained earnings as well as on dividends.[8] Consequently, given the technical details that would need to be ironed out before such a package could be put in place—not to mention the political controversy it would create—full integration could not be achieved quickly.[9]

The Withholding Rate

It is commonly assumed that under full integration the withholding rate applied to corporate-source income cannot fall very far below the top marginal rate of shareholders without creating untenable liquidity problems for investors in firms with low payout ratios.[10] This assumption requires careful scrutiny because if it is valid it has important implications. In the extreme case either the top personal rate would be reduced to about 50 percent or the corporate rate would be increased to 70 percent.[11] Reduction of the top rate would

determine the extent to which nominal gains that have been taxed actually represent real gains, see Martin Feldstein and Joel Slemrod, "Inflation and the Excess Taxation of Capital Gains on Corporate Stock," *National Tax Journal,* vol. 31 (June 1978), pp. 107–18.

8. The Canadian Royal Commission on Taxation, which has produced the most comprehensive proposal for total integration to date, did realize these implications; it recommended all these things except the inflation adjustment. See *Report of the Royal Commission on Taxation,* vol. 4 (Ottawa: Queen's Printer, 1967), pp. 3–93. The U.S. Treasury Department's *Blueprints for Basic Tax Reform* recommends all these except taxation of capital gains on an accrual basis.

9. There seems to be no point in repeating the well-known difficulties inherent in taxing all capital gains as they accrue; among these are liquidity problems and problems of valuing closely held businesses and real estate.

10. This view was expressed by the Canadian Royal Commission, *Report,* p. 35, and has been endorsed, for example, by Edwin S. Cohen in "Possible Solutions to Practical Problems in Integration of the Corporate and Shareholder Income Tax," *National Tax Journal,* vol. 28 (September 1975), p. 365.

11. It might appear that the top personal rate should be reduced to perhaps 36 percent, since preferences reduce the effective corporate tax rate to about that level. But (1) on liquidity grounds it would seem more reasonable to unify the personal rate with that paid by corporations with the *highest* effective rates, which are near 48 percent, and (2) if preferences were to be washed out (but not simply eliminated), a précompte would probably be used to bring the effective rate on distributed earnings up to the statutory rate. On the other hand, if preferences were

make it difficult to maintain an acceptable degree of progressivity in the income tax system.[12] On the other hand, an increase in the corporate rate to 70 percent would, in effect, constitute a forced dividend to all shareholders not in the top tax bracket. Given that one of the objectives of integration is to subject more funds to the test of the capital markets, this forced dividend might at first glance seem to be a positive effect; but, in fact, it would be an undesirable distortion of corporate financial policy. Moreover, it would contravene the spirit, if not the letter, of the law regarding the rights of owners of preferred stock (especially noncumulative stock). It is, after all, quite a different thing to discuss variations in rates of corporate tax (1) when that tax is a final burden and (2) when the corporate tax is "only" a withholding tax. In the extreme case the withholding tax might be raised to 100 percent, but be creditable or refundable to holders of common shares; in such an event there would be nothing left to distribute to "preferred" shareholders.[13]

The argument for unification of the two rates usually goes something like this:

if the individual rate goes as high as 70 percent and the corporate rate is 48 percent, a top bracket individual would have to pay out of his own funds 22 percent tax on corporate earnings never distributed to him or realized by him. Not only is there a possible constitutional issue on this score, but . . . such a system would seem unfair unless consented to by all shareholders.[14]

to be passed through, the effect on cash flow would depend on the type of preferences involved. Creditable preferences that were passed through would have no effect on the amount of gross-up and credit taken at the shareholder level. (See chapter 4.) But deductible preferences would actually *reduce* the amount of additional tax owed at the personal level by taxpayers with marginal rates above the corporate rate. (See table 4-3.)

12. Note, however, that in George F. Break and Joseph A. Pechman, *Federal Tax Reform: The Impossible Dream?* (Brookings Institution, 1975), chap. 6, and U.S. Treasury Department, *Blueprints for Basic Tax Reform,* chap. 5, total integration is combined with thorough tax reform in such a way that existing progressivity is maintained with marginal personal rates of no higher than 53 percent and 38 percent respectively.

13. This is one instance of the importance of the choice of rules under which undistributed earnings would be allocated to owners of various classes of stock. For an especially cogent statement of some of the points made in this paragraph, see Stanley S. Surrey, "Reflections on 'Integration' of Corporation and Individual Income Taxes," *National Tax Journal,* vol. 28 (September 1975), p. 336. See also the next section of this chapter.

14. Cohen, "Possible Solutions," p. 365.

Daniel Holland has presented a particularly powerful rebuttal to this generally held opinion. Most relevant for publicly owned corporations, it is worth quoting at length:

in principle, under an accrual income tax retained corporate earnings should be taxable to the shareholder at the time of reinvestment. This is the main issue, and considerations of shareholder's liquidity a secondary matter. To the extent that earnings are retained stock prices should rise, and stockholders could pay taxes by realizing the increment. Or, if they prefer, they could borrow to pay the tax. For most high-bracket taxpayers borrowing would not be necessary, however, since they would have savings out of current income, and could, therefore, meet the tax due on their pro rata share of retained earnings, thereby choosing to save in this form vis-à-vis other forms of saving. Finally, the stockholder always has the option of selling his shares in a given corporation, and buying those of corporations whose distribution policy accords more with his needs.

Therefore, political considerations and a possible constitutional issue aside, withholding need not be at the maximum rate of personal income tax.[15]

Holland's case can be made even more forceful if the standard liquidity argument is paraphrased something like this: When the shareholder receives distributed corporate-source income, he wants to reinvest it, or part of it, in the same corporation. But if he does so, he will not have enough cash flow to pay his income tax. Therefore, either the top bracket rate must be cut or as much as could conceivably be due from a taxpayer in the existing top marginal bracket must be withheld at source—even if it means vastly overwithholding on taxpayers in lower tax brackets—so as not to thwart his reinvestment goals.

An analogous argument that wage earners should have their tax liabilities reduced so that they could meet saving objectives would, despite the beginnings in that direction implied by individual retirement accounts and tax-sheltered annuity plans, probably be met with general derision.[16]

There is another side to the liquidity issue that has seldom been mentioned. It seems likely that in many instances firms would reduce

15. Daniel M. Holland, "Some Observations on Full Integration," *National Tax Journal,* vol. 28 (September 1975), p. 355.

16. Note that Cohen's argument, carried to its logical conclusion, is the case for an expenditure tax, something that has not been warmly endorsed by policymakers.

cash dividends if the corporate withholding rate were raised to 70 percent. If they did so, the low-income shareholder would find his own cash flow adversely affected, since he would be able to obtain benefit for the tax withheld on his behalf only at the end of the year, when he filed his tax return. Of course, it might be possible to let shareholders take provisional credit on their estimated tax for corporate taxes being withheld in their favor (as is done in West Germany) and even to alter withholding on wages to take account of corporate withholding (as is not the case in West Germany). But it seems unlikely that provision would be made for those with little labor income or other capital income, and therefore little tax liability, to receive credit for overpayment of the tax before they file their annual income tax returns.[17] Finally, the same basic argument could be made even if the withholding rate were maintained at or near 50 percent.

As Holland has rightly noted, so long as the basis for taxation is income rather than expenditure, no reason exists to put such high priority on the high-income shareholder's reinvestment plans, particularly since other options are open. This is especially true because under the envisaged integration scheme, part, and perhaps all, of long-term capital gains would have already been taxed as ordinary income at the corporate level; thus, though there would be transaction costs in realizing gains in order to pay taxes, no tax penalty (or much less of one than under the present system) would be involved. In fact, to the extent that share prices failed to reflect retained earnings, the shareholder realizing gains to pay taxes would, because of the write-up of basis, actually have a partial offset to his liability for the tax on retained earnings attributed to him.

On the other hand, it would seem unwise to have no withholding tax, at least if the effectiveness of information returns is not improved. Given the notable lack of success of self-enforcement of the income tax on dividend income, both equity and revenue would

17. It must also be remembered that the corporate withholding rate is a final tax for tax-exempt organizations unless they are granted the benefits of integration. Although there has been considerable discussion of whether to allow such organizations those benefits, hardly anyone has suggested that an unrelieved tax of 70 percent would be appropriate. But a 70 percent credit, though no different in concept from a 50 percent credit, would create greater political problems if extended to these organizations. Thus tax-exempt organizations would probably receive only partial credit if the rate were raised to 70 percent.

probably suffer if taxpayers had to be relied on to remit tax on retained as well as distributed earnings.

In short, then, achieving similarity of corporate and top personal rates would create problems whether the unification were achieved at too high or too low a rate. Thus it would seem most appropriate to choose some intermediate withholding rate, such as 40 to 50 percent, as a rough compromise,[18] and leave the top personal rate to be determined by equity objectives once integration and other reforms were in place, instead of "making the individual rate a hostage to the corporate rate and inseparably linked to it."[19] If that were done, the need to coordinate the two rates should not be a major obstacle to full integration.

Technical Problems of Full Integration

The case for integration based on the conduit view of the corporation is essentially the case for treating the corporation, for tax purposes, like a partnership. Seen in this light, dividend relief is at the most only a second-best alternative forced upon a nation by administrative realities. This section examines the administrative problems that might, in fact, render full integration administratively infeasible and narrow the choice to providing dividend relief, retaining the present classical system, or repealing the corporate tax and taxing capital gains on an accrual basis. The "pure partnership" approach to full integration would be very difficult to implement, indeed, and even a compromise approach would face serious problems.

The "Pure Partnership" Approach

The pure partnership approach would give rise to many problems. Under a purist interpretation of the partnership approach to total integration each shareholder would have attributed to him a pro rata share in the earnings of a corporation during the part of the year he owned its stock. Moreover, the various components of the earnings would retain their identity in the hands of the shareholder and be

18. It is of particular interest that the Office of Tax Analysis of the U.S. Department of the Treasury, while recognizing the liquidity problem, did not seem to regard a corporate withholding tax as an essential ingredient of its January 1977 integration scheme. See *Blueprints for Basic Tax Reform,* pp. 73–74.

19. The quotation is from Surrey, "Reflections," p. 338.

taxed to him as such, instead of being lumped together.[20] That is, capital gains and interest on state and local securities, for example, would be segregated from ordinary income so that the shareholder could take advantage of the special tax treatment of the first two.[21] Moreover, tax preferences would be allocated to the shareholder, so that there would be no question of whether they should be passed through or washed out; the very logical foundation of the partnership approach would require the former. Finally, a withholding tax could be applied at the corporate level, but doing that might be somewhat more questionable than if all forms of corporate income were simply lumped together.[22]

The possibility of flowing through all income identified by origin and passing through all preferences raises the possibility of widespread tax-shelter problems as well as administration and compliance ones. Whereas some high-income taxpayers must now be concerned about the prohibition of borrowing to carry tax-exempt securities, under integration all shareholders of firms holding such securities would have this worry. Likewise, other provisions of the U.S. tax code that currently impinge only on a taxpayer's personal

20. This description of the partnership approach is essentially a simple interpretation of the corporate partnership seen as an aggregate of its owners rather than as a separate entity. Though it has benefited from William A. Klein, "Income Taxation and Legal Entities," *UCLA Law Review,* vol. 20, issue 1 (1972–73), pp. 13–74, it is not intended to be an exhaustive study of the subject. Nor is it necessarily meant to be consistent with current interpretation in the taxation of partnerships under U.S. tax law. These shortcomings have little practical relevance, since it seems unlikely that the pure partnership approach is feasible, regardless of what reasonable interpretation is used.

21. That the capital gains and ordinary tax rates might be unified as part of a package containing integration does not affect this general argument, which applies equally to other types of preferentially taxed income.

22. Under the compromise approach described below, the corporate tax would retain more aspects of a separate-entity tax. Thus it is somewhat more reasonable from a conceptual point of view that under the compromise approach the withholding tax should be levied at a flat rate that is independent of the marginal rates of shareholders. If, as under the partnership approach, the corporation tax ceases to be a sensible part of the tax system, any withholding tax that is imposed would ideally be geared to the composition of the firm's income and to the marginal tax rates of shareholders. Given the existence of mutual funds, the use of street names, and so forth, such a requirement might be administratively very difficult to meet, though the issue deserves further study. However, this possible fault of the partnership approach is not considered further or weighted very heavily here, since its very existence depends on a stringent interpretation of that approach.

actions might come into play if he held shares in corporations engaged in tax-sheltered activities. Perhaps more important, if losses were simply flowed through to shareholders, corporations would very likely come to be used extensively for tax-shelter purposes, much as partnerships have been, unless such practices were constrained (as they recently have come to be in partnerships). The necessary constraints might seriously complicate the tax law.[23]

If some shareholders in corporations were themselves corporations, the corporate shareholders could not file their tax returns until informed of their portion of the profits (and other income) of the firms whose shares they own. Clearly, this would make it hard to get information to shareholders on a timely basis. Moreover, in some instances of interlocking corporate ownership, it would be impossible for one firm to determine the income to be reported to its shareholders until all firms determined theirs; for example, through a system of simultaneous equations.[24] The problem is not that the mathematics would be difficult; rather, the stumbling block is the need to transmit and utilize substantial amounts of complicated information on a timely basis.

Even in the absence of corporate shareholders, the data processing problem of the partnership approach would be enormous, since it would be necessary to report to each person who held stock in a given corporation during any part of the year his pro rata share of the firm's earnings for the year. This problem would be aggravated by the existence of stock held for shareholders by mutual funds or in the name of brokers.[25] Moreover, each of the shareholders would be responsible for adjusting his basis in the stock of the corporation for undistributed earnings attributed to him. Though this might not be a major problem in true partnerships, which are usually characterized by few partners and generally nonmarketable equity interests, it could be one in large, widely held firms with readily marketable securities. Certainly experience with record-keeping for reinvested income by owners of shares in mutual funds does not make one optimistic.

23. See Warren, "Integration." This aspect of integration, like most others involving preferences, has hardly been examined.

24. See Richard B. Goode, *The Postwar Corporation Tax Structure* (U.S. Treasury Department, Division of Tax Research, 1948), p. 20, n. 35.

25. Fortunately the United States is not plagued by bearer shares, which would tend to make any approach to integration unworkable.

The issuing of more than one class of stock by a corporation also complicates the implementation of the partnership approach to full integration. As Goode noted:

profits retained in one year in excess of accumulated claims of preferred stockholders would presumably be allocated to holders of common stock. Yet in a later year these funds might be used to pay dividends on preferred stock. Correction of this situation would require reopening returns or adjusting current year's income for all stockholders of the earlier year. . . .

In the interest of administrative feasibility at least the largest corporations with the longest lists of stockholders and the most complicated capital structures would probably have to be excluded from partnership treatment.[26]

Excluding large firms with complicated capital structures from integration would, of course, make integration a shell not worth the effort. But not much has been written suggesting that there is a feasible solution to the problems of multiple issues of stock since Goode, in 1948, made the statement above. As will be seen, this problem plagues less ambitious approaches to integration as well as the pure partnership approach.[27]

Audit adjustments and amended returns create additional problems.[28] Literal interpretation of the pure partnership approach would suggest that when audit adjustments or amended returns resulted in modification of the income figures for a corporation, each taxpayer who had held shares of the firm during the year in question would be required to file an amended return for that year. Under present law the Internal Revenue Service would be required to undertake litigation against each of the "shareholder-partners." This would clearly be unworkable, and it is almost certain that the IRS would proceed only against the corporation. But even if it did that, the search for an easy and proper solution would appear to be doomed.

It is not uncommon for litigation in complicated corporate tax

26. Goode, *Postwar Corporation Tax Structure,* pp. 20–21.

27. Under subchapter S, which is the closest thing to the partnership approach found in the U.S. tax code (outside of partnerships themselves), complications are avoided by specifying that only one class of stock may be issued and that all shareholders must be individuals or estates. Moreover, under subchapter S not all items of income retain their identity in the hands of shareholders.

28. I wish to thank Bernard Wolfman for suggesting this example and the next one.

cases to take eight or ten years. Thus either the statute of limitations would run out on shareholder liabilities or the shareholder would be deemed to be a party to the litigation. In the former case the outcome of the litigation would be academic. In the latter case the situation would be impossible, since millions of individual returns for a period long since past would have to be reopened. In addition, adjustment of allocated income for that period would involve adjustment to the basis of shares, including some that had been sold in intervening years, so that returns for yet other years would have to be amended. Furthermore, averaging provisions, provisions for carry-over of investment tax credits, and such, could result in further ripples to other years. But impossible as that seems, the situation would be even worse if there were corporate shareholders in the firm filing the amended return or subject to audit adjustment. In that case the corporate shareholders would be required to reopen *their* returns for the year in question. Even if one ignored the possibility of having to solve simultaneously for retrospective corporate tax liabilities in the case of interlocking ownership, one still would face the specter of all the shareholders in the shareholding company filing amended returns, with all the problems detailed above, and so on for other layers of corporate ownership.

Another source of difficulty would arise if the special treatment of long-term capital gains were not abolished. Suppose that a partnership owned some real estate that it sold at a gain. Though there might be a presumption that such a gain would be taxed as a capital gain if the partnership were not in the real estate business, the gain could be taxed as ordinary income to all the partners if any one of them were in that business. Carrying this rule over to the partnership taxation of corporations would, of course, cause administrative headaches and inequities. Thus it would appear that the distinction between capital gains and ordinary income would have to be applied at the firm level. But if this were done, the room for abuse would be enormous, since members of the real estate industry could use the corporate form to do what they could not do as individuals (have gains on real estate transactions treated as capital gains).[29] Of course, there might be ways around these abuses, but if separate rules had to

29. Collapsible corporations can now be employed in this way.

be made for corporations, depending on the composition of their ownership, the tax law would become further complicated.

Another problem involving tax preferences would occur when the fiscal years of corporations and shareholders did not coincide. In such a case the firm ideally would tell the shareholder-partner how much of the investment tax credit, for example, fell in each of his fiscal years that overlapped the fiscal year of the firm. But in the extreme case in which a firm had shareholders with fiscal years starting throughout the year, it would be necessary to report the investment tax credit (or investment eligible for the credit) on a day-by-day basis rather than in total for the year.[30] Moreover, it would no longer make sense to compute the limits for the credit at the corporate level, since the credit, if it existed at that level, would only reduce the provisional withholding tax and would have no effect on the ultimate tax liability at the shareholder level, where ideally the limitation should be applied. Thus each shareholder would be responsible for the calculation of his own investment tax credit (as affected by his own limitation), based on information supplied by the firm.

A final problem, similar to the one just described, involves the foreign tax credit. Under the literal interpretation of the partnership approach, the foreign tax credit, like the investment tax credit, would not exist at the corporate level in any important sense. Instead, it would be passed through to shareholders. But this means that all shareholders of firms paying taxes to foreign countries would have to file the requisite forms in order to take advantage of the foreign tax credit, even if they had no other foreign-source income. Therefore, it is possible that over 20 million taxpayers would be required to calculate limitations on the credit and be concerned with carry-backs and carry-forwards of the foreign tax credit.

In short, the pure partnership method would be difficult to administer if it suffered from only one of the problems outlined above. Since it could be afflicted with all of them, it does not seem to be a viable alternative. At most, the general objectives of the partnership approach might be achieved. Thus in what follows, any references to total integration (except where the contrary is stated) are to an

30. The present treatment under subchapter S, in which it is assumed that all income is attributed to shareholders on the last day of the corporation's tax year, does not seem entirely appropriate here.

impure system that involves allocation of retentions to shareholders, but attempts to avoid the problems described in this section.

A Less Ambitious Approach to Full Integration

The most commonly discussed approach that would approximate the results of the pure partnership is that proposed in Canada by the Royal Commission on Taxation and in slightly different form in the United States in *Blueprints for Basic Tax Reform*. After concluding that the partnership approach would be impossible to implement, the Royal Commission proposed a system that would entail optional "allocation" of retained earnings to shareholders, grossing up both dividends and allocated retentions, allowing the shareholder credit against his personal tax for the corporate tax, and writing up the basis of shares by the amount of allocated retentions.[31] The authors of *Blueprints for Basic Tax Reform* followed a similar course. The question, then, is whether the commission and the authors of *Blueprints* were correct in thinking that their proposals could be implemented; if not, the relevant choice is between the present classical system and dividend relief.[32] In answering this question, it will be useful to consider whether the problems that plague the partnership approach can be handled under the Canadian Royal Commission's and Treasury Department's methods of full integration. But first I note one slight difference between the administrative feasibility of the Royal Commission's approach and that of the U.S. Treasury's.

The objective of integration is (1) to include all corporate-source equity income in the income for tax purposes of shareholders, and (2) to increase the basis of corporate shares by the amount of earnings taxed to the shareholders but not distributed to them; the second

31. For a further description of the basics of the Royal Commission's approach, see Charles E. McLure, Jr., "Integration of the Personal and Corporate Income Taxes: The Missing Element in Recent Tax Reform Proposals," *Harvard Law Review*, vol. 88 (January 1975), pp. 558–61, 569–74. Though the Canadian Royal Commission's approach would have made allocation of retained earnings optional, that part of the plan does not seem desirable and is therefore discussed primarily in footnotes.

32. Another approach, mentioned in chapter 1, is to eliminate the corporate income tax but tax all capital gains on corporate stock as ordinary income on an accrual basis. Since this approach is not usually included within the scope of integration, it is not discussed further here. For a presentation of this system, see Carl S. Shoup, *Facing the Tax Problem: A Survey of Taxation in the United States and a Program for the Future* (Twentieth Century Fund, 1937), pp. 464–91.

step is needed to prevent such retentions from being taxed twice, once as income and once as capital gains. This result can be achieved in two broadly equivalent ways. Under one approach, retained earnings would be added to dividends and become part of shareholder income, with a basis adjustment being made for retentions. Under the other, all corporate income would be taxed to the shareholder (with no distinction between retentions and dividends) and result in an upward basis adjustment. Then dividends would not constitute taxable income to the shareholder; rather, they would be treated as a distribution of capital and result in a reduction of basis.[33] Algebraically the two approaches are identical; but as a practical matter they may differ considerably.

The first approach would seem to have the advantage that integration and its complexities might not need to be legislated. That is, only dividend relief would need to be provided, but for tax purposes corporations would be allowed the option of treating part of retained earnings like dividends, without actually making the distribution.[34] Given the pressures for "allocation" of retained earnings for tax purposes, integration would be achieved in many cases de facto, but would not be required.

The second approach, however, would seem to be preferable to the first. It would codify the basic principle that corporate-source income should be treated like other income, whether distributed or not. Adoption of the first approach, under which retentions and dividends would continue to be treated as two different types of income, would encourage differential treatment of dividends and retentions (where tax preferences were concerned, for example).[35] Thus in what follows I focus the discussion on a system based on the second approach, though occasionally I comment on the implications of the alternative method.

33. The first approach was proposed by the Canadian Royal Commission in its *Report,* pp. 6–9; the second by the U.S. Treasury Department in *Blueprints for Basic Tax Reform,* pp. 69–70.

34. This approach might avoid any constitutional issues of taxes being collected on unrealized income. But it might open the way for lawsuits by shareholders in low tax brackets any time the maximum amount of retentions were not "allocated" for tax purposes.

35. It would not be possible to make the allocation of retained earnings for tax purposes an optional matter under the second approach, as it was in the proposal of the Canadian Royal Commission (*Report,* p. 7).

If income had to be attributed to shareholders in the year in which it was earned, the same problems of providing information on a timely basis and needing to solve simultaneously for the tax liabilities of interrelated corporations would arise as under the pure partnership method.[36] But it would appear to be feasible to allow firms to allocate earnings of a given year to shareholders at a given date (or dates) in the following year or years. Though there would be some chance for delay of tax liability at the shareholder level, a corporate withholding tax could be collected so that the advantages of delay would be minimal.

It is usually agreed that, because of record-keeping requirements, allocating corporate income to shareholders on a pro rata basis, depending on the number of days that stock has been held, is unworkable. Hence it would be necessary to choose a day of record on which to allocate corporate earnings to shareholders. Since choosing the last day of the corporate fiscal year as the date of record paves the way for "trafficking in losses" between shareholders in different marginal tax brackets, the U.S. Treasury Department's *Blueprints* would make the first day of the corporate fiscal year the day of record.[37] But the choice is not without problems. *Blueprints for Basic Tax Reform* demonstrates that if capital gains are taxed as ordinary income, events occurring after the sale of stock have no effect on the calculation of the taxable income of the seller.[38] But this story is incomplete.

First, even if capital gains are taxed as ordinary income, they may

36. Under the alternative (Canadian) approach this problem would exist only for the retained part of earnings. Note, however, that if preferences were to be passed through (which involves grossing up retentions and dividends by the amount of taxable income and allowing shareholders credit for tax before credits at the firm level), administrative problems might arise if corporate income resulted in dividends one year but in allocated retentions the following year. It would be necessary to split corporate income into a distributed and a retained part and allocate the preferences between the parts. Besides involving unnecessary complications, this would invite differential treatment of the two parts of income.

37. *Blueprints for Basic Tax Reform*, p. 70.

38. If, for example, $100 of income earned after the sale is attributed to the seller, his basis in the stock he has sold is increased by $100. The $100 reduction in his capital gain on the stock just offsets the $100 of corporate income incorrectly attributed to him. See ibid., pp. 71–72. It is noted (p. 72) that the alternative method in which dividends and allocated retained earnings are treated as taxable income (with no reduction of basis on distribution) would create the anomalous situation in which the purchaser of shares who received dividends before the next record date would incur a tax liability, even though only a change in the composition of his portfolio were involved.

not be taxed as they accrue; if they are not, it will not do to offset capital gains against allocated retentions on a dollar-for-dollar basis. Though in total the taxable income of the seller is unaffected by post-sale events, the buyer does not pay tax on income attributable to the remainder of the year in which purchase is made until he disposes of the stock.[39] It seems unlikely that the market could exactly compensate for this, given the uncertainty involved in predicting income.

Second, even if it is agreed that the calculation of taxable income is unaffected, the amount of shareholder credit attributed to the shareholder of record is not independent of events after the sale. Therefore, he maintains an economic interest in the economic performance of any company whose stock he sells in a given year. Moreover, the credit goes to the wrong person (the seller rather than the buyer).[40]

As a compromise solution the last day of the fiscal year could be made the date of record, but shareholders would be allowed only an amount of deduction for losses based on a prorating of losses by the number of days the stock had been held.[41] Even this approach would

39. Ibid., p. 75.
40. See ibid., p. 74. In the example of note 38 the shareholder credit would be $50 higher (assuming a corporate withholding rate of 50 percent) if $100 were earned after the sale. Though capital markets could allow for expected post-sale income, they could not prevent severe inequities from occurring when income differed substantially from expected levels.
41. This is essentially subchapter S treatment. It might be desirable to append a provision that "extraordinary losses" would be allocated to actual shareholders on the day the loss occurred. Thus there would be no advantage in buying stock of loss companies for the loss deduction.
An interesting but generally neglected obverse side of the liquidity problem discussed earlier is worth mentioning. Under one interpretation of the flow-through of losses, the government would refund tax on losses to the firm at the same rate at which it taxes income. Then the shareholders would take gross-up and credit for the *negative* corporate tax. Shareholders subject to marginal rates above the corporate rate would receive refunds, but those in lower marginal rate brackets would *owe tax*. Given this anomalous result, it is more likely that no corporate tax would be refunded on losses. But if this were the case, gross-up and credit could not be applied to the loss at the shareholder level. That is, a shareholder to whom $100 of income and $100 of losses had been attributed would have no net corporate-source income and therefore should not be eligible for any gross-up and credit. But if losses were to be ignored, he would have a gross-up and credit on the income and no negative offset on the loss. More substantial problems could arise in the case of a parent company with both profitable and unprofitable subsidiaries. Disallowing offset of losses against gains in such cases would seem grossly unfair and unpopular, but distinguishing between direct and portfolio investment would further complicate the tax law.

not deal satisfactorily with the problem that the wrong shareholders might be getting the shareholder credit. If it were thought that this was not something that the market could handle, the withholding tax could be prorated among those who held stock during the year. But if this were done, there would seem to be little real reason not to pro-rate income as well.

Yet another way to prevent trafficking in losses would be simply not to pass losses through to shareholders. Instead, losses could be carried forward to offset earnings in future years.[42] Since the alternatives described above all suffer from major flaws, this may be the best approach, even if it is imperfect.[43]

For much the same reasons that they would make the pure partnership method unworkable, audit adjustments and amended returns would create almost insuperable problems if they meant reopening the returns of shareholders for the years affected by the resulting changes in income.[44] Thus there would seem to be no alternative but to reflect the results of adjustments and amended returns in the year in which the adjustments were made rather than in the year to which the adjustment referred.[45] This approach would, of course, place a substantial burden on accountants and financial analysts to make certain that contingent liabilities for taxes resulting from audit adjustments were set forth with sufficient clarity.[46]

42. It would make no sense to carry losses back, since all previously earned income would have been allocated to shareholders, unless the allocation of earnings were optional, as in the Canadian Royal Commission proposal. If allocation were optional, carry-back could be allowed to the extent of unallocated retentions. But recall that optional allocation is inconsistent with the decision not to distinguish between retentions and dividends, that is, the decision simply to allocate all corporate income and treat dividends as distributions from capital.

43. Presumably under such a system it would be firms (owned in large part by high-bracket shareholders) with other income, rather than shareholders, that would traffic in losses by absorbing firms with accumulated losses.

44. If allocation of retentions were optional, and substantial unallocated retentions were commonplace, results of such adjustments could simply be absorbed by unallocated retained earnings. But not all companies would have enough unallocated retentions to absorb adjustments, even if they had exercised the option not to allocate.

45. See U.S. Department of the Treasury, *Blueprints for Basic Tax Reform*, p. 74.

46. This burden may not be much greater than under present law. But whether present rules on disclosure would be adequate is not clear, since the entire area of financial disclosure under integration is largely unexplored and probably fraught with problems.

Under the hybrid version of full integration it would be easier to deal flexibly with the investment tax credit, other preference items, and the foreign tax credit than under the pure partnership approach. That is, under the latter it is illogical not to pass these items through to the shareholder to the extent that they would be available if invesment were made in a noncorporate form. But once the ideal of the partnership method has been qualified, it may do relatively little further conceptual damage to apply limits to the investment tax credit and the foreign tax credit, for example, at the firm level instead of at the shareholder level.[47] Moreover—and this may be either a plus or a minus, depending on one's point of view—whereas the pure partnership approach demands that tax preferences be passed through, a somewhat more persuasive case can be made for washing out preferences under the hybrid approach.

Finally, there seems to be no ready solution to the problem of allocating earnings to shareholders who might not actually benefit from the dividends traceable to the allocated earnings.[48] And though the hybrid approach may be somewhat simpler and administratively less demanding than the pure partnership method, it is clearly more complicated than the present tax system, because of the need to allocate all corporate-source income and make basis adjustments, both when corporate income is attributed and when it is distributed to shareholders.[49]

47. The results would, of course, be quite different under the two approaches if the averages of individual and corporate effective rates differed substantially.

48. This problem can be illustrated by the following example. Suppose that a firm with both common and cumulative preferred stock had alternative years of income and no income. In the first year the owners of common stock would include in taxable income their pro rata part of corporate income after payment of dividends on preferred stock and write up the basis of their shares by the same amount (and reduce it by the amount of any dividends on common stock, assumed to be zero). Owners of preferred stock would simply pay tax on dividends actually received. In the second year dividends would be paid to owners of preferred stock. But by assumption these dividends are paid from income previously taxed to owners of common stock. Special provisions would be needed to reverse the previous attribution to common shareholders for tax purposes. In this example reversal might be achieved by allowing deduction for dividends on preferred stock. (But recall the previous discussion of losses; in the case at hand deduction for dividends on preferred stock would create a tax loss.) Other cases seem not to be so tractable.

49. West German misgivings about the feasibility of full integration are described in Harry G. Gourevitch, *Integration of Corporate and Shareholder Taxes on Income: The European Experience* (Library of Congress, Congressional Research Service, 1977), pp. 48–54. A particularly interesting reason why West Ger-

On balance, it appears that full integration, even under this compromise approach, would not be easy to implement; certainly the record-keeping requirement and the problems of multiple issues of stocks and near stocks give one pause. But a definitive statement on feasibility must probably await further analysis. For this reason, if no other, full integration is not something that should be—or could be—rushed into. But by the same token, it should not simply be dismissed as an academician's pipe dream.

Problems of Dividend Relief

Most of the problems described in the previous section do not occur or are much attenuated if only dividend relief is attempted.

First, dividend relief can be proposed with or without unification of the capital gains rate and the tax rates on ordinary income. Moreover, there is less need to worry about the unification of the corporate rate and the top marginal rate applied to personal income. A corporate rate below the top personal rate simply means that tax is under-withheld; it cannot cause a cash flow problem of the type described earlier. Thus the corporate rate can be set with an eye primarily on equity in the taxation of retained corporate-source income, with due consideration of the tax regime applied to capital gains and effects on corporate liquidity. But it must be kept in mind that for foreign shareholders and tax-exempt organizations the withholding rate under the imputation approach is (or can be) a final tax.

many considered integration infeasible involves the treatment of nonresidents. Simply treating the corporation tax as a nonrefundable final tax would discriminate against foreigners and be inconsistent with the logic underlying integration, even in the unlikely event that it would pass muster under existing or model tax treaties. But if the tax were seen as a prepayment of tax for nonresidents, and therefore refundable, all corporate income might reasonably be treated as dividends now are; in that case only a withholding tax could be collected. Besides resulting in severe revenue loss, this treatment could be disadvantageous to West German firms competing with foreign investment in West Germany. (If, instead, the income were treated as coming from a permanent establishment in West Germany, any foreign shareholder would have to file a West German tax return and pay tax at progressive rates to keep the corporate tax from becoming a final tax.) West Germany seems to have decided that the corporate tax could only be considered a withholding tax that should be refunded to nonresidents, and therefore that full integration with denial of benefits to nonresidents would be infeasible under existing tax treaties. Though tax treaties might be renegotiated, doing this would not be a short-run activity.

Second, many of the technical problems encountered in the discussion of the partnership approach are unlikely to be important under dividend relief. Since dividends are amounts declared as of a certain date, timing would not seem to be a problem in determining the amount of personal income to include for tax purposes.[50] But, as noted in chapter 4, there would be problems of income measurement unless preferences were stacked last. Corporate shareholding would create problems (as noted in chapter 3 and below), but not of the type or magnitude of those found under full integration. Furthermore, though there would be important requirements for flows of information and for record-keeping, the requirements would be much less demanding than under full integration.

Nor would the existence of several classes of stock cause the same problems as under integration; all that would be needed, for example, would be conventions for whether certain types of payments were treated as dividends or interest. Under the most likely treatment of tax preferences, losses and changes in liabilities resulting from amended returns and audit adjustments would present no major new problems, since they could generally be absorbed by retained earnings, as now, rather than affect dividends, especially if the concept of earnings and profits is eliminated. Finally, the foreign tax credit would probably not be passed through to shareholders, as it should be under full integration. More likely it would be stacked last but washed out if distributed, as in Europe. But the proper treatment of income flowing across national borders remains a crucial question (see also chapter 6).

Of course, that dividend relief would be easier than full integration does not mean that problems would not exist. The remainder of this section is devoted to some of these problems.[51] Treatment of

50. Recall, however, the discussion of earnings and profits in the previous chapter.

51. The discussion draws on Committee on Corporations of the Tax Section of New York State Bar Association, "Report on the Integration of Corporate and Individual Income Taxes" (July 1977). Though that report follows too closely and with inadequate appraisal the alternatives outlined in *Tax Policy and Capital Formation,* prepared for the Task Force on Capital Formation of the House Committee on Ways and Means by the Staff of the Joint Committee on Taxation (GPO, 1977), it does provide a useful catalog of modifications of existing law that would have to accompany integration or dividend relief. Of course, most of chapter 4, dealing with tax preferences, is germane to a discussion of administrative difficulties of dividend relief.

tax-exempt organizations, foreign shareholders, resident share-
holders in foreign firms, and intercorporate dividends are discussed
separately, later in the chapter and in chapter 6.

Much of corporate and individual income tax law in the United
States is concerned with defining the boundaries between interest
payments, dividends, capital gains, and tax-free return of invested
capital. Dividend relief or integration would significantly affect many
of the current provisions intended to prevent the taxpayer from
taking unfair advantage in borderline cases of definition. A few of
these are discussed here. Though I have argued earlier that full inte-
gration, even along the lines proposed by the Canadian Royal Com-
mission and in *Blueprints for Basic Tax Reform,* would be difficult
if not impossible to administer, in several instances I consider the
effects of integration as well as the effects of two kinds of dividend
relief.

A deduction for dividends paid would reduce the present differ-
ence in the tax treatment of interest and dividends; in the extreme
case dividends and interest would be treated identically. But (as
noted in chapter 4) rules might still be needed to differentiate be-
tween dividends, capital gains, and return of investment. Moreover,
the existence of tax preferences that were not washed out on divi-
dends would constitute an important difference between dividends
and interest payments.

From the standpoint of aggregate tax burdens, the imputation
method should produce exactly the same results as the dividend-paid
deduction. But from the standpoint of the firm, the shareholder, and
the public, the two methods may seem quite different. Whereas inter-
est payments are deductible under either kind of dividend relief,
dividends are not deductible under the imputation approach. But
the relief to the shareholder is most visible under that approach.
Under either approach distributions result in a form of forced divi-
dend if a précompte system is used to bring the effective rate on
dividends up to a fixed rate at which the shareholder is allowed credit.
On the other hand, a variable credit approach adjusts the gross-up
and credit for taxes actually paid. Whereas the bondholder pays full
tax on interest received, the shareholder can take the imputation
credit against his tax liability on dividends received. Thus the inter-
ests of shareholders and those of corporate managers may conflict,
with the former preferring to be paid dividends and the latter to pay
interest.

Present tax laws are geared to preventing the conversion of ordinary (dividend) income to long-term capital gains. The importance of these provisions should be much less under dividend relief because the taxation of dividends would be reduced.[52]

Of course, as noted earlier, under full integration, earnings on equity capital would be taxed as earned, whether distributed or retained. Thus interest and earnings on corporate equity would be treated quite similarly. Moreover, redemptions of shares, like dividends, would be treated like return of capital and not like income. Finally, retentions, being taxed currently, would not result in tax-preferred capital gains.

Under the imputation method the gross-up would be treated as part of the adjusted gross income of the taxpayer. Similarly, the shareholder credit, including any creditable preferences that were passed through, would presumably be treated as part of taxes paid (in calculating the minimum tax, for example).

Interest paid for the purpose of carrying tax-exempt securities and certain forms of insurance contracts cannot now be deducted. Consistent treatment may demand that corporate deduction be disallowed for dividends paid in the same circumstance. But it would be inconsistent to argue that this tax preference should be disallowed if dividend relief were provided through the dividend-paid deduction approach, but not if it were provided through the imputation approach. However, if the firm can finance tax-exempt securities through dividends but not interest, does present law make sense? This way of looking at tax preferences calls into doubt either the analogy between interest and dividends or the basic tax preference under discussion.

Tax-exempt Shareholders

In a world in which all shareholders were resident individuals, integration and dividend relief would be relatively simple, despite all the complications cited thus far. But such is not the real world. As soon as one considers the possibility of intercorporate sharehold-

52. Under certain circumstances the individual taxpayer may prefer dividends to capital gains if dividend relief is provided. This would occur under rather unusual circumstances: full corporate rates on retentions, short periods between accrual and realization of capital gains, and preferential rates of dividends. The discussion of chapter 4 suggests that this constellation of rates is unlikely, because of the choice of stacking rules.

ing, resident ownership of shares of foreign firms, foreign ownership of shares in American firms, and ownership of shares by tax-exempt organizations, another layer of complexity is added. In this section I discuss the ownership of shares by tax-exempt organizations, and in the next section intercorporate dividends. The complications that arise because of international flows of corporate capital are the subject of chapter 6.

Because dividend relief under the imputation method must be provided at the shareholder level, it is a relatively simple matter to deny its benefits to tax-exempt organizations.[53] Such organizations can be allowed to take advantage of the full gross-up and credit, none of it, or any percentage between 0 and 100.[54] A similar comment applies to the proposals for complete integration made by the Canadian Royal Commission and by the U.S. Treasury Department in *Blueprints for Basic Tax Reform*.[55] The situation is, however, somewhat different if dividend relief is provided at the firm level through a deduction for dividends or a split-rate system. Under such an approach the benefits of dividend relief could not feasibly be denied

53. Note, however, that though it may be simple to write a law that excludes tax-exempt organizations from the benefits of integration or dividend relief, making the exclusion economically effective may be more difficult. Most obviously, the benefits of integration or dividend relief may be capitalized in the prices of shares and convertible debentures and therefore made available to tax-exempt organizations through the sale of corporate stocks. Technical devices, such as selling the rights to receive dividends to taxable individuals or organizations, can also be employed to circumvent the intent of such a law. (For other examples, see chapter 7.) Hence the revenue loss involved in extending the benefits to tax-exempt organizations would be less than usually thought. Some observers have suggested that it would be preferable simply to extend the benefits to tax-exempt organizations and avoid the socially wasteful shuffling of portfolios and legal maneuvers that denial of benefits would stimulate.

54. Note that it has been customary to discuss this issue as though the gross-up and the credit were equal. As seen in chapter 4, this is not necessarily the case, at least from a conceptual point of view. For the sake of simplicity—and because credit and gross-up are, as a practical matter, likely to be equal—I ignore this complication in what follows. (Moreover, it is the credit—not the gross-up—that is crucial for tax-exempt organizations.) Allowing for unequal gross-up and credit would be relatively straightforward.

55. This result does, however, depend on whether the corporate tax is retained as a withholding tax. If it is not, the tax-exempt organization would initially pay no tax on its share of corporate-source income. But if the corporate tax were retained as a withholding device, it (or some part of it) could be treated as a final tax that would not necessarily be fully refunded to tax-exempt organizations. The statement in the text reflects the usual assumption that there would be a withholding tax.

Table 5-1. **Taxation of Tax-exempt Organizations under Two Methods of Dividend Relief, Assuming 100 Percent Payout Rate**[a]
Monetary units

	Imputation method		Dividend-paid deduction method	
Item[b]	Credit permitted (1)	Credit denied (2)	No special tax (3)	Special tax levied (4)
1. Corporate-source income[c]	100	100	100	100
2. Deduction for dividends[d]	100	100
3. Taxable corporate income [1 − 2]	100	100	0	0
4. Corporate income tax [50% of 3]	50	50	0	0
5. Net corporate income (equals dividends) [1 − 4]	50	50	100	100
6. Gross-up [from 4]	50	50
7. Taxable income [5 + 6]	100	100	100	100
8. Gross income tax [0% of 7]	0	0	0	0
9. Credit [from 6]	50	0
10. Net income tax [8 − 9]	−50	0	0	0
11. Tax on dividends [50% of 5]	50
12. Total taxes [4 + 10 + 11]	0	50	0	50

... Not applicable to this method.
a. Terms relating to integration systems are explained in the glossary.
b. Except for percentages, the numbers in brackets refer to the lines in this table.
c. All corporate-source income is assumed to be taxable.
d. All net income is paid out as dividends (see line 5).

tax-exempt organizations, but it would be a simple matter to levy a separate tax on the dividends received by such organizations, thereby duplicating the results under the imputation method.[56]

This potential equivalence of treatment under the two methods of dividend relief is illustrated in table 5-1, for the simple case in which the firm pays out all its net income as dividends. If the tax-exempt organization receives the gross-up and credit under the imputation approach (column 1) or no special tax is levied on its dividend income under the dividend-paid deduction (column 3), it is treated like

56. It is common to treat tax-exempt organizations and foreign shareholders as equivalent in that neither could be excluded from the benefits of dividend relief provided at the firm level. But policy toward tax-exempt organizations is not constrained in the way that taxation of dividends paid to foreigners is constrained by treaty obligations and demands for "mirror-image" withholding taxes on dividends. See also chapter 6.

the individual in the zero marginal rate bracket.[57] If, however, under the imputation approach it is denied the gross-up and credit, it pays the corporate tax as a final tax (column 2). Or under the dividend paid deduction an equivalent special tax on dividends may be levied (column 4).

Of course, whether tax-exempt organizations would be denied the benefit of dividend relief under either scheme is a political question. It might seem more consistent (and might be politically easier) to deny the gross-up and credit than to levy a tax on the dividends of such organizations. Alternatively, the tax on income of erstwhile tax-exempts might not be limited to dividends, once it were instituted. A tax levied on the entire investment income of tax-exempt organizations at the current corporate tax rate would, of course, constitute a marked increase in burden on these organizations.[58]

Even if taxation of only distributed earnings on corporate equities held by tax-exempts were under consideration, it would be worth noting one possible crucial difference in the two approaches. Under the dividend-paid deduction cash dividends would probably increase relative to present levels, since otherwise all the tax saving of dividend relief would be retained by the firm. On the other hand, under the imputation approach cash dividends would probably fall, since the shareholder credit is, in a sense, a form of dividend and since otherwise the full benefits of the credit would accrue to shareholders. From a theoretical point of view, which approach were chosen would not much matter in a world of resident individual shareholders, because the payout policies under the two systems would probably converge. (That is, tax payments and retained earnings would be similar under the two schemes.) But the choice would clearly be important to tax-exempt organizations if they were denied the benefits of dividend relief under the imputation method but not under the dividend-paid deduction. For the total amount of "effective dividends" (cash dividends plus shareholder credits) received by tax-exempt organizations would presumably be greater under the

57. Yet another variant would involve collection of no withholding tax at the corporate level on dividends paid to tax-exempt organizations. See also the appendix to chapter 4.

58. Note that if tax-exempts were simply denied the benefit of the imputation credit, the rate of tax on their corporate-source income might rise. This would occur if a précompte were used to raise the effective rate of tax on preference income distributed to them. But see the discussion in note 55.

dividend-paid deduction (without special dividend tax) than under the imputation approach (with credit denied to tax-exempts). Naturally, the effects would go the opposite way if benefits were denied tax-exempts under the dividend-paid deduction but not under the imputation method. Finally, the treatment accorded tax-exempt organizations might well influence the feasibility of denying relief to foreign shareholders. In particular, if the corporate tax (or the part of it applied to distributed earnings) were treated as a withholding tax, for tax-exempt organizations as well as for individual shareholders, it would be difficult to argue persuasively that foreign shareholders should not receive the shareholder credit under integration or dividend relief.

The question then arises of what the proper treatment of dividends paid to tax-exempt organizations should be. There can be no categorical answer without some prior decision as to whether tax-exempt status makes sense. But if tax-exempt status is deemed sensible, the answer is clear. Gross-up and credit should be allowed under the imputation method, and no dividend tax should be levied under the dividend-paid deduction. If it is felt that such a solution goes too far, then a special income tax should be levied on the income of such organizations. But such a tax should not be limited to dividend income. It would be more sensible to tax all income at the chosen rate. (There is, of course, no reason to believe that the present corporate rate is the optimal rate for this purpose.)[59]

Intercorporate Dividends

One primary objective of integration and dividend relief is the reduction of tax-induced distortions of corporate financial structures. To be completely neutral, the tax system should always treat in the same way a given quantity of income that is retained within the corporate sector, regardless of whether it has simply been earned by one firm and retained, or earned by one firm, distributed to a second (and possibly redistributed one or more times), and then retained. Similarly, the aggregate tax levied on a dollar of distributed corporate equity income should be independent of the number of times the

59. For further discussion of some of the points raised in this section, see Charles E. McLure, Jr., and Stanley S. Surrey, "Integration of Income Taxes: Issues for Debate," *Harvard Business Review,* vol. 55 (September–October 1977), pp. 169–81.

income has been distributed from one corporation to another. Under full integration this result is, in principle, achieved automatically. Since at every level both retained and distributed earnings are attributed to shareholders, all earnings are eventually attributed to individual shareholders and taxed to them (and only to them).[60] Under dividend relief special provisions are necessary if complete relief is not granted and if some income is tax-preferred. These are discussed first for the imputation system and then for the dividend-paid deduction.

Table 5-2 shows that no special provisions are needed if dividend relief under the imputation method is complete and there are no tax preferences. In this table, and in tables 5-3 through 5-9, it is assumed that 300 of economic income is earned by and taxable to a subsidiary of a parent firm.[61] Equal parts of this gross income flow are assumed to result in net income flows that are (1) retained by the subsidiary, (2) distributed to the parent and then retained, and (3) distributed to the parent and redistributed to an individual shareholder in the 60 percent marginal rate bracket. Both parent and subsidiary are assumed to be subject to a 50 percent corporate tax rate.

In table 5-2 I assume that the corporate parent, like any other shareholder, grosses up dividends by the amount of the corporate tax and takes an equal credit against its corporate tax liability. When this is done, both the part of income directly retained by the subsidiary and the part distributed to the parent and then retained are subject to a tax of 50, as they ideally would be (see target tax, line 17). Moreover, the part distributed to the parent and then redistributed is subject to an aggregate rate of 60 percent, which is the individual shareholder's marginal rate. These results occur because the shareholder credit available to the parent exactly offsets the tax paid by the subsidiary.

Table 5-3 illustrates that the neutrality of table 5-2 does not carry over to the case in which dividend relief is incomplete. In table 5-3 the imputation credit (and the gross-up) is equal to only half the net dividend received, but is allowed to corporate as well as to individual

60. Recall, however, the many problems created for full integration by corporate shareholding.

61. Though "parent" and "subsidiary" are adopted to simplify exposition, most of the schemes discussed here are potentially applicable to intercorporate dividends paid on portfolio investments. Deviations of taxable from economic income are discussed briefly below.

Table 5-2. Taxation of Intercorporate Dividends at the Subsidiary and Parent Levels under the Imputation Method, Assuming Complete Dividend Relief[a]

Monetary units

Item[b]	Subsidiary		Income distributed to parent by subsidiary		
	Total income (1)	Income retained (2)	Total (3)	Retained by parent (4)	Redis-tributed by parent (5)
1. Subsidiary's income	300	100	200	100	100
2. Subsidiary's corporate tax [50% of 1]	150	50	100	50	50
3. Subsidiary's net income [1 − 2]	150	50	100	50	50
4. Parent's gross-up [from 2]	100	50	50
5. Parent's gross dividend [3 + 4]	200	100	100
6. Parent's gross corporate tax [50% of 5]	100	50	50
7. Parent's shareholder credit [from 4]	100	50	50
8. Parent's net corporate tax [6 − 7]	0	0	0
9. Parent's net income [3 − 8]	100	50	50
10. Shareholder's gross-up [from 6]	50
11. Shareholder's gross dividend [9 + 10]	100
12. Shareholder's gross tax [60% of 11]	60
13. Shareholder's credit [from 10]	50
14. Shareholder's net tax [12 − 13]	10
15. Net income[c]	140	50	90	50	40
16. Total tax [1 − 15]	160	50	110	50	60
17. Target tax[d]	160	50	110	50	60

... Not applicable at this level.

a. Terms relating to integration systems are explained in the glossary.

b. Except for percentages, the numbers in brackets refer to the lines in this table.

c. Columns 4 and 5 = line 9 − line 14; column 3 = column 4 + column 5; column 2 is from line 3; column 1 = column 2 + column 3.

d. Target taxation would prevail in case of direct ownership by individual.

shareholders. It can be seen that when double taxation of dividends is only partially relieved it becomes triple taxation, and income retained by the parent is taxed twice, resulting in heavier taxes than would be paid if the individual shareholder directly owned stock in the subsidiary (compare lines 16 and 17). This is essentially the

Table 5-3. Taxation of Intercorporate Dividends at the Subsidiary and Parent Levels under the Imputation Method, Assuming 50 Percent Dividend Relief[a]

Monetary units

| Item[b] | Subsidiary | | Income distributed to parent by subsidiary | | |
	Total income (1)	Income retained (2)	Total (3)	Retained by parent (4)	Redis-tributed by parent (5)
1. Subsidiary's income	300	100	200	100	100
2. Subsidiary's corporate tax [50% of 1]	150	50	100	50	50
3. Subsidiary's net income [1 − 2]	150	50	100	50	50
4. Parent's gross-up [50% of 2]	50	25	25
5. Parent's gross dividend [3 + 4]	150	75	75
6. Parent's gross corporate tax [50% of 5]	75	37.5	37.5
7. Parent's shareholder credit [from 4]	50	25	25
8. Parent's net corporate tax [6 − 7]	25	12.5	12.5
9. Parent's net income [3 − 8]	75	37.5	37.5
10. Shareholder's gross-up [50% of 6]	18.75
11. Shareholder's gross dividend [9 + 10]	56.25
12. Shareholder's gross tax [60% of 11]	33.75
13. Shareholder's credit [from 10]	18.75
14. Shareholder's net tax [12 − 13]	15
15. Net income[c]	110	50	60	37.5	22.5
16. Total tax [1 − 15]	190	50	140	62.5	77.5
17. Target tax[d]	170	50	120	50	70

... Not applicable at this level.

a. Terms relating to integration systems are explained in the glossary.

b. Except for percentages, the numbers in brackets refer to the lines in this table.

c. Columns 4 and 5 = line 9 − line 14; column 3 = column 4 + column 5; column 2 is from line 3; column 1 = column 2 + column 3.

d. Target taxation would prevail in case of direct ownership by individual. Column 5 = 25 + (75% of 60).

French treatment of intercorporate dividends on portfolio investment.[62]

A common way of overcoming this problem is to exempt intercorporate dividends in the hands of the parent but allow the parent's shareholders to take advantage of the credit resulting from the subsidiary's payment of corporate tax.[63] This approach is illustrated in tables 5-4 and 5-5. In table 5-4 dividend relief is complete, and in table 5-5 relief is provided for only half of the double taxation of dividends. In both cases corporate-source income bears the same amount of tax as it would bear if the individual shareholder owned stock in the subsidiary corporation directly. This would be true regardless of the number of corporate steps through which the income had passed. This treatment is basically what prevails in the United Kingdom, where income that has paid tax at a higher corporate level is known as "franked investment income." In the United Kingdom there is no minimum requirement for the percentage shareholding necessary to obtain this tax treatment.[64] It would, however, be possible to reserve the treatment described here for parent-subsidiary dividends and have dividends on portfolio investment taxed like other income of the parent firm (thereby generating the distortion illustrated in table 5-3).

Tables 5-6, 5-7, and 5-9 duplicate the results of tables 5-2, 5-3, and 5-5, but in the context of the dividend-paid deduction or split-rate system.[65] To make the examples comparable to the previous ones,

62. See Richard M. Hammer, "The Taxation of Income from Corporate Shareholders: Review of Present Systems in Canada, France, Germany, Japan and the U.K.," *National Tax Journal,* vol. 28 (September 1975), p. 328.

63. If the parent's dividend income were simply exempted (or if a deduction were granted for dividends received) and the subsidiary's credits were not passed through, a précompte would be due upon redistribution. In the example of table 5-4 only 33.33 could be redistributed, because the précompte would take the remaining 16.67 of net income of the parent resulting in distributions (line 7 of column 5).

64. Hammer, "Taxation of Income," p. 332. Canada employs a similar rule, but with significant exceptions. See ibid., p. 325. France also uses this approach for dividends from subsidiaries, but assumes that 5 percent of cash dividends are costs and not excludable. See ibid., p. 328.

65. Table 5-8 illustrates a variant of the affiliation privilege under partial dividend relief, rather than complete dividend relief under the split-rate approach (the analogue to table 5-4). In these examples the split-rate system is employed rather than the equivalent dividend-paid deduction simply because it seems expositionally more convenient.

Table 5-4. Taxation of Intercorporate Dividends under Imputation Method at Subsidiary Level, with Exemption at Parent Level and Parent's Shareholders Receiving Credit for Subsidiary's Taxes, Assuming Complete Dividend Relief[a]
Monetary units

	Subsidiary		Income distributed to parent by subsidiary		
Item[b]	Total income (1)	Income retained (2)	Total (3)	Retained by parent (4)	Redistributed by parent (5)
1. Subsidiary's income	300	100	200	100	100
2. Subsidiary's corporate tax [50% of 1]	150	50	100	50	50
3. Subsidiary's net income [1 − 2]	150	50	100	50	50
4. Taxable income of parent	0	0	0
5. Parent's corporate tax [50% of 4]	0	0	0
6. Net income of parent [3 − 5]	100	50	50
7. Shareholder's gross-up[c] [100% of 6]	50
8. Shareholder's gross dividend [6 + 7]	100
9. Shareholder's gross tax [60% of 8]	60
10. Shareholder's credit [from 7]	50
11. Shareholder's net tax [9 − 10]	10
12. Net income[d]	140	50	90	50	40
13. Total tax [1 − 12]	160	50	110	50	60
14. Target tax[e]	160	50	110	50	60

... Not applicable at this level.
a. Terms relating to integration systems are explained in the glossary.
b. Except for percentages, the numbers in brackets refer to the lines in this table.
c. Shareholder credit equals net dividend since corporate tax rate is 50 percent and dividend relief is complete.
d. Columns 4 and 5 = line 6 − line 11; column 3 = column 4 + column 5; column 2 is from line 3; column 1 = column 2 + column 3.
e. Target taxation would prevail in case of direct ownership by individual.

rates of 50 percent on retained corporate income and 25 percent on distributed earnings (without a "shadow effect") are used.

As before, if dividend relief is complete (table 5-6), interposition of one or more intermediate corporate layers between the shareholder and the "subsidiary" is irrelevant for the ultimate tax burden, whether the corporate shareholder is a parent firm or a portfolio investor; thus no special treatment of "affiliates" is needed. Since

Table 5-5. Taxation of Intercorporate Dividends under Imputation Method at Subsidiary Level, with Exemption at Parent Level and Parent's Shareholders Receiving Credit for Subsidiary's Taxes, Assuming 50 Percent Dividend Relief[a]

Monetary units

	Subsidiary		Income distributed to parent by subsidiary		
Item[b]	Total income (1)	Income retained (2)	Total (3)	Retained by parent (4)	Redistributed by parent (5)
1. Subsidiary's income	300	100	200	100	100
2. Subsidiary's corporate tax [50% of 1]	150	50	100	50	50
3. Subsidiary's net income [1 − 2]	150	50	100	50	50
4. Taxable income of parent	0	0	0
5. Parent's corporate tax [50% of 4]	0	0	0
6. Net income of parent [3 − 5]	100	50	50
7. Shareholder's gross-up[c] [50% of 6]	25
8. Shareholder's gross dividend [6 + 7]	75
9. Shareholder's gross tax [60% of 8]	45
10. Shareholder's credit [from 7]	25
11. Shareholder's net tax [9 − 10]	20
12. Net income[d]	130	50	80	50	30
13. Total tax [1 − 12]	170	50	120	50	70
14. Target tax[e]	170	50	120	50	70

... Not applicable at this level.

a. Terms relating to integration systems are explained in the glossary.

b. Except for percentages, the numbers in brackets refer to the lines in this table.

c. Shareholder credit is 50 percent of net dividend since corporate tax rate is 50 percent and 50 percent dividend relief is provided.

d. Columns 4 and 5 = line 6 − line 11; column 3 = column 4 + column 5; column 2 is from line 3; column 1 = column 2 + column 3.

e. Target taxation would prevail in case of direct ownership by individual. Column 5 = 25 + (75% of 60).

this is true under both the split-rate and imputation systems, it is true when the two are combined, as in West Germany.[66]

Table 5-7 demonstrates that a simple split-rate system applied at both (all) corporate levels is not neutral if dividend relief is not complete. As in table 5-3, double taxation of dividends results in (at

66. See Hugh J. Ault, "Germany: The New Corporation Tax System," *Intertax: European Tax Review* (August 1976), p. 268.

Table 5-6. Taxation of Intercorporate Dividends under the Split-Rate System at the Subsidiary and Parent Levels, without Affiliation Privilege, Assuming Complete Dividend Relief[a]

Monetary units

	Subsidiary		Income distributed to parent by subsidiary		
Item[b]	Total income (1)	Income retained (2)	Total (3)	Retained by parent (4)	Redistributed by parent (5)
1. Subsidiary's income	300	100	200	100	100
2. Subsidiary's corporate tax [50% of retained]	50	50
3. Subsidiary's net income [1 − 2]	250	50	200	100	100
4. Parent's corporate tax [50% of retained]	50	50	...
5. Net income of parent [3 − 4]	150	50	100
6. Shareholder's tax [60% of 5]	60
7. Net income[c]	140	50	90	50	40
8. Total tax [1 − 7]	160	50	110	50	60
9. Target tax[d]	160	50	110	50	60

... Not applicable at this level.
a. Terms relating to integration systems are explained in the glossary.
b. Except for percentages, the numbers in brackets refer to the lines in this table.
c. Columns 4 and 5 = line 5 − line 6; column 3 = column 4 + column 5; column 2 is from line 3; column 1 = column 2 + column 3.
d. Target taxation would prevail in case of direct ownership by individual.

least) triple taxation of dividends and double taxation of retentions when there is a layer of intercorporate dividends. It is for this reason that the old West German split-rate system used the affiliation privilege (Schachtelprivileg).[67] It is illustrated in table 5-8 (for the case without the additional tax, or Nachsteuer, on intercorporate dividends retained by the parent), and in table 5-9 (with Nachsteuer).

Under the affiliation privilege, dividends received from affiliates are exempt from corporate tax to the parent firm. For income that is redistributed by the parent firm this produces the correct result; in both tables 5-8 and 5-9 the aggregate tax on income ultimately distributed to individual shareholders is exactly what it would be if the

67. See Hammer, "Taxation of Income," p. 318, for further discussion of this aspect of the previous West German system.

Table 5-7. Taxation of Intercorporate Dividends under the Split-Rate System at the Subsidiary and Parent Levels, without Affiliation Privilege, Assuming 50 Percent Dividend Relief[a]

Monetary units

	Subsidiary		Income distributed to parent by subsidiary		
Item[b]	*Total income* (1)	*Income retained* (2)	*Total* (3)	*Retained by parent* (4)	*Redistributed by parent* (5)
1. Subsidiary's income	300	100	200	100	100
2. Subsidiary's corporate tax [50% of retained, 25% of distributed]	100	50	50	25	25
3. Subsidiary's net income [1 − 2]	200	50	150	75	75
4. Parent's corporate tax [50% of retained, 25% of distributed in 3]	56.25	37.5	18.75
5. Net income of parent [3 − 4]	93.75	37.5	56.25
6. Shareholder's tax [60% of 5]	33.75
7. Net income[c]	110	50	60	37.5	22.5
8. Total tax [1 − 7]	190	50	140	62.5	77.5
9. Target tax[d]	170	50	120	50	70

... Not applicable at this level.

a. Terms relating to integration systems are explained in the glossary.

b. Except for percentages, the numbers in brackets refer to the lines in this table.

c. Columns 4 and 5 = line 5 − line 6; column 3 = column 4 + column 5; column 2 is from line 3; column 1 = column 2 + column 3.

d. Target taxation would prevail in case of direct ownership by individual. Column 5 = 25 + (75% of 60).

individual shareholder owned stock in the subsidiary company. But in table 5-8 the affiliation privilege produces an additional undesirable effect. Because of the exemption from the parent's corporate tax, income that is distributed by the subsidiary and then retained by the parent is subject only to the subsidiary's tax on distributions, which is, by assumption, less than the tax ordinarily collected on retained earnings.

To avoid this problem, West Germany used a Nachsteuer in its previous system. Thus in table 5-9 a Nachsteuer of 25 is collected when income that has previously been subject to only the 25 percent rate on distributed income is retained by the parent. (In the West German case the 36 percent Nachsteuer brought the 15 percent rate on dividends up to the 51 percent rate levied on retained earnings.) The

Table 5-8. Taxation of Intercorporate Dividends under the Split-Rate System at the Subsidiary and Parent Levels, with Affiliation Privilege but No Nachsteuer, Assuming 50 Percent Dividend Relief[a]

Monetary units

	Subsidiary		Income distributed to parent by subsidiary		
Item	Total income (1)	Income retained (2)	Total (3)	Retained by parent (4)	Redis- tributed by parent (5)
1. Subsidiary's income	300	100	200	100	100
2. Subsidiary's corporate tax [50% of retained, 25% of distributed]	100	50	50	25	25
3. Subsidiary's net income [1 − 2]	200	50	150	75	75
4. Parent's corporate tax	0	0	0
5. Net income of parent [3 − 4]	150	75	75
6. Shareholder's tax [60% of 5]	45
7. Net income	155	50	105	75	30
8. Total tax [1 − 7]	145	50	95	25	70
9. Target tax	170	50	120	50	70

a. The notes for table 5-7 are applicable to this table.

system with affiliation privilege and Nachsteuer described in table 5-9 is equivalent to that described in table 5-5.[68]

The discussion to this point has proceeded under the assumption that economic and taxable income are equal, that is, that the subsidiary has no preference income. If indeed the subsidiary does have preference income that is deemed to be distributed, some of the systems described above do not automatically produce the proper result. Suppose, for example, that in table 5-2 the entire 300 of income of the subsidiary were preference income. There would be no corporate tax on the income retained directly by the subsidiary (column 2) and the full 100 would be available for retention. But under common European practice a précompte of 66.67 would be collected on the preference income in column 3 and only 133.33 would be distrib-

68. An important respect in which they are not identical was, however, crucial in West Germany. Note that if the parent in the example were a foreign firm, income distributed to it and reinvested in West Germany might be treated more favorably than a similar income flow retained by a family of West German firms, because the foreign firm would not pay the Nachsteuer. This so-called Auslaendereffekt (foreigner-effect) and its role in the switch to the present system of full dividend relief are discussed in more detail in chapter 3.

Table 5-9. Taxation of Intercorporate Dividends under the Split-Rate System at the Subsidiary and Parent Levels, with Affiliation Privilege and Nachsteuer, Assuming 50 Percent Dividend Relief[a]

Monetary units

	Subsidiary		Income distributed to parent by subsidiary		
Item[b]	*Total income* (1)	*Income retained* (2)	*Total* (3)	*Retained by parent* (4)	*Redistributed by parent* (5)
1. Subsidiary's income	300	100	200	100	100
2. Subsidiary's corporate tax [50% of retained, 25% of distributed]	100	50	50	25	25
3. Subsidiary's net income [1 − 2]	200	50	150	75	75
4. Parent's corporate tax	0	0	0
5. Nachsteuer [25% of 1 for retained]	25	25	...
6. Net income of parent [3 − 4 − 5]	125	50	75
7. Shareholder's tax [60% of 6]	45
8. Net income[c]	130	50	80	50	30
9. Total tax [1 − 8]	170	50	120	50	70
10. Target tax[d]	170	50	120	50	70

... Not applicable at this level.

a. Terms relating to integration systems are explained in the glossary.

b. Except for percentages, the numbers in brackets refer to the lines in this table.

c. Columns 4 and 5 = line 6 − line 7; column 3 = column 4 + column 5; column 2 is from line 3; column 1 = column 2 + column 3.

d. Target taxation would prevail in case of direct ownership by individual. Column 5 = 25 + (75% of 60).

uted in cash. This washing out of preferences would be consistent with the desired result under standard European practice if the parent redistributed the income (column 5). But because of the précompte the income retained by the parent after distribution by the subsidiary (column 4) would be taxed more heavily than that retained directly by the subsidiary.[69] The same result would occur even if, as in table 5-4, intercorporate dividends were exempt to the parent, because the précompte is collected at the subsidiary level. This would be true to a lesser extent if, as in table 5-5, dividend relief were only partial.

69. This anomaly was noted in chapter 3 in the discussion of the West German system.

It would be possible to avoid this result for income remaining in the corporate sector by not requiring payment of the précompte on dividends paid to affiliated companies from preference income.[70] Preference income treated in this way and redistributed by the parent would be classified as preference income of the parent and subject to précompte at that level, so that the proper results would be maintained.

Under the dividend-paid deduction approach of table 5-6 the same problem would be encountered as in the discussion of tables 5-2 and 5-4; preferences would be washed out even though the preference income remained in the corporate sector. On the other hand, if the affiliation privilege were provided, as in tables 5-8 and 5-9, the correct result would be achieved, but only if there were no Nachsteuer (as in table 5-8) or if the Nachsteuer did not apply to retained preference income received as dividends from subsidiaries.

Under different stacking rules (preferences stacked first or prorated between dividends and retentions) or a different treatment of preferences (that is, pass-through), the relevance of intercorporate stock ownership would vary, depending on (1) the general scheme adopted for the relief of double taxation (imputation versus split-rate or dividend-paid deduction), (2) the chosen treatment of a particular preference, and (3) whether income is ultimately distributed or retained in corporate solution. Since a system that stacks preferences last and washes them out seems to be the most likely one to be adopted, there seems to be little reason to examine exhaustively all the many possible permutations. But by combining the methodologies in chapter 4 with those in the last three paragraphs, the reader should be able to determine the complications that would be encountered under a given scheme.

70. It seems possible, but unlikely, that this treatment would be extended to dividends paid to portfolio investors.

International Aspects
of Integration

MOST DISCUSSIONS of full integration and dividend relief have tended to concentrate on the domestic implications. But because of the importance of multinational corporations to the U.S. and world economies, it is not enough to focus solely on domestic issues. International aspects of integration and dividend relief are significant, and they are complex.

This chapter explores the international issues that will arise in any consideration of integration or dividend relief.[1] For several reasons it is oriented more toward policy issues and less toward administrative problems than earlier chapters are. First, the policy issues, having been relatively neglected, are not well understood. Little can be gained from detailed analysis of how to achieve alternative targets until one at least knows which of them are reasonable goals of public policy. Second, any useful discussion of administrative feasibility in the international sphere would be conducted in the context of guide-

1. For an excellent discussion of issues in this area, see Hugh J. Ault, "International Issues in Corporate Tax Integration," Georgetown University Law Center, *Law and Policy in International Business,* vol. 10, no. 2 (1978), pp. 461–94.

lines (and perhaps alternative ones) for the treatment of tax preferences, a context in which analysis is, as shown in chapter 4, very complicated. It simply does not seem worthwhile to attempt a comprehensive discussion that would consider (1) alternative approaches to international taxation in the context of (2) alternative treatments of tax preferences in (3) alternative schemes for integration and dividend relief.

International corporate investment can be carried out in at least four distinct ways: through individual purchase of the stock of foreign corporations (individual portfolio investment), through corporate purchases of (noncontrolling interest in) the stock of foreign corporations (corporate portfolio investment), through direct corporate investment implemented through branches of a domestic corporation, and, most important of all for U.S. foreign investment, through direct corporate investment in the stock of foreign subsidiaries. Moreover, there are at least five methods of providing various degrees of integration: the classical system; the split-rate, the dividend-paid deduction, and the imputation systems of dividend relief; and full integration. Any country could have any one of these. Thus, even if differences arising from variations in the definition of income, in the treatment of tax preferences, and in the degree to which dividend relief is provided are ignored, there are twenty-five conceivable ways in which the tax systems of two countries could be paired (classical with full integration, dividend-paid deduction with imputation, and so forth). An exhaustive examination of the ways in which the four types of foreign investment could be treated in each of the twenty-five cases would be a major undertaking.[2] Therefore, to reduce the problem to manageable size, I concentrate primarily on two types of investment: individual ownership of shares in foreign firms and corporate ownership of foreign subsidiaries. I chose the former because it is useful for understanding the principles involved, the latter because it is the form of most U.S. foreign investment. And instead of attempting to go systematically through the twenty-five possible combinations of tax systems, I focus largely on cases in which both countries in the analysis provide dividend relief. But to

2. For such an exhaustive analysis, see Mitsuo Sato and Richard M. Bird, "International Aspects of the Taxation of Corporations and Shareholders," International Monetary Fund, *Staff Papers*, vol. 22 (July 1975), pp. 384–455.

a limited degree I also consider cases in which both countries have fully integrated income taxes and those in which a country providing dividend relief is dealing with a country with a classical system.

I have also placed several additional restrictions on the discussion.

First, for the most part I do not consider the complications resulting from the simultaneous occurrence of tax preferences and international ownership claims. Given the complexities of each subject in itself, a comprehensive discussion of the problems arising from the two combined is beyond the scope of this book.

Second, in discussing dividend relief I generally consider only the tax treatment of distributed corporate-source income; qualifications based on taxation of retained earnings appear in footnotes. Although cases occur in which a careful discussion of dividend relief requires analysis of tax treatment of retentions, these chiefly involve earnings retained by a foreign subsidiary of a domestic firm. Then the question is whether or not domestic tax on such earnings should be deferred.[3]

The answer to that question can be important for both equity and efficiency, especially given the possibility of abuse when subsidiaries are chartered in tax-haven countries.[4] But for present purposes it is relatively unimportant, since much of the discussion is equally valid whether taxes on earnings retained by foreign subsidiaries are taxed currently or are deferred. This is clearly true for discussion that deals

3. Whereas deferral would have no place in a system of full integration and, indeed, would be basically inconsistent with the underlying principles of integration, it can be argued that it is inconsistent not to allow deferral in a system based on the classical, or separatist, view of the corporation. Since dividend relief is a halfway approach that accepts the classical view on retained earnings, deferral seems more appropriate in a system with dividend relief than in a fully integrated system. But if one uses the separatist view of the corporation to justify deferral, one is forced to argue as well that the foreign tax credit makes no more sense for direct investment than for portfolio investment. And it can be argued that viewing the corporate family as a unit (which calls for the foreign tax credit, but not deferral) *is* consistent with the separatist view of the corporation. An alternative approach would be to require full integration for subsidiaries. In such a case deferral would not be an issue, but many of the technical issues raised in chapter 5 would occur. Though they might be more manageable if encountered only within the corporate sector, they would be compounded by intricacies of international fiscal relations.

4. In the absence of clear standards in the tax-preference field, low foreign taxes are not presumptive evidence of abuse.

just with the administrative feasibility of dividend relief. Current taxation of retentions of foreign subsidiaries may cause administrative problems, but these would occur even under a classical system with no deferral and are generally independent of the problems involved in dividend relief.

Where equity and efficiency effects of dividend relief are concerned, the choice between deferral and current taxation does matter. Arguments that are valid in a world of current taxation may be questionable in a world of deferral. The prime example—discussed later in the chapter—involves what is called capital-export neutrality. For ease of exposition I adopt as my basic assumption the continuation of deferral, but in footnotes I draw attention to the most important allocational consequences of that choice.

Third, I do not consider the role of withholding taxes, except as they are potentially part of schemes to withhold benefits of dividend relief from foreigners. This tends to happen and become a controversial issue when two countries have unequal degrees of dividend relief (including a country with a classical system and one with dividend relief).

I have divided this chapter into four major sections. In the first section I outline some alternative conceptual approaches to the taxation of dividends (or corporate-source income, in the case of full integration) attributable to individual shareholders in foreign firms. I do this primarily to isolate technical questions of administrative feasibility. Then, in the second section, I discuss direct corporate investment through foreign subsidiaries, again focusing on the same technical questions. The discussion of the taxation of intercorporate dividends in chapter 5 is also relevant here, since the tax treatment of intercorporate dividends received from domestic and from foreign subsidiaries (or paid to foreign and domestic parents) should be consistent with each other. The third section briefly reviews criteria of neutrality, equity, and nondiscrimination that are commonly found in discussions of the taxation of international capital flows. (Some readers may prefer to reverse the order in which they read the first and second sections and the third section.) The final section attempts a synthesis in which various approaches to dividend relief and integration are appraised on the basis of their neutrality, equity, administrative feasibility, and probable political acceptability.

Table 6-1. Tax Treatment of Corporate-Source Income Attributable to, or Dividends Paid to, Individual Investors under Alternative International Systems[a]
Monetary units

Item[b]	Classi-cal (1)	Divi-dend-paid deduc-tion[c] (2)	Source (3)	Resi-dence (4)	Neither (5)	Both (6)
			Country providing credit under integration or imputation system			
1. Corporate income[d]	100	100	100	100	100	100
2. Corporate tax in source country [40% of 1]	40	...	40	40	40	40
3. Net corporate income or cash dividend [1 − 2]	60	100	60	60	60	60
4. Gross-up [from 2]	40	40[e]	0[f]	40[g]
5. Gross income or dividend [3 + 4]	60	100	100	100[e]	60[f]	100[g]
6. Personal tax [70% of 5]	42	70	70	70	42	70
7. Imputation credit [7a + 7b]	40	40[e]	...	80[g]
a. Source country [from 4]	40	40
b. Residence country [from 4]	40[e]	...	40[g]
8. Net personal tax liability [6 − 7]	42	70	30	30	42	−10
9. Net personal income or dividend [3 − 8]	18	30	30	30	18	70
10. Total tax collections [1 − 9]	82	70	70	70	82	30
a. Source country [2 − 7a]	40	...	0	40	40	0
b. Residence country [6 − 7b]	42	70	70	30	42	30

... Not applicable.

a. Terms relating to integration systems are explained in the glossary.

b. Except for percentages, the numbers in brackets refer to the lines in this table.

c. Corresponds to exemption of income in the country of source in the case of complete integration.

d. Assumed to be fully taxable and to be fully distributed in the case of dividend relief.

e. Gross-up and credit are assumed to be equal to tax paid in source country, even if provided by country of residence.

f. Assumed that gross-up is not required if no credit is granted.

g. Gross-up is as in note e, that is, grossed-up income includes source-country tax only once. But credit is given by both countries.

Alternative Approaches: Individual Shareholder

Table 6-1 describes the aggregate tax burden that would be imposed on international flows of imputed corporate-source income (under full integration) or distributed income (under two forms of dividend relief) under several alternative schemes of taxation. Strictly speaking, the table is applicable only to portfolio investment by individual shareholders and therefore may not be descriptive of

some of the most important problems in the international sphere.[5] Yet even for these it is a useful starting place, since it permits the isolation of a number of trouble spots in a way that would not be possible if direct corporate investment were examined first.

In the example of table 6-1 and others that follow, it is assumed that the country of source of corporate equity income or dividends has a corporate income tax of 40 percent and that the marginal personal income tax rate on the shareholder in question in his country of residence is 70 percent. Where I examine dividend relief I assume a 100 percent payout rate (or deal only with the distributed portion of corporate-equity income). I begin with a presumption that any country providing dividend relief would bear the fiscal cost of doing so, but recognize that arrangements might be worked out for the source and residence countries to share those costs.

Dividend-paid Deduction

As a benchmark, the tax treatment in the classical system is presented in column 1. Because the personal tax in the country of residence of the shareholder is levied on dividends paid out of income net of the corporate tax in the country of source, with no integration or relief from double taxation of dividends, the tax treatment is exactly what it would be in a classical system involving only one country.[6] In column 2 dividends are assumed to be deductible to the corporation in the country of origin of dividends. The result is, of course, that dividend relief is complete and is provided entirely by the country of origin. That is, the 70 percent personal tax is collected on dividends by the country of residence and the country of origin collects nothing on distributed corporate-source income.[7] It would be impossible for a dividend-paid deduction system to operate

5. Although most U.S. foreign investment occurs through subsidiaries of U.S. firms, foreigners make substantial portfolio investments in the United States.

6. Though the tax *treatment* is the same in the two cases, the *result,* in terms of aggregate tax rates, may be different if the corporate tax rates in the two countries are not identical.

It is assumed that the corporate tax in the country of source cannot be credited against personal liability in the country of residence. If it were credited, the dividend would presumably be grossed up and the outcome in column 4 would result.

7. The country of origin does, of course, collect tax on retained corporate-source income. And to the extent that the deduction for dividends paid is not complete, the source country obtains the revenue from its tax on distributed corporate-source income.

otherwise, though one can imagine a treaty arrangement under which the residence country would rebate to the country of origin part of the personal tax proceeds on dividends received from abroad.[8]

If both source and residence countries have similar degrees of dividend relief and if dividend flows between them are of roughly equal magnitude, it should not matter much whether the source country bears the full fiscal cost of dividend relief or is partly or wholly compensated by the country of residence. But if the degree of dividend relief provided by various countries is different or if dividend flows are not roughly in balance, the arrangements for sharing fiscal costs can be important indeed.[9] And if the residence country has a classical system, even the presence of dividend relief in the source country can be controversial, and the residence country is unlikely to be willing to share any of the fiscal cost of dividend relief.

A country using the deduction or split-rate approach to provide the relief from double taxation of dividends paid to domestic shareholders could, in theory, limit the benefits of dividend relief to domestic shareholders, and thus the loss of revenue, by levying an extra withholding tax on dividends paid to nonresidents. If other countries using a similar approach to dividend relief followed the same course and if such withholding taxes were creditable in the country of residence of shareholders, the result would be the same as under an agreement that provided explicitly for the sharing of the fiscal costs of dividend relief.

The situation is, however, somewhat different when a country using the dividend-paid deduction is dealing with a country using a

8. Such an approach for sharing the cost of dividend relief is not so different in concept from that of the directive on harmonization proposed by the Commission of the European Communities in which the source country would compensate the residence country for imputation credits granted recipients of dividends paid from income taxed in the source country. See Commission of the European Communities, "Proposal for a Council Directive Concerning the Harmonization of Systems of Company Taxation and of Withholding Taxes on Dividends," *Bulletin of the European Communities,* Supplement 10/75: *Harmonization of Systems of Company Taxation* (Luxembourg: Office for Official Publications of the European Communities, 1975), especially article 13. For further thoughts on the use of such a "clearing-house" arrangement for the sharing of costs of dividend relief, see Ault, "International Issues," pp. 479–83.

9. Thus the directive proposed by the commission provided that both corporate tax rates and dividend relief should be in a narrow band centered at 50 percent. Commission of the European Communities, "Proposal for a Council Directive," articles 3, 8.

classical system. Neutrality of taxation of international investment flows would not be violated so long as the residence country allowed the withholding tax to be credited against the shareholder's personal tax liability. (See also the section below on principles of international taxation.) But the residence country might be unwilling to bear any of the cost of dividend relief provided by the source country and would object that any extraordinary withholding tax levied by the source country on dividends paid to foreigners violated the generally accepted tenet of international tax relations that withholding rates be "mirror images" (that is, equal in both countries).[10] It has been argued, however, that, whereas reciprocity of withholding rates can be defended in a world of classical systems, its applicability to a world of full integration or dividend relief is questionable.[11]

Column 2 of table 6-1 can also be used to illustrate one approach to full integration. Instead of dividends being deducted in calculating taxable income, corporate income might simply be exempt in the country of source and included in the personal income of shareholders. But foreign-source income would enter the personal tax return of the shareholder on somewhat different footing from income from domestic corporate sources, at least in systems involving corporate withholding of tax against personal liabilities. That is, whereas net (after-tax) corporate income from domestic firms would ordinarily be grossed up by the amount of a withholding tax, and credit given for the withheld tax, there would be no withholding tax on foreign-source income in the scheme depicted in column 2. Likewise, under such a scheme, corporate-source income would be exempt from corporate withholding tax in the source country if attributed to foreign shareholders, but not if attributed to domestic shareholders. These anomalies could be overcome, of course, if neither country employed withholding even on domestic-source corporate income— but only at a significant cost, including sacrifice in enforcement of collection. Moreover, barring any arrangement for rebates, this approach involves the relinquishing of all claim to tax revenue by the

10. This last situation, of course, describes the position of West Germany and the United Kingdom in their dealings with the United States (see also chapter 3). Both adopted imputation systems (at least in part) despite preferences for a split-rate approach.

11. See Sato and Bird, "International Aspects," and the final section of this chapter.

country of source of corporate income. As suggested by the discussion above (and in the final section), this would not be a major problem if international flows of imputed corporate-source income were roughly balanced. Since they are not, the probability of widespread acceptability of this approach would seem to be quite limited.

Imputation System

An alternative approach to full integration that would be more attractive to source countries would involve collection of withholding tax at the corporate level by those countries. This approach would, of course, require using the gross-up and credit technique. It is probable that source countries would not be willing to bear the entire fiscal cost of integration and that residence countries would not be anxious to integrate such foreign withholding taxes into their personal taxes by allowing shareholders unrequited credits for such taxes. It is therefore probable that arrangements might be created under which the source and residence countries shared the costs of the shareholder credits. Analysis of such arrangements and their difficulties under dividend relief is similar to their analysis under full integration, though perhaps simpler, and is therefore done primarily in the former context. Suffice it to say here that, for a reasonable result to be achieved under either dividend relief or full integration, gross-up and credit should be at the corporate tax rate levied in the source country.[12] Thus shareholders would be forced to use the tax rate prevailing in each source country to calculate gross-up and credit on imputed income or dividends originating there. That is, one of the primary simplifications of a purely domestic system—a fixed gross-up

12. I do not consider in detail the complication of tax preferences and alternative ways in which they might be treated; the 100 in the examples that follow is economic income and the 40 percent rate is the statutory rate.

Basing the gross-up and credit on the tax rate in the country of residence would generally be quite unsatisfactory, since the credit would bear no necessary relation to the taxes actually paid, even in the absence of tax preferences. It would not be feasible to overcome this by levying a précompte (equal to the difference in tax rates in the two countries) in the country of residence. In theory, the country of origin could levy a précompte that depended on the corporate tax rate in the country of residence of the shareholder. (Where the residence country's tax rate was higher than the origin country's, the précompte would be negative. Since any such arrangement would inevitably be the object of treaties, the revenue—or cost—of such an arrangement could well accrue to or be covered by the country of residence.) Even though such principles could be worked out in theory, it seems unlikely that they could be implemented.

and credit rate—would not be consistent with countries setting their own corporate tax rates.[13]

Columns 3 through 6 of table 6-1 describe alternative arrangements under which both the source and residence countries have full integration or imputation systems, and the source country, the residence country, neither country, or both countries provide the imputation credits necessary to implement the withholding approach for integration or dividend relief. For dividend relief (integration), in columns 3 and 4 the gross-up and credit, being based on the source country corporate tax, is 40, bringing the gross dividend (imputed corporate income) up to the 100 assumed to be the corporate income giving rise to the net cash dividend (corporate income) of 60. As in the purely domestic examples of earlier chapters, the personal tax on the 100 is 70, the imputation credit is 40, and the net liability for personal tax is 30. In column 3 the country of source provides the credits, and therefore (in the absence of rebates) reaps none of the tax revenue (except under dividend relief, when it obtains that on retained earnings), which goes entirely to the country of residence, as in the example of column 2. For dividend relief this example is roughly descriptive of the approach followed in the French and draft U.K. treaties with the United States.[14]

In column 4 the country of residence provides the imputation credits, so that the foreign corporation tax is "integrated" into the personal income tax of the country of residence. The aggregate tax burden is the same as in column 3, but it is split differently between countries of residence and source. In particular, the source country gets the revenues from the corporate tax on distributed earnings (under dividend relief—from the withholding tax under full integra-

13. If, however, the rates are similar, even if they are not identical, little damage would be done. Thus the requirement in the directive proposed by the Commission of the European Communities that corporate rates fall within the range of 45–55 percent. ("Proposal for a Council Directive," article 3.) For the advantages of a uniform gross-up, see chapter 4.

14. Of course, in both these systems the dividend relief is only partial, and withholding taxes are applied to dividends. Note, moreover, that in the French treaty with West Germany the result is not achieved in the same way as in its treaty with the United States. In the Franco-German treaty, the West German shareholder takes credit against his West German personal liability and the West German treasury is compensated by the French treasury. In its other treaties France gives the credit directly to the shareholder, instead of passing it through the treasury of the country of residence.

tion) and, in a more realistic example, from the retained part of corporate-source income. The country of residence gets the revenue from the residual personal tax on dividends (or attributed income) after allowance for the imputation credit. In the case of shareholders in marginal tax brackets below the corporate rate in the source country, the credit would, of course, more than cancel the personal liability to the treasury of the residence country and be offset against liability for personal tax on other income or refunded. If the top personal rate in the residence country were to be reduced to the level of the corporate rate in the source country, the residence country would gain no revenue and, on balance, would lose to the country of source. Because this scheme involves personal credits for corporate taxes paid to foreign countries, it has limited chances of political acceptance except under very special circumstances.[15]

Moreover, the example of column 4 involves administrative complications that do not appear to be present in the example of column 3. In particular, shareholders in the country of residence must use the tax rate applicable in the source country in calculating the gross-up and credit. Alternatively, the firm paying the dividends can notify the shareholder and the fiscal authorities of the amount of imputation credit.[16] But these approaches would seem to be administratively unworkable, even in simple cases, since fiscal authorities in the residence country would have no power of corporate audit in the source country. In more complicated cases problems would be compounded. For example, suppose that both countries agreed that tax preferences should be stacked last and washed out (or simply washed out, in the case of integration), but disagreed on the definition of economic income and tax preferences. In such a case, which is relatively favorable to international cooperation, the source country would collect the précompte according to its own definition, but

15. For some reason this seems less palatable than the foreign tax credit currently allowed individuals for foreign personal taxes and parent firms for foreign taxes paid by foreign subsidiaries. Of course, limitations on the foreign tax credit are designed to prevent credits of taxes paid to foreign countries in excess of the effective domestic tax rate.

16. Recall, moreover, that this discussion is in the context of two countries both of which use the imputation approach. It takes little imagination to see that reliance on foreign firms would be difficult if the country of residence of the firm did not provide dividend relief or employed the dividend-paid deduction. See also Sato and Bird, "International Aspects."

the residence country, in accordance with its own tax laws, would presumably allow either more or less credit than the full amount of tax collected in the source country.[17] Under other even more complicated systems, such as selective pass-through of preferences or different stacking rules in the two countries, there would be no chance of integrating the source country tax into the residence country's personal income tax except in a very rough way.

By comparison, if dividend relief were provided by the source country for whatever taxes it had collected, it would be simpler to provide the requisite information to foreign shareholders and to police the shareholder credits. Yet the advantages that the approach of column 3 in table 6-1 has over that of column 4 can easily be exaggerated. That is, a system in which the residence country accepts whatever dividend relief the source country chooses to offer, so far as tax preferences are concerned, is not totally satisfactory, either. But the failure to grant equivalent dividend relief to all resident shareholders, inherent in the approach of column 3, might be somewhat more tolerable than the distortions and inequities that would occur when the residence country was attempting unsuccessfully to provide the same degree of dividend relief for both its own corporate tax and that of the country of source, even though the definition of income and other important features of the two corporate tax systems differ considerably.

No country currently tries to implement the approach described in column 4 of table 6-1. The mechanics of the approach proposed in the directive on harmonization by the Commission of the European Communities are more akin to those of column 4 than to those of column 3.[18] Though the proposed directive would minimize the problems created by widely differing rates of corporate tax and degrees of dividend relief by placing 45 to 55 percent limits on both the tax

17. One theoretically conceivable approach would involve calculating an effective tax rate on source-country income for each definition of economic income used by a residence country. Gross-up and credit could then be based on these effective tax rates. Any potential advantages of a uniform gross-up and credit would be lost. Moreover, one could not realistically expect corporations to use every residence country's definition of economic income to calculate the effective tax rates they pay on income originating in the source country.

18. The country of source would, however, transmit to the country of residence funds to cover the imputation credits, so that the internation split of the revenues would be more in line with what is shown in column 3.

rate and the percentage of relief from double taxation, not enough attention was devoted to the issues raised by international differences in the definition of taxable income and in the treatment of tax preferences.[19]

The situation shown in column 5 of table 6-1 is typical of the present arrangement between countries that allow dividend relief—except as modified by tax treaties such as those granted by France and the United Kingdom.[20] The country of source normally does not provide imputation credits to nonresidents, except by treaty, and foreign taxes are not integrated into the personal taxes of the country of residence; in short, neither country extends relief to international capital flows. The result is, of course, tax treatment that is exactly what it would be under a classical system, as shown by comparing columns 1 and 5. In such a world, tax administration is fairly simple, but there is clearly a substantial disincentive against foreign investment.

In column 6 of table 6-1 a case is presented in which both source and residence countries allow dividend relief.[21] It does not describe a real situation or a practice likely to occur, but is included primarily for completeness.[22] In such a case there would, of course, be a substantial distortion in favor of foreign investment.[23]

19. As noted in chapter 3, differences in taxable and economic income are not as great in Europe as in the United States. Moreover, all members of the European Community providing dividend relief stack preferences last and wash them out. (But see the discussion in chapter 3 of differences in the French and British systems of treating preferences.)

20. Strictly speaking, column 5 pertains only to relations between two countries with imputation systems or fully integrated systems. But it can also be used to illustrate relations between a country with a classical system and one with an imputation system. In a world of full integration, column 5 would seem a bit crazy. That is, corporate equity income would be attributed to shareholders, whether distributed or not, but there would be no gross-up and credit. Such a system is so unlikely that there is little need to discuss it further.

21. Exactly the same result would occur if the source country employed the dividend-paid deduction and the residence country allowed an imputation credit.

22. A condition of the French grant of the imputation credit to foreign shareholders is that the dividends must not be exempt or eligible for imputation credit in the country of residence of the shareholder. This condition is to some extent inconsistent with France's express intent to use the credit to attract foreign investors, since it implies that foreign treasuries are necessarily beneficiaries of the credit.

23. The undertaxation is equal to the rate of the corporate tax for which credit has been allowed twice. If the residence country exempted foreign dividends and the source country nonetheless granted the imputation credit, the undertaxation would be even greater.

A final case (not included in table 6-1) is one in which dividends (or income) are taxed in the source country, without benefit of credit, but are exempt in the country of residence. In this case the corporate tax of the source country becomes a final tax—and the only tax. If, however, the source country also extends the credit, there is no tax at all.

Column 1 in table 6-1 describes only the situation in which dividends are paid. Earnings retained by the corporation in the source country are, of course, taxed at the corporate rate in that country. Under a system of dividend relief, columns 2 through 6 also apply just to distributed earnings; retained earnings pay only the source-country corporate tax. But these same columns could generally apply as well to a system of full integration.

Summary

In summary, then, there are important reasons for basing integration or dividend relief on the corporate tax rate of the source country.[24] If that is the aim, the approach of column 3, which involves an imputation credit provided by the source country, is probably administratively feasible. But this objective can be achieved more easily for dividend relief if the dividend-paid deduction approach of column 2 is used. Integration or dividend relief provided by the residence country, but at the source country's tax rate (column 4), involves considerable administrative handicaps. The approach of column 5, which provides relief in neither country, is clearly feasible, but it discourages foreign investment, at least to the extent distribution is expected. The opposite approach of allowing relief in both countries, as in column 6, is not a likely candidate for adoption and is probably best ignored. On balance, given the limited perspective of this section —administrative feasibility—the dividend-paid deduction method is the preferred means for providing dividend relief. For full integration, the imputation approach with credits granted by the source country is a decidedly better alternative than the other approaches; however, it is probably politically infeasible in the absence of rebates from the residence country to the source country.

24. For now, the issue of which country should bear the fiscal cost of dividend relief is brushed aside; it is assumed that international agreements would determine shares in costs. It may be somewhat easier to work out these shares under the imputation approach than under the dividend-paid deduction.

Alternative Approaches: Subsidiary Investment

The bulk of U.S. foreign investment is made through subsidiaries. Tables 6-2 and 6-3 show some alternative ways in which international flows of dividends from subsidiary to parent to shareholder could be treated. In these examples it is assumed that a foreign subsidiary incorporated in the country of source is owned by a parent incorporated in another country.[25] The individual shareholders of the parent company are assumed to be residents of the country of residence of the parent company. The corporate rate in the country of residence is assumed to be 60 percent; other tax rates are the same as those in table 6-1.

Suppose that both countries have systems involving dividend-paid deductions (table 6-2). If earnings of the subsidiary are not taxed to the parent until distributed to it (as now), retained earnings of the subsidiary are taxed at the corporate rate prevailing in the country of source, which obtains the revenue from the tax on those earnings.[26] Intercompany dividends are taxed only to the parent firm, so that retained earnings of the parent bear the corporate tax in the country of residence.[27] Earnings distributed by the parent company are deductible to the parent but are taxed to individual shareholders at the marginal tax rates applicable to their income in the residence country, which receives the revenue from this source.

The same result can be achieved if both countries use the imputation method and the country of source provides the imputation credits for tax paid by the subsidiary (table 6-3).[28] Thus, instead of

25. That some countries do not base residence on incorporation has no operational significance for present purposes.

26. Retained income that is subsequently distributed may be a problem under the dividend-paid deduction; this is one of the standard problems of this approach, though one that could rather easily be overcome.

27. Recall, however, the problem encountered in West Germany under the split-rate system because income distributed by West German firms to foreign parents but reinvested in West Germany would pay less tax than income retained by groups of West German firms (see chapter 3 for a discussion of this Auslaendereffekt and chapter 5 for a discussion of ways to avoid it).

28. Under this scheme the residence country will not collect précompte when dividends are paid from foreign-source income. Since the source country will be providing the imputation credits and the corporation will be paying tax at the full rate to the country of residence, the issue does not arise.

The same result described in the text could also be achieved if one country had

Table 6-2. Taxation of Foreign Subsidiary and Domestic Parent and Shareholder, with 100 Percent Dividend-paid Deduction in Both Countries[a]

Monetary units

Item[b]	Disposition of income of 300 by subsidiary		
	Retained	Paid to parent as dividend	
1. Attributed income	100	200	
2. Dividend-paid deduction [from 6]	...	200	
3. Taxable income of subsidiary [1 − 2]	100	0	
4. Corporate tax of subsidiary [40% of 3]	40	0	
5. Retained earnings [1 − 4]	60	...	
6. Dividends paid to parent [1 − 4]	...	200	
		Paid by parent	
		Retained	to shareholder
7. Attributed dividend income of parent [from 6]	...	100	100
8. Dividend-paid deduction [from 12]	100
9. Taxable income of parent [7 − 8]	...	100	0
10. Corporate tax of parent [60% of 9]	...	60	0
11. Retained income of parent [7 − 10]	...	40	...
12. Dividends paid by parent [7 − 10]	100
13. Personal tax liability [70% of 12]	70
14. Total tax collections [14a + 14b]	40	60	70
a. Source country [from 4]	40	0	0
b. Residence country [10 + 13]	0	60	70

... Not applicable.
a. Terms relating to integration systems are explained in the glossary.
b. Except for percentages, the numbers in brackets refer to the lines in this table.

simply allowing a deduction for dividends paid, the source country collects the tax from the subsidiary and then returns it to the parent as an imputation credit.

This result may, in some sense, be thought reasonable, though one could not expect unanimous agreement from source countries. But one can easily be too sanguine, even if the split of the fiscal cost of dividend relief were not an issue.

First (as chapter 5 shows), even in a purely domestic context the results of direct ownership are replicated for intercorporate ownership only under very special circumstances. Allowing relief based on dividends paid by subsidiaries to parents can result in substantial

an imputation system and the other a dividend-paid deduction. But it would be much more complicated. There are clearly substantial advantages if all countries use the same approach to dividend relief.

Table 6-3. Taxation of Foreign Subsidiary and Domestic Parent and Shareholder, with Imputation Method in Both Countries[a]
Monetary units

	Disposition of income of 300 by subsidiary		
Item[b]	*Retained*	*Paid to parent*	
1. Attributed income	100	200	
2. Corporate tax of subsidiary [40% of 1]	40	80	
3. Retained income of subsidiary [1 − 2]	60	...	
4. Net dividends paid by subsidiary [1 − 2]	...	120	
		Retained	*Paid by parent to shareholder*
5. Attributed dividend income of parent [from 4]	...	60	60
6. Gross-up for dividends received by parent [from 2]	...	40	40
7. Grossed-up dividend received by parent [5 + 6]	...	100	100
8. Gross corporate income tax of parent [60% of 7]	...	60	60
9. Imputation credit [from 6]	...	40	40
10. Net tax of parent[c] [8 − 9]	...	20	20[c]
11. Retained earnings of parent [5 − 10]	...	40	...
12. Net dividends paid by parent [5 − 10]	40
13. Gross-up for dividends received by shareholder [from 8]	60
14. Gross dividends of shareholder [12 + 13]	100
15. Gross liability of shareholder [70% of 14]	70
16. Imputation credit of shareholder [from 13]	60
17. Net liability of shareholder [15 − 16]	10
18. Total tax collections[d] [18a + 18b]	40	60	70
a. Source country [from 2]	40	0	0
b. Residence country [from 8 and 8 + 17, respectively, for last two columns]	0	60	70

... Not applicable.
a. Terms relating to integration systems are explained in the glossary.
b. Except for percentages, the numbers in brackets refer to the lines in this table.
c. Assumes that no précompte is required when the residence country provides relief and dividends are paid from foreign-source income; this is contrary to common European practice.
d. Assumes that imputation credits are paid by the country of source. See also the discussion of table 6-1.

undertaxation if the income in question is not redistributed to individual shareholders. When there is partial dividend relief and parents and subsidiaries reside in different countries, special arrangements are needed to achieve the desired result.

Second, though the results illustrated in tables 6-2 and 6-3 appear reasonable at first glance, they hold the possibility for substantial tax

avoidance and economic distortion through the use of firms incorporated in tax-haven countries. Suppose, for example, that the parent company is chartered in a tax-haven country that has only minimal corporate taxes, which can be ignored for practical purposes. In such a case, the column that shows the income retained by the parent will show no tax liability on income earned by the subsidiary in the source country but retained by the parent—an extreme form of the deferral problem familiar to students of the international aspects of the present tax system. Moreover—and this is something with which U.S. observers have been less concerned—the "foreigner-effect" that bothered the West Germans under the old split-rate system will be accentuated. (See chapter 3.) That is, whereas the domestic firm in the source country which wants to retain earnings for reinvestment would pay the corporate rate on income yielding retentions, the parent firm in the tax-haven country would benefit from the dividend-paid deduction or imputation credit, but would pay little or no residence-country tax on the earnings before reinvesting them in the source country.

One possible solution to this problem, which could be adopted unilaterally by source countries, would be to differentiate between direct investment through subsidiaries and portfolio investment. For the latter the tax treatment suggested by tables 6-2 and 6-3 might be appropriate and more or less free of abuse. But for direct investment the burden of providing dividend relief might better be left to the country of residence of the parent.[29] Denial of deduction for dividends paid or imputation credits by the source country, combined with dividend relief and the continued availability of the foreign tax credit in the residence country, would tend to achieve this result.[30] Though the administrative difficulties described in the section above on the individual shareholder might exist to a limited degree, they would appear to be much less serious for direct investors than for portfolio investors. A more far-reaching approach would be to im-

29. Ault, "International Issues," reaches basically the same conclusion, though for somewhat different reasons.

30. This would be true only if credits for taxes paid to foreign governments could be passed through to shareholders; that is, if précompte did not nullify such credits. Moreover, such technical questions as how many layers of subsidiary-parent relations to pierce in deciding whether to provide the credit under the rules for portfolio investors or the parent-subsidiary rule would need to be settled, presumably by treaty. Note, in addition, that use of the indirect foreign tax credit in its present form would result in the washing out of tax preferences created by the source country, since credit would be granted only for taxes actually paid.

pose a requirement of integration on families of related corporations. This is, of course, substantially more controversial.

Another approach would be to allow dividend relief in the country of source, but only on the basis of treaty; no relief would be allowed parents (first-tier subsidiaries) in tax-haven countries.[31] Under the dividend-paid deduction the equivalent restriction would be to disallow deduction for dividends paid to parents resident in tax-haven countries. Thus the tax-haven problem could be overcome under either approach to providing dividend relief. If full integration were the goal, the imputation method and its restrictions would be the only feasible approach.[32]

In summary, dividend relief would be best provided to individual shareholders and corporate portfolio investors by the country of origin of income, through either the dividend-paid deduction or the imputation method. If the goal were full integration, only the imputation method would do. In the case of direct investment effected through corporate subsidiaries, on the other hand, it would appear preferable to leave the task of providing dividend relief or full integration to the country of residence of the parent firm. Such a distinction between portfolio and direct investment should be feasible.

Practice has in large part followed the pattern just described. No country currently integrates foreign corporate income taxes into their personal income taxes; nor is this situation likely to change. Rather, portfolio shareholders must look to the country of source for relief from double taxation of dividends.

For direct investment, there has been a tendency for the country of residence to provide relief, through exemption of foreign earnings or provision of a foreign tax credit.[33] But because of the précompte on distributions from foreign-source income, this relief is generally

31. Under the directive on harmonization proposed by the Commission of the European Communities, the imputation credit would not be available to the parent; it would pass through to individual shareholders and be available only upon distribution by the parent to such shareholders. This approach might be workable within the European Community and in the context of similar corporate rates. But if applied on a broader basis it might prove to be administratively infeasible. Moreover, there is room for problems if corporate tax rates and degrees of dividend relief are not similar between countries.

32. Note, however, that integration within a family of corporations is substantially simpler than that for widely held corporations, especially if subsidiaries are wholly owned.

33. Note, however, that not all countries allowing foreign tax credits allow them for deemed taxes, that is, taxes paid by subsidiaries.

available only for foreign earnings that are not distributed to share-holders of the parent firm.[34] On closer examination, then, this relief might better be seen as a vestigial remnant of the classical system instead of as a well-constructed and consistent part of the imputation system.

No country has been willing to provide relief to foreign share-holders automatically under an imputation system.[35] But France and the United Kingdom have been willing to provide relief by treaty to portfolio investors, and the United Kingdom has even agreed to extend (at a 50 percent rate) the relief granted under treaty to direct investors in the United Kingdom. Presumably, the United Kingdom will not extend this relief to tax-haven countries by negotiating treaties with countries with corporate tax rates substantially lower than its own.

Principles of International Taxation

Economists commonly refer to economic arrangements that result in the maximization of economic welfare as "efficient." Moreover, if certain (rather stringent) conditions are met, neutral taxation—that is, taxation that does not interfere with marginal decisions on the allocation of economic resources—can be expected to result in efficient outcomes. In the international context, however, efficiency and neutrality can take on different meanings, depending on whose welfare is the target of maximization. Furthermore, equity no longer involves simply the distribution of tax burdens among individuals; it involves the allocation of tax revenues among various national treasuries as well. It is useful, therefore, to have a working knowledge of commonly used concepts of neutrality, efficiency, and equity as a background for the discussion of policy decisions on the treatment of international flows of capital income under an integrated income tax system.[36]

34. But stacking rules tend to keep the credits intact (see chapter 3).

35. Germany has, of course, provided such relief through its split rate.

36. For more on these concepts, see Sato and Bird, "International Aspects," pp. 406–11; Lawrence B. Krause and Kenneth W. Dam, *Federal Tax Treatment of Foreign Income* (Brookings Institution, 1964), pp. 44–56; and especially Peggy B. Musgrave, *United States Taxation of Foreign Investment Income: Issues and Arguments* (Harvard University Law School, 1969), chap. 7. Other useful references are the papers by Carl S. Shoup ("Taxation of Multinational Corporations," pp. 3–42)

Efficiency and Neutrality

Maximization of economic welfare for the world as a whole requires *worldwide efficiency*. This is achieved when taxes do not distort choices of where to invest; that is, when taxes exhibit *capital-export neutrality*. In principle, capital-export neutrality can be realized under a classical system if the source country relinquishes claim to tax revenues or if the country of residence of the corporation grants foreign tax credits.[37]

Maximization of the national welfare of one particular country requires *national efficiency*. It is achieved if the total return to a capital-exporting country (that is, the sum of private income and fiscal revenue) does not depend on where investment is made. It can be realized in a classical system when the country of residence allows deduction of foreign taxes in calculating taxable income. Since capital-export neutrality involves equality of net (after-tax) returns and national efficiency involves equal gross (inclusive of tax) returns, the two principles are generally incompatible.

Finally, another concept of neutrality appeals to many businessmen, but has little attraction from a welfare point of view. Under

and Peggy B. Musgrave ("International Tax Differentials for Multinational Corporations: Equity and Efficiency Considerations," pp. 43–57) in United Nations, Department of Economic and Social Affairs, *The Impact of Multinational Corporations on Development and on International Relations; Technical Papers: Taxation* (New York: United Nations, 1974).

37. Throughout the rest of this chapter I ignore international differences in the provision of public services. At this point I consider only neutrality through the corporate level of the tax system; the personal level of taxes is considered afterwards.

In practice, there are several reasons why the use of foreign tax credits may not suffice to achieve capital-export neutrality. Tax rates may be higher in the source country than in the residence country, so that not all foreign taxes can be credited; tax on income of foreign subsidiaries may be deferred by the country of residence of the parent firm; the definitions of taxable income and various incentive provisions may differ between countries; investment incentives may be available only for domestic investment in the residence country; foreign losses may not be deductible against income for tax purposes in the country of residence; and subnational taxes may be treated differently, depending on whether they are paid in the country of residence (for example, deducted) or the country of source (for example, credited). For further discussion, see G. C. Hufbauer, "A Guide to Law and Policy," in *U.S. Taxation of American Business Abroad: An Exchange of Views* (American Enterprise Institute for Public Policy Research, 1975), pp. 1–6. These important qualifications are largely ignored in what follows.

capital-import neutrality the same tax is applied to the income of all firms competing in the same country. For it to be achieved in a classical system, capital-exporting countries must exempt foreign-source income from taxation or capital-importing nations must provide credits for taxes levied in residence countries; except for the use of the territorial principle in some countries, neither of these practices is common. In general, capital-export neutrality and capital-import neutrality are not compatible unless taxes are identical in all countries.

Table 6-4 illustrates the above three principles in the context of a classical corporate tax system. In each column it is assumed that the parent company, located in the country of residence of the shareholder, owns stock in a foreign subsidiary incorporated in the country of source of the corporate income and that all income is distributed. Column 1 shows that the aggregate corporate tax burden on foreign-source income paid by the parent firm and its subsidiary is the same as would be paid on an equal gross return earned in the domestic market, provided the entire foreign tax can be credited in the country of residence. Moreover, in such a case, even if account is taken of personal taxes, the return that can be earned on corporate equities in various countries is independent of differences in taxes.[38] Thus, if all corporate income is distributed, capital-export neutrality is achieved for corporate investment, regardless of whether one looks at only the aggregate corporate (subsidiary and parent) tax burden or at the burden including both corporate and personal taxes.[39]

Consider now column 2, in which foreign income is exempt from corporate tax in the country of residence. Capital-import neutrality seems to be achieved by such a policy, since all corporate income earned in the country of source (the capital-importing country) is taxed at the same corporate rate. Note, however, that the equality of taxation extends only through the corporate (subsidiary-plus-parent) level. Once tax rates levied on dividends at the individual level are considered, the equality of rates naturally vanishes.

38. Of course, investment made through the corporate sector is taxed more heavily than investment made directly by individuals in noncorporate organizations. No further account is taken of this qualification, which is generally ignored in literature on international tax considerations.

39. If not all income is distributed and the corporate tax rates in the two countries are not the same, capital-export neutrality will not be achieved unless income retained by the subsidiary is taxed to the parent firm.

Table 6-4. Illustration of Capital-Export Neutrality, Capital-Import Neutrality, and National Efficiency under the Classical Corporate Tax System[a]
Monetary units

Item[b]	Foreign tax credit available in residence country (1)	Foreign income exempt from tax in residence country (2)	Taxes paid to source country deductible in residence country (3)
1. Corporate-source income	100	100	100
2. Source-country corporate tax on subsidiary [40% of 1]	40	40	40
3. Net income of subsidiary [1 − 2]	60	60	60
4. Taxable income of parent[c]	100	0	60
5. Gross residence-country corporate tax on parent [60% of 4]	60	0	36
6. Foreign tax credit [from 2]	40
7. Net residence-country corporate tax [5 − 6]	20	0	36
8. Total corporate level taxes [2 + 7]	60	40	76
9. Net income of parent [1 − 8]	40	60	24
10. Personal income tax [70% of 9]	28	42	17
11. Total tax collections [11a + 11b]	88	82	93
a. Source country [from 2]	40	40	40
b. Residence country [7 + 10]	48	42	53

... Not applicable.

a. Capital-export neutrality is illustrated in column 1, capital-import neutrality in column 2, and national efficiency in column 3. All income is assumed to be distributed at each level.

b. Except for percentages, the numbers in brackets refer to the lines in this table.

c. Column 1 is from line 1; column 3 is from line 3.

The situation in which there is a deduction in the residence country for taxes paid in the country of source of income is illustrated (somewhat less satisfactorily) in column 3. It is readily seen that taxes are higher here than in either column 1 or column 2. Thus the deduction for taxes paid to the source country results in less foreign investment than under a capital-export neutral tax or under a tax that exhibits capital-import neutrality through the corporate level.

It is now time to ask how these various concepts of efficiency fit into a world of full integration or dividend relief. Throughout I generally take a conduit view of the problem, as is appropriate in a world of integration. That is, I do not merely examine the tax burden through the corporate level, as in the earlier discussion of the classical system; instead I ask about aggregate tax burdens, including those incurred by individual shareholders. When full integration is dis-

cussed, I attribute income of foreign subsidiaries to shareholders in the domestic parent corporation. When dividend relief is at stake, I initially accept, as noted earlier, the basic tenet of U.S. taxation of foreign-source income: income of subsidiaries should be taxed to the parent only when distributed. Many would, of course, argue that it is impossible to discuss neutrality and efficiency adequately without attacking deferral head-on, and that this analysis is therefore biased. Hence, in footnotes I consider the implications of deferral of domestic tax on retained earnings of foreign subsidiaries.

Either of the arrangements described in columns 3 and 4 in table 6-1 could, in principle, achieve worldwide efficiency in a world of full integration. Under either approach the taxpayer would pay the same total income tax, regardless of where he invested his capital.[40] Similarly, so far as the taxation of the *distributed* portion of corporate-source income is concerned, the dividend-paid deduction approach of column 2 or either of the imputation approaches just described (columns 3 and 4) would achieve capital-export neutrality in a world of dividend relief.[41] To the extent that dividend relief were incomplete, the result would lie somewhere between the result for complete dividend relief and that for the classical system.

None of the options for integration or dividend relief considered in table 6-1 generally achieves capital-import neutrality; so long as individual tax rate schedules differ among countries, competition among individual investors in a given market must usually be on unequal terms.[42] Similarly, national efficiency is inherently incon-

40. This would not be true if the imputation credit were based on the tax rate in the country of residence instead of on the rate in the source country. Note, however, that unequal pass-through of tax preferences in the two countries (to either portfolio or direct investors) would interfere with worldwide efficiency. This implication has not been generally recognized. For further discussion, see Charles E. McLure, Jr., "International Aspects of Dividend Relief," paper delivered at a conference on the imputation method of dividend relief at Erasmus University, Rotterdam, November 24, 1978.

41. If the foreign corporate tax differed from the domestic tax, capital-export neutrality would not be achieved if domestic tax on earnings retained by foreign subsidiaries were deferred. Naturally, neither of the systems described in columns 5 and 6 would produce capital-export neutrality, even for distributed earnings, when the concept is interpreted to include personal as well as corporate taxes on distributed income.

42. It may be worth mentioning in passing that capital-import neutrality, in the sense of a lack of differential taxation, has no important analogue in the purely domestic context. Corporations sometimes complain about unfair competition from

sistent with the results of integration and dividend relief, as well as with their basic purpose.[43]

In summary, then, neither capital-import neutrality nor national efficiency is fully consistent with integration or dividend relief. But that is no great loss, since neither concept is a high-priority goal. Capital-export neutrality, on the other hand, which *is* an important goal because it implies maximum worldwide efficiency, can be achieved in any of several ways.[44]

Adding layers of foreign subsidiaries to the example of table 6-1, though it seriously complicates the problem, does not change the fundamental conclusions of the previous paragraph. Capital-import neutrality and national efficiency remain impossible to achieve in an integrated system, but capital-export neutrality is inherent in a consistent system of full integration or dividend relief.

Equity

Both *national equity* and *international equity* involve the relative tax burdens on resident individuals of a given country. The former considers only taxes levied by the country of residence, while the latter also considers taxes imposed by other countries. In general, they are consistent with national efficiency and worldwide efficiency (capital-export neutrality), respectively, and therefore need not be discussed further. *Intercountry equity,* on the other hand, involves equity in the division of tax revenues between national treasuries. More particularly, it involves both the distribution of claims to such tax revenues *between* countries of source and countries of residence and the allocation of income *among* countries of source.[45] I concentrate solely upon the former distribution, leaving aside the complex questions involved in using either the separate-entity (separate-

cooperatives, and objections to competition from firms owned by tax-exempt organizations led to the passage of the tax on unrelated business income. But there is little record of complaints about competition from firms owned predominantly by individuals in low tax brackets.

43. This is rather ironic, since more than one country seems to have adopted dividend relief in order to encourage domestic investment (see chapter 3).

44. Note, however, that the efficiency argument has been made in the context of complete dividend payout. As mentioned above, capital-export neutrality will not generally be achieved if tax on earnings retained by foreign subsidiaries is deferred.

45. For more on this issue, see Musgrave, "International Tax Differentials," and Peggy B. Musgrave, "International Tax Base Division and the Multinational Corporation," *Public Finance,* vol. 27, no. 4 (1972), pp. 394–413.

accounting) approach or formula apportionment among countries of source.[46]

As in so many matters of equity, there are, unfortunately, no scientific guidelines in this area. If all countries had similar levels of per capita income and similar levels and types of public services and no country were a significant net importer or exporter of capital, the choice of whether the source or residence country received the tax revenue would be relatively unimportant. But, in fact, some countries are important net exporters of capital and others are important net importers, so that the choice matters a great deal. (How much it matters depends, of course, on the way income is allocated among source countries.) Moreover, it simply will not do to overlook differences in the types and levels of public service provided in various countries. In addition, differences in the levels of per capita income suggest that the equity rules for division of tax revenues that apply between advanced and developing countries should not be the same as those that apply among developed countries.[47] Finally—and this is not so much a matter of equity in the distribution of tax proceeds as it is one of political power—some arrangements are simply likely to be unacceptable as a practical matter. It might, for example, be thought that on equity grounds the members of the Organization of Petroleum Exporting Countries have no particular claim to the vast amounts of fiscal revenues they receive.[48] But little short of warfare could change the present distribution of tax revenues. Other examples, though less extreme, less dramatic, and less important, might nonetheless be significant.

International Fiscal Relations

International tax treaties have been guided by two overriding principles: *nondiscrimination* and *reciprocity*.[49] The first of these

46. Musgrave, "International Tax Base Division," treats these issues. For preliminary thoughts on the transference of experience in the interstate sphere to the international arena, see Charles E. McLure, Jr., "Taxation of Multijurisdictional Corporate Income: Lessons of the U.S. Experience," in Wallace E. Oates, ed., *The Political Economy of Fiscal Federalism* (Heath, 1977), pp. 241–59.

47. For a more extensive discussion of the issues raised here, see Richard A. Musgrave and Peggy B. Musgrave, "Inter-nation Equity," in Richard M. Bird and John G. Head, eds., *Modern Fiscal Issues: Essays in Honor of Carl S. Shoup* (Toronto: University of Toronto Press, 1972), pp. 63–85.

48. But see the discussion of the national rental criterion in ibid., pp. 72–75.

49. See Sato and Bird, "International Aspects," pp. 403–06 and 424–26. My discussion in the next few paragraphs draws heavily on pp. 424–29.

provides that countries cannot discriminate in their taxation of domestic and foreign firms; the second that withholding taxes applied to dividends should be "mirror images" of those applied by the treaty partner. But these rules, which are sensible enough in a world of classical income taxes, lose their attraction if some countries provide dividend relief or integration. A strict interpretation of the reciprocity requirement, for example, would demand that a source country providing a dividend-paid deduction should use mirror-image withholding rates on foreign shareholders, regardless of the tax regime applied to corporate-source income in their country of residence. (As noted in chapter 3, the United States has indeed adopted this line in its negotiations with West Germany and the United Kingdom.)

It has been argued that "effective reciprocity" constitutes a more reasonable approach in a world in which some countries use a classical system and others provide integration or dividend relief.[50] When two countries with similar systems (classical, integrated, or dividend relief) were involved, effective reciprocity would become actual reciprocity. But when dissimilar systems were involved, treaties would cover the basic corporate tax as well as withholding rates and would aim for equivalent total taxation of corporate-source income of foreigners rather than formal equality of withholding rates. Thus a country that provided dividend relief to domestic shareholders could deny relief to shareholders residing in countries that used the classical approach and were unwilling to make any reciprocal concession in withholding rates.

Synthesis

On balance, much can be said for an international system of taxing corporate income in which aggregate tax rates are based on the residence of individual shareholders rather than on the source of the income. Only such a system is fully consistent with the rationale for integrated income taxes: the taxation of the global income of individuals, regardless of source. By comparison, source-based taxation is inherently schedular; under it integration of corporate taxes and the personal taxes of shareholders is conceptually impossible. Moreover, residence-based taxation is consistent with worldwide efficiency (capital-export neutrality), whereas source-based taxation generally

50. See ibid., pp. 426–29.

is not.[51] Finally, because benefits of public services are usually more household-related than business-related, it is reasonable to believe that benefit taxation, to the extent that it is a function of income taxation, is better served by taxing income at residence than at source.[52]

In a world of full integration, residence-based taxation would require that shareholders include in their income for tax purposes their grossed-up corporate-source income, regardless of the country in which that income originates. The shareholder would then take credit for taxes paid at the corporate level on the corporate-source income attributed to him.[53] In a world of dividend relief, residence-based taxation could be implemented by using either the imputation method or the dividend-paid credit, but it would not extend to the undistributed portion of corporate-source income. Thus capital-export neutrality would not ordinarily be achieved if taxes were deferred on foreign-source income that was retained by foreign subsidiaries.

In theory, the capital-export neutrality implied by residence-based taxation of distributed corporate-source income could be achieved with either the source country or the residence country granting the imputation credits necessary to achieve integration or dividend relief. But, as argued above, for technical reasons it seems unlikely that residence countries would grant imputation credits except for direct investment in subsidiaries. Rather, at least for portfolio investment, imputation credits allowed by the source country seem to be the more

51. This statement is strictly true only for an integrated system or for dividend relief under either 100 percent dividend payout or current taxation to parents of income retained by foreign subsidiaries.

52. That the benefit principle provides no support for a separate corporation income tax has been argued in Charles E. McLure, Jr., "Integration of the Personal and Corporate Income Taxes: The Missing Element in Recent Tax Reform Proposals," *Harvard Law Review*, vol. 88 (January 1975), pp. 532–82. At best, when benefits are business-related, benefit taxation is likely to be achieved by the use of a tax on production (such as an origin-principle tax on value added); because benefits are more likely household-related, a consumption-based tax (such as a retail sales tax or a destination-principle tax on value added) may be more appropriate. But the marginal cost of most of the services provided for business firms may be reflected better by user charges (or use-related taxes) than by broad-based taxes like income and sales taxes.

53. In such a system, basis in corporate shares would be written up by the amount of corporate-source income, and dividends would be tax-free and would reduce the basis in such shares. Any capital gains tax would presumably be paid to the country of residence.

promising avenue for progress, and the dividend-paid deduction inherently involves the source country's granting relief.[54] As for direct investment, the foreign tax credit would seem to take care of the problem of double taxation, at least roughly.

Source countries may, of course, balk at such an arrangement, since it would seem to deprive them of revenue. In particular, it can be expected that developing countries would object strongly to a system of either full integration or dividend relief that called for source countries to provide the tax credits or refunds. These capital-importing countries would have hardly any corporate tax base under such a system, even if the principle of effective reciprocity were adopted.

But the problem is easily overstated. First, the source country would continue to derive the revenue from the retained portion of corporate-source income under a system of dividend relief.[55] Only under full integration would the source country lose all its revenue. Given the dim prospects of the adoption of integration on a worldwide scale, the problem of internation distribution of revenues is much diminished. Furthermore, a great deal of foreign investment is done through subsidiaries. For this type of investment the residence country is likely to grant the relief from double taxation of dividends, as now. Finally, it is possible that some sort of international compensation arrangement could be established under which the cost of imputation credits would be shared more equitably by source and residence countries, especially when the former is a developing country.

In short, the system envisaged would be one in which dividend relief is provided at the rate of tax paid in the source country. In part for administrative reasons it would be provided by the source country in the case of portfolio investment and by the country of residence in the case of direct investment in subsidiaries. This implies that the foreign tax would not be integrated into the domestic tax in the case of portfolio investors. It also means that the residence country would not follow current European practice of applying the précompte to

54. Note that this discussion abstracts from the nature of public goods and the implied choice of the proper country to provide the relief.

55. Royalties, which usually are not eligible for the foreign tax credit, could, to some extent, also be used to overcome this problem in the case of source countries rich in natural resources.

dividends paid out of foreign earnings of parent firms, since the pré-compte currently has the effect of washing out the advantage of dividend relief.

A final question remains: how should the United States deal with countries that retain classical systems when the United States adopts dividend relief? Two problems are involved: the proper treatment of foreign portfolio investors in U.S. corporations and the proper treatment of U.S. portfolio investors in foreign firms. (The treatment of direct investment would not seem to be a problem, since it would involve little change from present arrangements unless the United States were to follow the British lead in this area.) There are no "correct" answers to these problems. But the French approach to the first one is a reasonable place to start. That is, the imputation credit could be extended by treaty to foreign investors in U.S. corporations. This would not imply that the imputation, rather than the dividend-paid deduction, approach should be used to provide relief. If international recognition of "effective reciprocity" could be gained, either approach could serve.[56]

For incoming dividends the proper approach is somewhat clearer. Since it would be an administrative nightmare to try to integrate the foreign tax into the domestic personal tax, it would seem to be best simply to tax portfolio shareholders on their net dividends (that is, dividends after payment of foreign corporate tax, without gross-up) from countries with classical systems (as is done now).[57] Withholding taxes would ideally be based on effective reciprocity. This approach would tend to discourage portfolio investment in such countries. But direct investment would not be discouraged so long as the foreign tax credit were allowed for taxes paid by subsidiaries of U.S. firms. Thus the presence of countries using the classical system would probably complicate the picture, but should not be a major obstacle to achieving an acceptable method of dividend relief.

56. For a forceful statement of the argument for effective reciprocity, see Sato and Bird, "International Aspects," especially pp. 426–29. See, however, Ault, "International Issues," pp. 483–92, for difficulties with this approach.

57. Note that this approach would be consistent with national efficiency and would hinder international investment.

Conference Discussion

THE CONFERENCE discussion was limited primarily to the technical questions that would be encountered in a move to full integration or dividend relief; questions of the desirability of integration or dividend relief, though they occasionally arose, were off limits.[1]

Full Integration

The conference began with an attempt to isolate the problems of implementing full integration.[2] Eight problems were noted:

1. As explained fully in chapter 1, "dividend relief" is used to describe systems that involve only distributions, and not imputation of retained corporate earnings to shareholders for tax purposes. "Integration" (except when occasionally used in a broad sense) refers to schemes for taxing corporate equity income that try to replicate the taxation of partnerships by imputing retained corporate income to shareholders for tax purposes. Thus, contrary to much recent usage of the term, "partial integration" is not a synonym for dividend relief. Nor does "dividend relief" carry any pejorative connotation.

It should be noted that the conference discussion preceded the announcement of the proposal for partial dividend relief by Congressman Al Ullman, chairman of the House Committee on Ways and Means, in early 1978. However, some participants were aware of the similar proposal made to the White House by the Treasury Department in September 1977 (see chap. 1, n. 1).

2. Early in the conference the combination of accrual taxation of capital gains and elimination of the corporate income tax was ruled out for purposes of the discussion. Several participants thought that this approach (with periodic evaluation

215

1. Basis adjustment would be required to prevent retained corporate earnings from being taxed twice—once when they were earned and once when they resulted in capital gains. Some participants thought that this problem could be handled through the issuance of taxable stock dividends.

2. The need to allocate corporate income among various classes of stock would cause problems, since it is not always clear until actual distribution occurs which class of stock will in fact benefit from earnings. (For example, it is possible that income would be allocated to owners of common stock, who would therefore be liable for tax, even though dividends were ultimately paid to owners of preferred stock.)

3. No date for the allocation of corporate losses would be totally satisfactory. Allocation on a daily basis would be unworkable for administrative reasons, but allocation of losses to the owner of shares on the last day of the firm's fiscal year was generally seen as unacceptable because it would create the possibility of "trafficking" in losses by wealthy individuals. Allocation to shareholders of record on the first day of the year, on the other hand, though it would result in income being allocated to the right person, would give the imputation credit to the wrong person (see chapter 5). One compromise solution suggested was to allocate income and losses to the shareholder of record on the last day of the year, but to allow him a share in losses equal to only the fraction of the year he had held the stock, except in the case of "catastrophic" losses occurring late in the year.

4. Any attempt to reflect in shareholder returns for the taxable year in question the results of subsequent audit adjustments and amended returns would appear to be hopelessly complicated, because of the need to reopen thousands of shareholder returns. But allowing the results to be taken in the year in which the final liability was settled could lead to abuse through manipulation.

5. Chains of firms would create difficult administration and compliance problems; these would be magnified if there were losses, amended returns, or audit adjustments.

of shares and constructive realization of gains and losses) would be a more promising one than the taxation of undistributed corporate-source equity income under integration. Because their chances of political acceptance were said to be remote, schemes for integration that do not include withholding at the corporate level were also ruled to be beyond the purview of the conference—but not without dissent.

6. The treatment of tax preferences would further complicate the system; for example, preferences might be disallowed to the extent that they were distributed.[3] Whereas under present law it is necessary to know current and accumulated earnings and profits, this new scheme would require the firm to keep accounts for accumulated and current taxable income and for accumulated and current preference income.

7. If the investment tax credit (ITC) and foreign tax credit (FTC) were to be attributed to shareholders, as they would be under a pure partnership approach, limitations should be applied at the shareholder level rather than at the corporate level. But this would create an unacceptable burden of compliance for most shareholders.

8. Full integration would involve taxation of the shareholder on income that he had not yet received. At the very least, this could cause cash-flow problems for shareholders in marginal rate brackets above the corporate rate.

It was noted, however, that many of these problems would exist even under dividend relief and that the administrative feasibility of full integration should be appraised on the basis of only those difficulties that are unique to it. Problems caused by tax preferences, audit adjustments and amended returns, chains of corporations, and perhaps the limitations on the ITC and FTC would be encountered in some schemes for dividend relief.[4] Only the problems of basis adjustment and losses and the cash-flow problem that would be created when the individual shareholder's marginal tax rate exceeded the corporate withholding rate were thought to be unique to full integration.

On the possibility of overcoming these various problems, and especially the latter three, the discussion was inconclusive. Some participants believed that the integration scheme outlined in the Treasury Department's 1977 *Blueprints for Basic Tax Reform* (which relied on capital markets to reflect losses in stock prices) would be adequate to take care of the problem of losses. But others contended that the *Blueprints* scheme, by allocating losses to the stockholder of

3. As defined in chapter 4, preferences are provisions that reduce the amount of tax to below that which would be collected if the statutory rate were applied to economic income; they can be "deductible" or "creditable." Whether the foreign tax credit should be treated as a preference is unclear.

4. See chapter 5 for a discussion of these difficulties.

record on the first day of the year,[5] would work only if there were no withholding tax at the corporate level; if there were withholding, the wrong shareholder would get credit for the tax. As for audit adjustments, the view was expressed—but was hardly unanimous—that equity in taxation would probably not be much impaired by a scheme that reconstructed corporate income for the year in question, but attributed the adjustment in tax liability to shareholders in the year in which the adjustment occurred, since any untoward effects would be eliminated by capital markets. Many participants felt that the result would not be much different from that which occurs in similar circumstances today.

Some participants thought that problems of basis adjustment (increase for imputation; decrease for distribution) could be handled by relying on the electronic data-retrieval capabilities of brokers and investment institutions. But others thought that the experience of mutual funds made for a pessimistic assessment. Whereas basis adjustment due to reinvestment would be easy in principle (as is that due to other investment), the real problem is one of making the requisite adjustments to all the individual share lots held by investors unless they are allowed to employ an average cost basis. Although some participants thought that it should be possible to deal with the problem of more than one class of stock by promulgating simple, if arbitrary, rules, no one ventured to say what such rules might be.

It was suggested that the cash-flow problem of shareholders whose marginal tax rate exceeded the corporate tax rate could be handled by allowing the shareholder to sell stock to the firm whose shares he owned, without incurring capital gains tax. (In essence, the basis adjustment would be applied first to sales or redemptions of stock to which retained earnings had been allocated, rather than pro rata to all such shares, whether sold, redeemed, or held.) But others cautioned that besides opening the way for abuse, this approach might run afoul of state corporate laws controlling repurchase of stock. Finally, it was noted that there would be no cash-flow problem if the top personal rate were no higher than the corporate rate. But even this result would depend on the treatment of tax preferences. (If preferences were to be washed out on distribution, under some approaches a shareholder subject to a marginal rate above the effective corporate rate could encounter cash-flow problems.)

5. U.S. Department of the Treasury, *Blueprints for Basic Tax Reform* (Government Printing Office, 1977), p. 69.

To the extent that problems created by tax preferences and the foreign tax credit had their genesis in limitations on the use of such preferences and credits, they could be solved, it was said, by taking away the limitations (which some proponents of this view contended make no sense to begin with). But, though this view may have been generally accepted for investment tax credit and other preferences, there was reluctance to allow unlimited credit for the taxes imposed by foreign countries.

The appraisal of full integration was mixed. The problems to be overcome in implementing full integration appear to be real and serious. Some participants felt that, since a great deal of attention had been devoted to these problems in the United States and elsewhere, still further study of the feasibility of full integration might be unproductive. But others thought that with more study it might be possible to surmount many of the problems.[6] Some stressed the fact that only quite recently has a concerted effort been made to deal with the problems and that even now the surface has barely been scratched. Some felt that, at the very least, the eight problems outlined above deserved further attention before a definitive verdict was possible. Moreover, it was noted that anyone examining the prospects for a corporate income tax in 1913 would almost certainly have concluded that a system such as the present "classical" one would be administratively impossible. And one observer said that many Canadian accountants and lawyers who had originally been against the proposals of the Royal Commission on Taxation for full integration, in part for administrative reasons, have now concluded that such a system would have been simpler than the dividend-received credit actually adopted. A general feeling existed, however, that even if the complications of full integration could be handled adequately, integration would not make the tax code less complex. Nor would all the added complications be lodged at the corporate level, where they could be handled most easily.

Integration by the Back Door

Some of the conference participants expressed the view that whether full integration is feasible or not may be largely immaterial,

6. Attention was drawn to the apparent success of cooperatives in achieving a form of integration. In cooperatives, it was said, there is no distinction between taxable income and earnings and profits, and the imputation problem is handled by issuing scrip.

since under certain circumstances its effects can be achieved simply by allowing dividend relief and relying on stockholder pressures to force an increase in dividend payout rates. To understand this viewpoint, make the simplifying assumptions that (1) the top personal tax rate is no higher than the corporate rate, and (2) there is no foreign income or tax preferences. (Taxation of long-term capital gains as ordinary income strengthens the conclusion, but is not essential to it.) In a world of complete relief from double taxation of dividends no shareholder would have any tax incentive to prefer retained earnings to dividends, and, so far as tax considerations were concerned, most shareholders would have a strong interest in having high payout rates. In such a case, it was argued, payout rates would probably be near 100 percent except when constrained by law or debenture agreements, and integration would, in effect, be nearly complete.[7] And yet it would not have been necessary to deal with the troublesome problems unique to full integration (cash-flow, basis adjustment, and so forth). But it was noted that, strictly speaking, the argument that equal corporate and top personal rates lead, in effect, to full integration is applicable only if dividend relief is complete, as in the Federal Republic of Germany. If, as in France and the United Kingdom, only about half the corporate tax were allowed as a credit (or an equivalent amount of relief were provided under the dividend-paid deduction or split-rate system), high-income shareholders could be expected to continue to prefer retentions over dividends, so that back-door integration would not be achieved.[8] More-

7. The revenue effects under 100 percent payout would approximate those under full integration. The efficiency objective of integration (avoidance of discriminatory taxation of equity income originating in the corporate sector) would be achieved if the payout rate were 100 percent, but not if it were less. Even if payout rates fell below 100 percent, the equity objective of integration—taxation of corporate-source income like ordinary income—would be achieved at the top of the income scale, though not at the bottom. One objection to this view is that equity would be achieved at the top of the scale by reducing top marginal rates, thereby diminishing the progressivity of the income tax; it is hardly ever suggested that equality between the corporate rate and the top personal rate be achieved by raising the former. On the other hand, the progressivity of the tax system would be increased to the extent that preferences were washed out; but this would require that dividends would indeed be paid from preference income—which is unlikely to occur. Finally, because it would encourage dividend payout, integration by the back door would lack the neutrality toward corporate financial policy that is a hallmark of full integration.
8. The alternative of legally required 100 percent distribution of earnings was rejected as inconsistent with existing statutes and corporate obligations.

over, it was noted that in West Germany preliminary indications are that even complete relief from double taxation of dividends has not resulted in an increase in dividend payout rates.

The view that integration can be achieved by the "back door" is further strengthened, it was said, by consideration of the response of many small firms that would qualify for treatment as subchapter S corporations (that is, be taxed as partnerships, though incorporated). For if the surtax exemption were eliminated at the same time that the top marginal personal rate were reduced to the level of the corporate rate, there would be no tax advantage in continued use of the "normal" (nonsubchapter S) corporate form of business organization. Since the corporate form could not be used to shelter retained earnings, dividend rates for small firms would be expected to rise, as they have in Canada. Or such firms could just be operated as subchapter S corporations or perhaps even as partnerships. But for both of these forms of organization full integration is, with some exceptions, already provided under present law. Thus full integration would be spurred by the move to dividend relief to the extent that it was accompanied by a reduced top personal rate and elimination of the surtax exemption. An interesting policy question is whether large firms with more complicated capital structures than are currently allowed under subchapter S should be allowed to elect full integration on an optional basis. If the use of subchapter S or partnerships increased, the problems of full integration, which some participants felt have not been adequately handled under present law, would be accentuated.

Once the likely treatment of tax preferences and foreign-source income is admitted, one cannot be so sanguine about integration by the back door. Given the tax implications of distributing preference income under a stack-last, wash-out system for preferences, it would be highly unlikely that firms would normally pay out more than their taxable income (or the analogue for creditable preferences). Thus back-door integration would not be completely achieved in a system that treated preferences in this way.[9] Moreover, if preferences were

9. But, as argued in chapter 4, in one sense the equity effect of deductible preferences would be preserved in such a system, since retained preference earnings would be exempt from tax, just as preference income would be exempt in a fully integrated system with full pass-through. But dividends would tend to equal taxable income; the nonneutral impact on dividend policy is in marked contrast to the complete neutrality in the fully integrated system.

stacked last and washed out for regular corporations, but passed through for partnerships and (in large part) for subchapter S corporations, the choice of form of business organization would be distorted.

The discussion of the possibility of achieving integration by the back door highlighted an important shortcoming in previous treatments of integration and dividend relief and the need for empirical research. Too much of the previous analysis has occurred in an implicit framework in which the dividend payout rate is fixed, even though one of the expected effects of integration, and especially of dividend relief, is an increase in corporate distributions. (Revenue loss, for example, has been assumed to be much larger under dividend relief than under integration, though with 100 percent dividend payout the cost of dividend relief should equal that of integration.) Unfortunately there is almost no direct empirical evidence on how U.S. firms would respond to dividend relief or full integration; at best, what exists is survey responses showing expected reaction to dividend relief in the United States and evidence resulting from the recent West German shift to full dividend relief and from the British movement to and from a classical system since 1965. But the effects of the most recent British change will be clouded by the fact that it occurred simultaneously with imposition of an incomes policy limiting increases in dividends. Experience in France and West Germany seems to contradict the rise in dividend payouts expected by the theoretical analysis.[10] But if the French and West German experience is to be relevant, it must be subjected to more sophisticated analysis than has thus far been used—in the West German case after enough time has passed for something resembling equilibrium to be reached.[11]

Complicating any attempt to determine how firms would respond to full integration or dividend relief is the difference in the situations in which various shareholders, companies, and industries would find themselves. Managers of firms that had traditionally paid out small

10. As noted below, it is not easy to interpret this experience, since cash dividends may be reduced while gross (inclusive of the credit) dividends rise. And the reduction in taxes inherent in dividend relief makes it possible for both gross dividends and retained earnings to rise.

11. Of course, West German experience with dividend relief began with the establishment of the split-rate system in 1953. But it would be difficult, indeed, to separate statistically the effects of dividend relief from the other structural changes that were occurring in postwar Germany at that time.

portions of their income could not be expected to be happy about a tax reform that encouraged payout unless they could be confident that shareholders would reinvest. Yet they might find shareholder pressures for distribution irresistible. It is unclear whether they would be more likely to yield to such pressures—and regret doing so less— if they could declare taxable stock dividends or if there were nearly automatic dividend reinvestment plans. If they were denied the benefits of dividend relief, shareholders that are currently tax exempt would be adversely affected by a reduction in the *cash* dividend, even though the *effective* dividend (cash plus credit) received by shareholders eligible for the credit were increased. Finally, industries characterized by large amounts of tax preference income and high dividend payout rates, such as banks and regulated public utilities, would be adversely affected by any plan for dividend relief that involved washing out preferences, even if preferences were stacked last.

Participants familiar with European experience with partial (and more recently with complete) dividend relief noted that firms appear to treat the shareholder credit as a part of dividends and hence to reduce cash dividends in response to dividend relief. But such a response could be consistent with increased effective dividends (cash dividends plus credits), so the relief would appear to be split between the shareholder and the corporation. Though it is clear that firms would be loath to distribute tax-free income and thereby incur liability for the précompte or its equivalent—and indeed the précompte yields little revenue in France—some participants felt that the reduction in cash dividends was not merely the response to the possibility of précompte on foreign-source income. (In West Germany this would be the primary cause of a précompte liability, since book income and taxable income correspond more closely there than in the United States.) Be this as it may, foreign experience thus far suggests that dividend relief is not necessarily an easy route to full integration, though the general failure to allow complete relief from double taxation of dividends and to equalize the corporate and top personal rates clouds the issue.

Foreign Experience

Some participants who were familiar with European systems of dividend relief felt that European experience is instructive, in that it

raises serious questions as to what economic objectives are to be served by dividend relief and suggests problem areas that must be confronted. Others felt that the European experience with dividend relief is of only limited precedental value, except perhaps in the international field, where cosmetic differences in systems may have important implications for treaty negotiations. Although the same technical problems that were discussed at the conference were given as reasons for not adopting full integration in West Germany (basis adjustment, losses, audit adjustments and amended returns, and so forth), some observers believed that European discussions of integration had never approached the sophistication exhibited at the conference.

This difference in level of discussion may be traced in part to the difference in the way Europeans and Americans (at least the advocates of integration) view the corporation income tax. Whereas in the United States the case for full integration and even for dividend relief usually depends on the acceptance of the conduit view of the corporation, in Europe that view is generally discounted, and the appeal of dividend relief is more pragmatic. (See chapter 2.) The conceptual difference is usefully illustrated by the discussions of tax preferences in the two areas. In the United States academic concern began with the view that integration is a necessary component of a Haig-Simons definition of income and tax preferences are deviations from that definition; thus it is only natural that the proper treatment of tax preferences would be a crucial element of discussion. In Europe the frame of reference has been different. With the exception of West Germany, the European countries have been concerned primarily with removal of the double taxation of dividends rather than with integration per se. Given such an orientation, it is logical to arrive at a policy that would impose a précompte on any dividends from income not carrying the full corporate tax burden; in the absence of the précompte, relief from double taxation would be given when double taxation did not exist.

Other differences between the American and the European attitudes to integration and dividend relief include the following: Even though West Germany's concern about tax-induced leverage (debt finance) parallels the United States', the distortion that results from differentially high taxation of corporations is seen in West Germany to be a distortion of the form of business organization rather than of

sectoral investment, output, and consumption, as in America. And in the United Kingdom the fault of the overtaxation of dividends is seen as a loss in the "quality of investment" (excessive reinvestment of retained earnings), which is somewhat different from the additional U.S. concern over sectoral misallocation. In part, these differences may be due to the fact that, though European economists are generally familiar with Harberger's analysis of tax-induced sectoral misallocation of resources, some who are influential do not take seriously his estimates of the welfare losses resulting from an unintegrated corporate tax.

As in France, dividend relief has been seen in West Germany as a way to increase interest in the domestic stock market, a feature that was hardly ever mentioned in early discussions of dividend relief in the United States.[12] (In early West German proposals dividend relief would have been tied to initiation of a mandatory plan for employee stock ownership, so that the benefits of dividend relief would eventually be enjoyed by workers.) But whereas France does not provide 100 percent dividend relief, owing, in part, to the revenue loss involved and the politically controversial nature of dividend relief, West Germany does. Because a reduction in cash dividends represents a real loss to those not obtaining the credit (for example, tax-exempt organizations and foreigners), equity investment has become less attractive to such groups, and it appears to some observers that foreigners are selling their shares in German firms.[13]

In Canada the impetus for the dividend-received credit was not relief from double taxation of dividends, but stimulus for corporate investment. In that context the important issue was whether investment by non-Canadians should be encouraged, rather than whether tax preferences should be passed through; given the Canadian objective of dividend relief, it was taken for granted that preferences should be passed through, since a précompte would have "blunted incen-

12. More recently, considerable attention has been paid to the effect that reducing the differential taxation of equity income would have in increasing the attraction of investment in equity securities. This concept did not figure heavily in early discussions of integration in the United States.

13. Of course, one of the reasons for the West German reform that resulted in 100 percent dividend relief was the "foreigner effect"; under it the foreign parent taking funds out of the Federal Republic and reinvesting them in its West German subsidiary would pay less total West German tax than a West German firm that retained earnings and reinvested them. (See also chapters 3 and 5.)

tives." (But preferences are passed through only approximately, not exactly; see also chapter 4.)

For at least two reasons, West Germany chose a hybrid system involving elements of both the split-rate system and the gross-up and credit system: (1) though there was no desire to exempt "tax-exempt" organizations and foreigners from tax, it was felt that raising the tax on them to 56 percent would have been extreme, and (2) retaining the split-rate feature tends to avoid the so-called Chaban-Delmas effect (refunds to high-income taxpayers who have substantial dividend income, little other income, and substantial deductions) by keeping the corporate rate on distributed income below the top personal rate.[14]

In both the United Kingdom and West Germany the reliance on the imputation method (which in West Germany's case is partial) is largely the result of historical developments in international treaty negotiations. Though both countries would have preferred to employ a simple split-rate system, they felt that doing so in a world of treaties based on mirror-image withholding would have required that they extend the benefits of dividend relief to foreign shareholders in domestic corporations, something they did not want to do. Thus they were more or less forced to adopt the gross-up and credit system, which allows more latitude in denying relief to foreigners. There was agreement at the conference that the British system, with its advance corporation tax, was intentionally designed so that the tax would be treated as an advance payment against the corporate tax, not against the personal income tax. It was felt that this cosmetic difference can be important in international treaty negotiations.

European experience with the précompte is of some interest, since the tax treatment of preference income and foreign income is crucial to any decision about integration or dividend relief. First, there seems to be a general dislike for the précompte system as a way of washing out preferences on distributed corporate income, perhaps because it involves a mandatory distribution; in France, at least, business appears to prefer a variable credit geared to the firm's effective tax rate. (Along the same lines, many participants felt that any preference of U.S. business for a dividend-paid deduction would vanish if it were

14. In addition, maintaining a rate differential of at least 20 percent allowed West Germany to continue to collect a 25 percent withholding tax under its treaty with France.

linked to withholding, as in the scheme attributed to the Treasury Department.) In France little revenue is collected from the précompte; thus while in theory the précompte discriminates against corporations, the stacking rule mitigates the discrimination—though perhaps only because dividend policy is being distorted. On the other hand, it was said that in West Germany firms that had been rather casual about provisions for the précompte are finding out to their surprise that they have précompte liabilities.

Tax Preferences[15]

The existence of tax preferences raises two crucial questions. First, should preference income be passed through to shareholders on distribution or washed out (treated as taxable income to the shareholder)? Second, regardless of which treatment is accorded preferences, should it be assumed that preference income is the first to be distributed (stacked first), that preferences are the last component of income to be distributed (stacked last), or that preference income and fully taxed income are distributed and retained in proportion to their shares of net income (prorated)?

Some participants strongly supported the view that the only administratively feasible way to handle tax preferences would be to stack them last (against retained earnings) and wash them out when they were distributed. This was explained by the following example, said to be patterned after the plan considered by the Treasury Department in 1977.[16]

Suppose that there is a 46 percent corporate tax rate. The firm places 21/46 of the corporate tax in a refundable income tax account (RITA). The firm can, at its discretion, also withhold tax of up to 28 percent on gross dividends (dividends inclusive of the withholding tax).[17] The amount withheld is then allowed as a credit at the

15. See chapter 4 for a more extensive discussion of these issues.

16. For a detailed description of the similar plan proposed by Chairman Al Ullman of the House Ways and Means Committee, see the appendix to chapter 4.

17. A firm would not necessarily choose to withhold the full 28 percent if it distributed preference income. Suppose in the extreme case that it had no taxable income. It would then have nothing in its refundable income tax account and would actually have to remit any withheld tax to the Treasury. There might be conflict between shareholders, who would desire the credit generated by withholding, and corporate managers, who would prefer not to create a deficit in the RITA.

Table 7-1. Illustration of a Refundable Income Tax Account Approach to Dividend Relief, by Alternative Tax Rates[a]

Monetary units except where indicated

Item[b]	Marginal personal tax rate of shareholder (percent)	
	50	20
1. Corporate-source income	100	100
2. Corporate income tax [46% of 1]	46	46
3. Withholding tax [28% of 9][c]	21	21
4. Refundable income tax account [21/46 of 2]	21	21
5. Net withholding tax [3 − 4]	0	0
6. Corporate tax liability [2 + 5]	46	46
7. Cash dividend [1 − 6]	54	54
8. Shareholder credit [from 3]	21	21
9. Gross dividend [7 + 8]	75	75
10. Personal tax liability on gross dividend [marginal tax rate × 9]	37.5	15
11. Net personal liability [10 − 8]	16.5	−6
12. Total tax liability [6 + 11]	62.5	40
13. Total liability without dividend relief (46 plus marginal tax rate times 54)	73	56.8
14. Percentage of overtaxation removed[d]	45.65	45.65

a. Terms relating to integration systems are explained in the glossary.
b. Except for percentages, the numbers in brackets refer to the lines of this table.
c. This figure for withholding tax produces the dividend in line 9.
d. Calculated as (line 13 − line 12) as a percent of the excess of line 13 over the marginal tax rate × 100.

shareholder level. Funds in the RITA can be used to discharge corporate liabilities for withholding tax on dividends. (In the case of fully taxed income the RITA would be just adequate to offset liability for a 28 percent withholding tax on dividends.) Table 7-1 illustrates this approach in the simple case in which all corporate-source income is paid out and there are no preferences.

If the firm withholds the maximum amount on dividends, the 21 in the refundable income tax account can be seen either as a means of reducing the corporate rate on distributed earnings to 25 percent or as a prepayment of the withholding tax that the corporation must pay on its dividends to produce the shareholder credit. In either case, the corporation must pay to the government 46, the shareholder has a credit of 21, and gross dividends can be 75, composed of 54 of cash and the 21 credit. The shareholder calculates his liability by using his own marginal rate and takes the 21 credit; if this marginal rate is

below 28 percent, the shareholder's liability attributable to dividends falls short of the credit. In total, the amount of tax paid (line 12) is equal to the 46 paid at the corporate level plus whatever net liability exists at the personal level (line 11). Comparison of this aggregate rate with the aggregate effective rate that would prevail under a classical system (line 13) reveals that the same fraction of the over-taxation of dividends has been removed at all levels of marginal tax rates (line 14). Of course, for retained earnings, the 46 percent corporate tax is a final tax.

The effects of preference income can be seen by considering a case in which the firm has 54 of tax-exempt income as well as the 100 of taxable income assumed in the example above.[18] The example is not altered so long as the firm distributes only 54 in cash; the RITA just offsets the withholding at the firm level and the tax-exempt income is retained. Suppose however, that the firm wished to distribute not 54 in cash but 81. Since the cash dividend of 81 would result in with-holding of 31.50, the gross dividend would be 112.50 (28 percent of 112.50 is 31.50). This 31.50 would, of course, be creditable at the individual level, but only 21 of it would be offset by the RITA, so the firm would be liable for an additional tax payment of 10.50 (a form of précompte) over and above what it would pay if it only paid out fully taxable income (that is, retained an amount equal to the pref-erence income). Thus the scheme described above operates to stack deductible preferences last and wash them out, as in the European systems, but it does so in a way that does not require the definition of preferences or economic income. And if all distributions are treated as dividends, as in the proposal, there is no need for such a concept as earnings and profits to be used in differentiating between dividends and return of capital.[19]

Finally, it was claimed that it would be possible to pass creditable preferences through, at least in a rough way, by treating them as payments of tax and adding them to the refundable income tax

18. Though this example is useful for illustrating the problem, some observers felt that it does not convey the difficulty of dealing with preferences. It is easy to define preference income in the case of interest on municipal securities, but, they believed, in other cases it would be impossible to determine preference income—the difference between economic and taxable income.

19. Whether all distributions should be treated as dividends, as in the West German system, is an open question. If not, there would have to be rules to define when the corporation was returning capital, as in the present system.

Table 7-2. Treatment of a Creditable Tax Preference for an Individual and for a Corporation Using a Refundable Income Tax Account, Assuming Complete Dividend Relief[a]

Monetary units

Item[b]	Corporation Without invest- ment tax credit	Corporation With investment tax credit — RITA used for actual tax	Corporation With investment tax credit — RITA used for actual tax plus credit	Individual Without invest- ment tax credit	Individual With invest- ment tax credit
1. Income	100	100	100	100	100
2. Gross tax [50% of 1 or 70% of 1]	50	50	50	70	70
3. Investment tax credit	0	10	10	0	10
4. Net tax [2 − 3]	50	40	40	70	60
5. Net income [1 − 4]	50	60	60	30	40
6. Refundable income tax account [from 4 or 3 + 4]	50	40	50
7. Cash dividend [1 − 4]	50	60	60
8. Gross-up [equal to 6]	50	40	50
9. Taxable dividend [7 + 8]	100	100	110
10. Gross personal tax [70% of 9]	70	70	77
11. Shareholder credit [from 8]	50	40	50
12. Net personal tax [10 − 11]	20	30	27
13. Net personal income [7 − 12 or from 5]	30	30	33	30	40

... Not applicable to individuals.
a. Terms relating to integration systems are explained in the glossary.
b. Except for percentages, the numbers in brackets refer to the lines of this table.

account. But pass-through would not really be achieved, since the credit would be subjected to the personal income tax when distributed. This can be illustrated by using an example in which it is assumed that dividend relief is complete and a corporation taxed at a 50 percent statutory rate has an investment tax credit of 10 and distributes all its earnings to shareholders in the 70 percent marginal personal bracket (see table 7-2). If the investment tax credit is simply added to the RITA, its benefits are reduced upon distribution by the amount of the personal marginal rate times the investment tax credit (by 70 percent of 10, to 3, in the present case). If credits are to be preserved upon distribution, they must increase the shareholder credit, but not taxable income.

Flow-through of preferences was said to have many of the problems associated with full integration: lack of timely information for shareholders, problems created by audit adjustments and amended returns, and so forth. Thus some participants thought that only systems involving washout of preferences were workable alternatives. Moreover, some felt that any defense of pass-through must rest on the assumption that the preference in question is a "good" preference; others felt, however, that most preferences are not justified and that pass-through of preferences would offend commonly held notions of tax equity.

Some participants saw little compelling reason for prorating and washout, but others had liked the idea of prorating preferences between dividends and retentions and washing out preferences on preference income that is distributed, as a means of partially eliminating preferences thought to be undesirable. It was suggested that the knife-edged pattern of incentives, in which firms are induced to pay out all fully taxed income and avoid paying dividends from preference income, is undesirable and could be avoided by prorating. It was noted, however, that prorating of preferences adds considerably to the complexity of the tax system. Some felt that basically it is not even possible to define preferences (or at least implement such a definition) in the sense of deviations of taxable income from economic income. This being the case, it is not satisfactory, they stressed, simply to list tax preferences, as under current law, since the correspondence between items on the list and real deviations from economic income would not be close.

In addition, it was argued, prorating involves a serious administrative and compliance burden. Under current law some firms must be concerned about the dividing line between distributions from earnings and profits, which are taxed as dividends to shareholders, and distributions in excess of earnings and profits, which are return of capital. This distinction depends in part on the treatment of preferences; some are included in earnings and profits and some are excluded. But, under current law, the complicated calculation of earnings and profits is of little relevance to most firms, since distributions rarely exceed accumulated earnings and profits. By comparison, prorating would make it necessary for any firm with preference income (which might include the surtax exemption, receipts from term life insurance, and such) to calculate economic income (or its statu-

tory equivalent) on the first dollar of dividends. But under some systems of stacking preferences last, including the plan said to have been considered by the Treasury, it would not even be necessary to calculate economic income or preference income unless some preferences were explicitly chosen for pass-through. Furthermore, the information needed for prorating is not likely to be known on a timely basis. Thus prorating of preferences would be extremely clumsy, and it might render dividend relief administratively infeasible.

Even if such problems are ignored, it may not be possible to use prorating to attack preferences. The idea was suggested by the example of a dividend-paying firm with preference income. Such a firm might split into two firms, owned by the same shareholders, in response to the enactment of dividend relief involving prorating and washout of preferences on distributions. One of the new firms would have no preference income and would pay out a high percentage of its income as dividends. The other would have preference income but would pay no dividends. In such a case, even if preferences were prorated, the effect would be the same as if the law provided for preferences to be stacked last.

Some participants seemed quite content with a system that stacked preferences last and washed them out, since for many firms the relevant factor would be the stacking last, not the washing out. For even though preferences would be washed out if deemed to be distributed, such a result would occur only when the "last (preference) stack" was reached; for most firms preference income is less than retained earnings and therefore preferences would not be washed out. Moreover, there was some agreement that a system that stacks preferences last and washes them out has the advantage of preserving tax preferences that reverse over time (because they involve deferral rather than exemption), so long as the "last stack" is not reached. (If the last stack were reached, and such reversing preferences were distributed, basis adjustment might be required. It would not be required for outright exemptions.)

Other participants expressed the view that any system of dividend relief that washed out preferences was fundamentally undesirable. They felt that the distortions in the present tax system, which are already aggravated by various limitations on the availability of tax preferences, would be further accentuated if tax preferences were washed out on distributed earnings. Because of the tax-induced

pressure on firms not to distribute preference income (see chapter 4), these participants felt that integration under such a back-door approach would not be complete and the vaunted allocative advantages of integration would not be achieved. Since the washing out of preferences would, in addition, depend on the "mix" of income (taxed or preference) in a particular firm and on the firm's dividend policy, firms could be expected to try to avoid losing the advantage of preferences by combining with other firms. Firms with substantial preference income and high dividend rates would tend to merge with firms with low payout rates and/or little preference income. The end result would be that firms would, in fact, largely avoid washout, and the Treasury would collect less revenue than expected. The only tangible result would be the combination of firms in a manner that is not apt to be economically efficient. Washing out preferences in this context would serve only to penalize business in a highly erratic manner.

As an illustration of the disadvantage of washing out preferences, attention was called to the situation of banks and regulated public utilities. Because of the investment tax credit and accelerated depreciation, it was said, many utilities are paying dividends from preference income.[20] And for several reasons banks, too, are paying dividends from income that has not borne full U.S. tax. First, they are large investors in state and local securities. Second, they have large amounts of accelerated depreciation and investment tax credits, since Congress has so structured the investment tax credit that many companies cannot use it directly and, to get any benefit from the credit, are required to finance their new capital investments through bank leases. In such transactions the banks are, in effect, purchasers of the investment tax credit and benefit from it only to the extent that the credit exceeds what they pay their customers for it. Third, a substantial part of the earnings of the biggest banks comes from business that they conduct abroad and pay foreign tax on.[21] If dividend relief involved washout of preferences and the for-

20. Under the RITA system, as proposed, the investment credit would be treated as tax paid, would generate a RITA credit, and would therefore pass through, in part, to shareholders, whereas accelerated depreciation would be entirely washed out (but stacked last). But under alternative approaches to the problem both forms of preferences might be washed out completely.

21. Many participants felt that the foreign tax credit is not a preference, even though European systems of dividend relief commonly treat it like one.

eign tax credit, banks would probably change the mix of their investments over time so as to reduce the preferences and reliance on foreign income. In the case of tax-exempt interest, the investment credit, and accelerated depreciation, the state and local governments and the industrial firms and their customers that are currently the principal beneficiaries of the preferences would be the ones most adversely affected in the long run. But in the short run, washing out preferences and the transitional problems of adjusting their businesses to washout could be very expensive for the banks. Public utilities would have a more difficult problem than banks, since they would have no alternative to present investment patterns.

At least one participant expressed the opinion that the problem of public utilities could be handled fairly easily with a special provision: the owner of preferred shares of regulated utilities would be allowed to treat some portion of cash dividends as return of capital to be used to reduce basis (as, in effect, is the case under present law when only a small fraction of distributions comes from earnings and profits).

Another participant, who believes that preferences should be passed through to shareholders if they are to remain in the tax law, offered what he claimed to be a simple scheme for doing so. Under it, corporate income would be split into taxable and exempt income and distributions would be treated as coming from three sources, in the following order: income that had been taxed at the corporate level, income exempt to the corporation, and distributions from other sources. Distributions from income taxed at the corporate level would be taxed on a grossed-up basis at the shareholder level. Such distributions would be grossed up by the amount of taxes actually paid at the corporate level, but the shareholder credit would include creditable preferences. Distributions of income exempt from tax at the corporate level would also be exempt in the hands of shareholders. And distributions from depreciation and paid-in capital would not be subject to personal tax, but would reduce basis. This scheme, which was claimed to be administratively feasible, would stack deductible and exemption preferences after fully taxed income, but would pass them through. The investment tax credit would be passed through, but with the first dollars of dividends.

A view was expressed that the decision to provide dividend relief

did not imply a need to reexamine tax preferences. But the predominant view was that a system of dividend relief could not be designed without the designers squarely facing the issues of whether and how tax preferences would be passed through.

Some of those who were skeptical about the "stack-last and washout" treatment of tax preferences suggested a differential analysis in which the effects of integration were compared with those of a simple rate cut. According to this view, the results of the two policies might be quite similar except in the financial sphere. Since the knife-edged effects mentioned earlier could be avoided by a reduction in the corporate tax rate, as well as by dividend relief with prorating of preferences, it was argued that perhaps the rate reduction should be preferred to dividend relief with preferences stacked last. As a partial counter to this view, it was noted that dividend relief has an advantage from an equity standpoint because the shareholder credit —which some would see as a cut in the corporate tax—is taxed at the marginal rate of individual shareholders.

Finally, some participants felt that the refundable income tax account would be technically feasible and could be designed to achieve roughly any degree of dividend relief and treatment of tax preferences and foreign income desired, but that it might be comprehensible only to technicians—not to the legislator, the businessman, or the ordinary taxpayer.

Tax-exempt Organizations

Most participants agreed that, as a matter of principle, "tax-exempt" organizations should be given the benefit of dividend relief, but felt that the fundamental question of the propriety of tax exemption of various types of organizations should be examined closely. Though some thought that investment decisions of pension funds would be distorted if such funds were not given dividend relief, others felt that distortion would occur if this relief were provided. One advocate of the second view asserted that since 1950 there have been no completely tax-exempt organizations. The tax on unrelated business income introduced in that year applies to commercial ventures and perhaps to some income from real estate of tax-exempt organizations, and the corporate tax is levied (at the corporate level)

on income from corporate equities, so that only interest income of "tax-exempt" organizations is totally exempt. This being the case, it was said, it is not clear whether the shift toward equity investment that dividend relief for tax-exempt organizations would create would be a net gain for society. Certainly most firms would say that it would be totally unfair to have to compete with corporations whose stock is owned in large part by tax-exempt organizations. Though the same complaint could be levied against a corporation owned by low-income shareholders, the likelihood of substantial ownership by shareholders in low marginal tax brackets would be substantially greater for tax-exempt organizations and the reasoning underlying the tax on unrelated business income much more compelling.

In judging the propriety of tax exemption, some participants believed, one must look beyond the organization in question to the beneficiaries of its actions. In the case of pension funds, for example, some participants thought that the basic tax exemption makes no sense, since it is the vehicle for deferral of personal income tax. Moreover, as a short-term matter the benefits of extending dividend relief to pension plans would in the first instance be captured by the employing firms instead of accruing to the employees making contributions to the funds. This would occur because most pension plans specify benefits to be paid rather than contributions. A smaller group of participants thought that dividend relief should be withheld from tax-exempt organizations to compensate for the tax expenditures currently allowed institutions such as universities. But it was noted that most such institutions would pay no income tax if they were taxed on their net income after deduction of operating expenses. Lastly, another group viewed pension funds as corporations; to them intercorporate dividends would rightly be tax exempt, and taxes would be paid only when dividends were paid from the corporate sector to the household sector.

Considerable discussion was devoted to the effects of response by tax-exempt organizations to the denial of relief on the dividends they receive.

First, it was noted that it would be almost impossible to prevent such organizations from benefiting from dividend relief. For one thing, the benefits of integration would be spread by capital markets to owners of debt securities through an increase in interest rates on such securities. In addition, tax-exempt organizations would realize

capital gains on their holdings of equities when those securities rose in price as a result of the removal of the double taxation of dividends.

Second, it was noted that revenue projections that assume unchanged portfolio selection by such organizations are unrealistic. To the extent that these organizations shifted out of corporate equities if denied relief (the shares being bought by tax-paying investors), revenue loss would be substantially larger than has commonly been supposed. There is little evidence to show how strong the tax-induced shift from equities would be. But the fact that such organizations hold minimal amounts of state and local securities suggests that over time the shift would be substantial. (On the other hand, investment in equities has clear advantages for tax-exempt organizations: equities are traditionally thought to provide a hedge against inflation not available on debt issues, and it is usually thought easier to resist spending capital gains than interest income.) This being the case, it may be preferable to extend dividend relief to tax-exempt organizations directly, to avoid the distortions involved in not doing so.

On the last point it was also mentioned that it might be technically difficult to prevent charities from benefiting even more directly from dividend relief, even if public policy favored such a course. Most obviously, charities would invest in convertible debentures. Three other ways in which the purpose of the law could be circumvented were also suggested (with the implication that there were probably many more): (1) the charity could be the discretionary beneficiary of a trust; legally the trust, rather than the charity, would obtain the benefits of dividend relief, which would then be passed on to the charity; (2) it might be possible in a sale to split the dividends from stock, so that legally a taxable shareholder received the dividends and tax credit, but for the privilege compensated the tax-exempt organization that held the stock; (3) under a system with a discretionary withholding rate, two classes of stock would be issued; tax-exempt organizations would hold stock on which no withholding was assumed to occur.

The reasons for denial of dividend relief to tax-exempt organizations in foreign tax systems are of some interest. If the purpose of dividend relief is defined narrowly as eliminating the double taxation of dividends, it is not necessary to extend dividend relief to tax-exempt institutions, since no double tax is paid. Moreover, with-

holding the benefits of dividend relief from tax-exempt organizations gives countries a useful bargaining ploy in international negotiations: it can be said that if the corporate tax is not refunded to local tax-exempt organizations, it is not truly a withholding tax on shareholders and therefore need not be refunded to foreign shareholders.

Imputation versus Dividend-paid Deduction

One group of participants contended that the distinction between the dividend-paid deduction and imputation (withholding or gross-up and credit) methods of providing dividend relief is not useful and that there is only one method of providing dividend relief. Thus the dividend-paid deduction can be recast as the withholding method simply by adding to it withholding against tax liability on dividends at the corporate rate. If this is done, the gross dividend is reported to the shareholder, instead of the shareholder grossing up a cash dividend, as under the imputation method as usually described. Alternatively, under the imputation approach, if the corporate tax on distributed income is seen as withholding for the personal tax (so that *gross* dividends are stated), there is no corporate tax on dividends and a dividend-paid deduction results. In either event, the corporation remits tax on corporate income and the shareholder takes credit for the tax attributed to dividends.

According to this view, several commonly accepted ideas about the differences between the two basic systems of providing dividend relief involve fallacies. First, it makes no sense to ask whether the relief from double taxation of dividends occurs at the firm or the shareholder level; under either system it can be made to occur initially at either level. That is, the dividend-paid deduction method does not necessarily leave more funds initially at the corporate level than the imputation method; a withholding tax on dividends can be used with the former method to take funds from the corporate level and give credit to the shareholder level. Second, except for limitations imposed by existing tax treaties, the imputation method does not necessarily allow more flexibility in dealing with tax-exempt organizations and foreigners than the dividend-paid deduction method; though it may be politically easier to deny the benefits of dividend relief to those groups under the imputation system, there is nothing

inherent in the administration of the two systems that requires this. Moreover, the imputation method does not provide more flexibility in dealing with tax preferences than the dividend-paid deduction method; though techniques differ, anything that can be done under one system can be done under the other. Finally, it is not necessarily true that the dividend-paid deduction is mechanically simpler; the imputation method may be simpler in some cases (for example, when dividends are paid in years after income is earned).

The discussion up to this point raised the important question of what the rate of U.S. corporate income tax under the proposal considered by the Treasury Department would be taken to be in calculating foreign tax credits. In the European systems the corporate rate is taken to be the rate actually applied to corporate income at the corporate level. Under the French system, for example, it is 50 percent, even though an imputation credit is given for half the tax on dividends. In West Germany the rate depends on the level of distributions and varies between 36 and 56 percent. The interpretation of the U.S. rate might depend on how the U.S. proposal were structured. If, for example, tax-exempt organizations were granted the shareholder credit or its equivalent, it might be difficult to argue that there was not a tax on foreigners distinct from the corporate income tax. It was noted that the British system, in which it appears that the corporate tax is high and cash dividends low but subject to gross-up and credit, provides more leverage in international negotiations than would the equivalent interpretation in which corporate taxes were low and gross dividends were high but there was no gross-up.

A number of participants were reluctant to accept the full equivalence of the two methods of providing dividend relief. It appeared to the dissenters that one or the other of the methods would be simpler to implement, depending on what was decided about such issues as the tax treatment of foreigners and tax-exempt organizations and how to handle tax preferences. If, for example, it were decided to allow the benefits of dividend relief to all shareholders and to stack all preferences last and wash them out, the dividend-paid deduction might be easier to implement. But under almost any other set of policy decisions the two might differ and the imputation method might be easier to implement. Moreover, excluding tax-exempt organizations from the benefits of dividend relief would require a

politically difficult special tax under the dividend-paid deduction, whereas it would require simply disallowing the credit under the imputation method. (But if the dividend-paid deduction were combined with a withholding tax, the withheld tax would not be refunded, and this could be seen as a special tax on dividend income of these organizations.) And though, in theory, the two systems, or any combination of them, would affect dividend decisions identically, they might not, in fact, for there is no assurance that businessmen would view the systems as identical.

Another crucial set of differences involves the ways in which the two systems would be seen by third parties. Regulatory agencies might, for example, see relief provided at the shareholder level as having no relevance for their deliberations on rate-making for public utilities. Or they might see the credit available to the shareholder as part of the rate of return and adjust accordingly. Finally, they might be quite likely to adjust for the reduction in taxes paid at the corporate level because of the deduction of dividends. Depending on such decisions, the benefits of dividend relief might effectively be taken away from the regulated public utilities.

The second important group that would appraise the U.S. tax system would be foreign governments. Under existing international practice it seems likely that a simple deduction for dividends would benefit foreign shareholders in U.S. firms, because of the difficulty of denying the benefit in a world of mirror-image, or reciprocal, withholding rates on dividends paid to foreigners. On the other hand, it might be fairly easy to deny the benefit to foreigners under a simple imputation system, since many other countries have done so. But would it be possible under a dividend-paid deduction approach to treat the tax paid at the corporate level as a withholding tax (as in the RITA approach) and then not grant refunds to foreign shareholders? If the benefits of dividend relief provided in this way were allowed tax-exempt organizations, it might be hard to deny them to foreigners. In short, it is extremely difficult to define the "corporate income tax" under any form of dividend relief—and especially under the proposal considered by the Treasury.

The methods by which tax preferences would be handled under the two basic approaches are somewhat different. Whereas washing out preferences under the imputation method would require pré-

compte (or variable gross-up and credit based on the effective tax rate of the corporation), under the dividend-paid deduction it would be necessary only to limit deduction to dividends paid from fully taxed income;[22] in either case stacking rules would be required to dictate the order in which distributions were assumed to come from taxed and preference income. To pass preferences through under the imputation approach it might be necessary to have gross-up that could differ from the amount of credit. Under the dividend-paid deduction approach, pass-through would be achieved by treating distributions of preference income as a return (tax-free) of capital. But to preserve the preferences fully it would be necessary not to reduce the basis in shares by the amount of such distributions. Besides noting that this approach would require special rules for distributions paid from preference income, conference participants raised several questions about it. Would it work for creditable preferences as well as for deductible preferences? Are other rules needed in cases in which preferences involve advantages of deferral of tax liability rather than exemption? In particular, would basis adjustments be required in such cases? And how could the advantages of excessive early deductions be made to reverse themselves in later years?

A final difference between the two approaches involves administrative burdens and litigation by the government. Litigation would probably be against the corporation under the dividend-paid deduction approach, but in some circumstances under the imputation approach it might be against the shareholder. With fixed gross-up the compliance burden of audit adjustments could be placed on the firm, where it would be more easily handled, rather than on the shareholder; with variable gross-up this would not generally be the case.

Owing in part to the uncertainties about effects on corporate dividend policy, foreign reaction, and proper treatment of tax-exempt shareholders, the Ford administration's July 1975 proposal combined the dividend-paid deduction and imputation approaches. Some participants noted that, given the many uncertainties, it would be desirable to retain the flexibility afforded by such a dual system.

22. To some extent washout would be more or less automatic under the dividend-paid deduction, since the maximum tax that can be eliminated is the tax paid by the corporation. But it would be necessary to have rules to determine whether current preference income or accumulated income were distributed first.

International Flows of Income[23]

The tenets that commonly govern the taxation of international capital flows have evolved under a classical system in which there is a separate corporate income tax and little or no attempt to integrate the personal and corporate income taxes. These tenets are ill suited to a world of integration or dividend relief, and it is far from clear how they should be modified when one or more countries adopt a system that provides integration or relief from double taxation of dividends. In particular, in a system of dividend relief at least two questions must be answered: whether the country of source of corporate income should extend dividend relief to foreign shareholders in domestic firms, and whether the country of residence of shareholders should grant the imputation credit to shareholders receiving dividends from foreign corporations, thereby integrating the foreign corporate tax into the domestic personal tax. Analogous questions would arise if full integration were adopted. Ideally the answers to the two questions would be consistent. Of course, the issues would be considerably complicated if not all countries adopted integration, a given form of dividend relief, or a simple classical system.

It was noted that inherent in the case for integration is the case for residence-principle taxation; that is, taxation in which the shareholder is taxed on his worldwide income in his country of residence at the marginal rate determined there. This is commonly interpreted as requiring integration of the foreign corporate tax into the domestic personal tax. Yet most countries are understandably reluctant to allow shareholders credit for corporate taxes paid to foreign governments, because of the loss of revenue and control over the credits to be allowed. In fact, West Germany has not stressed worldwide efficiency or capital-export neutrality, which might require integration of foreign corporate taxes with the West German personal tax. Rather, West Germany, it was said, has embarked on a deliberate policy to encourage domestic investment relative to foreign investment. Thus it does not provide gross-up and credit for foreign corpo-

23. Chapter 6 was not available at the time of the conference. The discussion reported here related largely to Hugh J. Ault, "International Issues in Corporate Tax Integration," Georgetown University Law Center, *Law and Policy in International Business,* vol. 10, no. 2 (1978), pp. 461–94.

rate taxes and levies a précompte on foreign source income that is distributed by West German firms.

As an alternative it was suggested that the source country should provide the dividend relief. But it was noted that the stakes in this debate are quite asymmetrical, with the United States having about five times as much invested abroad as foreigners have invested in the United States. Thus, because of the potential loss of revenue, most countries could not be expected to agree readily to an arrangement whereby the United States gave imputation credits to foreign shareholders in U.S. firms in exchange for reciprocal treatment abroad. Only countries eager for foreign investment would be likely to enter into such a deal. Such an approach would almost certainly be unacceptable to the developing countries, especially those rich in natural resources. Nor would it be advantageous to most of the developed countries vis-à-vis the United States.[24]

Countries that have systems of dividend relief (and those that have considered full integration) tend to try to limit revenue loss by not extending the benefits of dividend relief (or integration) to foreign shareholders. In Canada, for example, the predominance of U.S. shareholding makes indispensable the denial of the benefits of either integration or dividend relief to foreigners. Given the prevalence of the convention that withholding tax rates should be mirror images (and the amount of time needed to negotiate new treaties, even if one were optimistic about gaining exemption from mirror-image withholding), the imputation method has been chosen over the dividend-paid deduction approach as a means of providing dividend relief. Whereas under the latter approach a special, or higher rate of, withholding tax would be needed to prevent foreign shareholders from enjoying the benefits of dividend relief, under the imputation method it has been thought acceptable simply not to extend the benefits of gross-up and credit to foreign shareholders. In fact, the British have gone so far as to employ an advance corporation tax, which is collected on the payment of dividends. Even though this tax is offset against corporate tax liability, and is there-

24. However, the present difference between the treatment of interest and of dividends was noted: there seems to be little dispute over whether interest should be taxed at the country of residence or the country of origin of the interest payments; residence is virtually the unanimous choice, though some developing countries do levy withholding taxes on interest payments.

fore argued by the British to be an advance payment of corporation tax that is not refundable to the shareholder, it could also be construed (less favorably) as a withholding tax collected on a gross dividend that includes the ACT as well as the cash dividend.

This difference in interpretation illustrates the point that once integration and dividend relief are examined in an international context, it is not always clear what the corporate income tax is. This point can be further illustrated with reference to the West German system. In its treaties the Federal Republic of Germany cedes jurisdiction to the country of source, exempting foreign income of West German corporations from West German tax. But to the extent that foreign source income is distributed, the précompte-type levy is due. West Germany's treaty partners claim that this practice violates West German promises not to impose the West German corporate tax on foreign source income. When West Germany counters that the précompte is merely a prepayment of the personal tax, it must face the objection that in such a case foreign shareholders in West German firms should receive refunds for the 36 percent collected on distributed earnings. Thus the crucial question: how to define the corporate tax for purposes of treaty negotiations and calculation of foreign tax credits in a system with dividend relief.

West Germany has also resisted the notion that the total dividend relief it provides domestic shareholders should be available to foreign shareholders and has argued that in appraising its corporate income tax (and its refusal to grant its shareholder credit to foreign investors) attention should be paid to the *aggregate* level of taxes collected on corporate income in West Germany and in other countries. If, for example, the United States collects taxes of 46 percent of income, West Germany feels that it should be allowed a similar overall level of taxation. The willingness of the United Kingdom to extend relief to foreign direct investors, some thought, may reflect an attempt to offset the adverse effects of the increase in the corporate tax rate from 40 percent to 52 percent.

Of course, the pressures are not entirely against extending dividend relief to foreign shareholders; balance of payments objectives and considerations of economic growth might dictate that a country grant dividend relief to foreign shareholders. Several countries have been ready to negotiate away their right to tax dividends paid to foreign shareholders: on the basis of bilateral treaties, the French have

extended the benefits of dividend relief to foreign portfolio investors, and the United Kingdom has even been willing, though reluctant, to allow dividend relief for direct investment by U.S. corporations. Yet no country wants to be in the position of being forced to provide dividend relief to foreigners; at the very least the imputation method gives a country bargaining strength that is sorely missing under the dividend-paid deduction approach. Complete reliance on the dividend-paid deduction method (or the equivalent split-rate system) was explicitly rejected in at least two important countries (West Germany and the United Kingdom) for precisely that reason.[25]

The difficulties of coordinating national tax systems involving dividend relief has led Professor van den Tempel of the Netherlands to state that a classical system is preferable to one providing dividend relief. Though some observers have stated that the van den Tempel approach has the international tail wagging the domestic dog, others have suggested that in this case perhaps the international problem, rather than domestic considerations, is the dog. In any event, the latest proposal for a directive on harmonization in the countries belonging to the European Community explicitly rejects the van den Tempel approach and takes as a starting point a situation in which all member countries levy corporate taxes of roughly 50 percent and relieve about 50 percent of the double taxation on dividends.[26]

Under this proposed directive, individual shareholders would receive an imputation credit in their country of residence based on corporate taxes paid to the source country. But the residence country would be compensated by the country of origin of the corporate-source income that had collected the corporate tax underlying the imputation credit. Conference participants noted, however, that this system would work only because the European countries levied corporate taxes at similar rates and only to the extent that they

25. The West German system does, of course, retain a split rate in conjunction with the shareholder credit. But West Germany would probably have preferred to rely solely on the split rate by exempting dividends from the corporate tax. And given the direction of recent treaty negotiations, under whose terms the United Kingdom would extend dividend relief to many foreign shareholders, this supposed difference between the two systems may be largely illusory.

26. West Germany's system of 100 percent dividend relief clearly does not accord with the scheme proposed in the draft directive. Note that in December 1977 the European Parliament failed to approve the draft directive. See *Intertax: European Tax Review* (January 1978), p. 1.

provided similar degrees of dividend relief. More generally, it might be necessary to choose between a system in which foreign corporate taxes were integrated into domestic personal income taxes (by allowing the foreign taxes as a credit against the domestic tax of the shareholder) and a system in which the country of source provided a dividend-paid deduction or extended credit to nonresident shareholders. At present, no resident country allows individual shareholders credit for foreign corporate taxes, but several source countries have, as mentioned before, provided credits for nonresident investors.

It was noted that the United States has at various times advocated positions that can be interpreted to suggest that relief should be given in both ways. Worldwide efficiency, one of the cornerstones of U.S. foreign tax policy, would require that shareholders investing in foreign countries should benefit from dividend relief based on source-country taxes. In its treaty negotiations with countries providing dividend relief, the United States has argued that any such relief should be provided by the residence country; that is, foreign corporate taxes should be integrated into the personal income taxes of such countries.[27] But in these negotiations the United States has also pressed for the extension of the shareholder credit to U.S. investors in foreign firms. Such a dual approach, if adopted in full, has little to recommend it on conceptual grounds, since it would mean that a country would tax neither income originating within its borders and flowing to foreigners or foreign-source income of resident shareholders. Because such an approach would involve giving up revenues from all international flows of capital income, it is unlikely to receive widespread support. Yet this approach, modified so that each country provides half the total dividend relief, is quite consistent with the approach in the draft directive of the Commission of the European Communities. Some participants seemed to feel that the latter approach held promise as a compromise solution. But it was noted that it would work best if all countries had similar degrees of integration or dividend relief. (See also note 26.)

Among the questions raised, but not answered fully, were the following: If the European Community had adopted the proposals for

27. Capital-export neutrality could also be achieved if source countries provided the credits. But as a country using a classical system the United States has been unwilling to follow this approach.

harmonization outlined in the draft directive and the United States had elected a dividend-paid deduction system, would harmonization of U.S. and European taxes be feasible? Since some participants believed that deferral really destroys capital-export neutrality, is it sensible to continue to make deferral available if choices about dividend relief are predicated on the achievement of capital-export neutrality? Under a system of dividend-paid deduction, could (and should) the United States have different withholding rates for various countries, depending on the benefits granted to U.S. shareholders by foreign countries? Finally, how should the imputation credit be treated in corporate financial statements and tax statistics: as reduction in the corporate tax or in the individual tax? (Although the British statute is written in such a way that the corporate tax is reported in financial statements at the 52 percent rate and the credit is treated as going to shareholders, under the Treasury proposal the credit might reasonably be interpreted as reducing the corporate rate. If so, the implications for international treaties might be adverse.)

Conclusion

It was clear from the discussion at the conference that integration of the corporate and individual income taxes presents many difficult problems. It may be useful, in conclusion, to review some of the many questions that should be addressed if full integration or dividend relief is to be adopted in the United States.

The case for integration. What are the economic effects of full integration? Of dividend relief? In particular, how would each system affect debt-equity ratios, dividend payout rates, stock prices, the allocation of resources, the distribution of tax burdens, and so forth? Can these effects be quantified with acceptable accuracy? Are the expected benefits enough to justify the considerable dislocation and administrative burden implicit in a shift to integration or dividend relief? Are the differences in the effects of the two systems great enough to justify attempting integration, or is it enough to implement dividend relief? To what extent does the answer to that question depend on the treatment accorded existing tax preferences? Would there be appreciable differences in dividend payout, depending on the treatment of tax preferences? On the treatment of tax-exempt organizations?

Feasibility of full integration or dividend relief. Granting that full integration is preferable, is it feasible? How can the eight problems of full integration discussed earlier be overcome? Or if dividend relief is the alternative, would the three or four administrative differences between dividend relief and integration tip the scale toward dividend relief? Is dividend relief feasible? In what form? What withholding (corporate) rate should be imposed if full integration is instituted? If dividend relief is the choice? What top personal rate is appropriate under a regime of integration? Under dividend relief? What changes in the capital gains law should accompany integration? Dividend relief?

Imputation versus dividend-paid deduction. Are the differences between these two approaches to dividend relief real or only apparent? Is the only difference one of perceptions and political realities? In particular, are there likely to be important differences[28] in (1) the treatment of public utilities, (2) dividend payout rates, (3) the ability to handle tax preferences flexibly, (4) the ease of handling losses; audit adjustments and amended returns, (5) how foreign governments will define the American corporate tax; restraints on treaty negotiations, (6) the ease of taxing or exempting chosen organizations (that is, the present tax-exempt sector), and (7) definitions of "dividends" for nontax purposes?

Tax preferences. How should tax preferences be treated under integration or dividend relief? In other words, should preferences be passed through to shareholders or washed out? And should they be stacked first or last? Is the answer the same for all preferences? For both tax credits and deductible (or exclusion) preferences? To what extent does the answer depend on technical questions of tax administration rather than on judgments about proper social or economic policy? What technical difficulties would be encountered in trying to implement various treatments of preferences? Are some approaches to dividend relief likely to be more easily administered than others, especially so far as preferences are concerned? Does the refundable income tax account approach (the approach considered by the U.S. Treasury Department), with its optional rate of withholding, make

28. The differences noted in the text were mentioned during the conference. Differences might also exist, for example, in rights of preferred shareholders, accounting practices, and dividend policy permitted under state law.

sense? Under any of the approaches, is it necessary to define economic income? Preferences? Earnings and profits?

International aspects. How should the United States treat dividends paid to foreign portfolio shareholders in U.S. corporations? Direct investors? Dividends paid to U.S. shareholders by foreign corporations? Are the answers the same for developed and developing countries? Should these matters be decided bilaterally or multilaterally? Is the answer different if (1) all countries provide integration or dividend relief, and (2) some retain classical systems? Is one method of providing dividend relief preferable in terms of the latitude it provides in the international sphere? How does the treatment of tax-exempt organizations reduce options in the international field? How would the refundable income tax account system be interpreted in foreign countries?

Glossary

Advance corporation tax (ACT) An advance payment of corporation tax levied on dividend distributions by firms in the United Kingdom. The tax (currently 33/67 of dividends), which is credited against the corporation's tax liability for the year, helps to assure that preferences on corporate-source income are washed out when preference income is distributed.

Affiliation privilege See Schachtelprivileg.

Auslaendereffekt The "foreigner effect" likely to occur under the split-rate system of dividend relief: the earnings of a foreign-owned subsidiary that are reinvested in the country of residence of the subsidiary are taxed less heavily than is income earned and retained by a firm or group of firms resident in the same country.

Avoir fiscal Credit against personal income tax of a stated percentage of dividends received (50 percent in France). The avoir fiscal is included in personal taxable income. (See also Shareholder credit.)

Capital-export neutrality The situation in which taxes do not distort the choices that firms make about where to invest.

Capital-import neutrality The situation in which the same tax is applied to the income of all firms competing in the same country.

Classical system An unintegrated system of taxation, such as that in the United States, which results in the double taxation of corporate dividends.

Conduit theory The view that the corporation has no independent tax-

paying ability and should be seen as a "conduit" through which earnings pass on the way to shareholders.

Dividend-paid deduction A method of dividend relief in which a tax deduction of up to 100 percent is allowed corporations for dividends paid to shareholders.

Dividend payout rate The proportion of profits that a corporation pays out as dividends.

Dividend relief Relief from the double taxation of dividends at the corporate and personal level. Under it (to be distinguished from *integration*), distributed income is free of tax at the corporate level and is taxed only at the shareholder's marginal personal rate. In *full* (or *total*) *dividend relief,* all distributed income is taxed only at the shareholder level; in *partial dividend relief,* only a portion of distributed income is so taxed, the rest being subject to double taxation.

Double taxation of dividends The classical method whereby the corporation pays tax on its net income and the individual recipient of dividends paid from the net income pays tax on the dividends he receives.

Earnings and profits The key concept in differentiating between dividends and other distributions under current U.S. tax law. Distributions are treated as dividends and taxed as ordinary income to the extent that they are paid from earnings and profits. Accumulated earnings and profits resemble retained earnings and are more inclusive than accumulated undistributed taxable income in that they include certain items of preference income.

Economic income See Haig-Simons income.

Foreign tax credit A credit allowed in the country of residence of a corporation for income taxes paid to foreign countries.

Gross-up and credit See Shareholder credit.

Haig-Simons income An ideal for the measurement of income for tax purposes. It consists of consumption plus increase in net wealth.

Imputation system A method of dividend relief in which all or part of the corporate tax liability on distributed earnings is "imputed" to the shareholders and treated as withholding against their personal income tax on dividends.

Integration Tax system in which all income earned at the corporate level—that is, both retained and distributed earnings—is attributed to shareholders and taxed at the rates applicable to the incomes of the various shareholders. Under *full* (or *total,* or *complete*) *integration,* all corporate earnings are used in calculating gross-up and credit.

Mainstream tax Under the British system of dividend relief, the excess of the corporation income tax over the advance corporation tax.

Nachsteuer Under the old West German system of dividend relief, a "back tax" collected from a parent firm on any earnings exempted under the Schachtelprivileg, but not distributed within the year. It was needed to prevent such earnings from benefiting unduly from the reduced rate on dividends under the split-rate system.

Neutral taxation Taxation that does not distort choices of production, consumption, or financial policy.

Ordering rules See Stacking of preferences.

Partnership method The conceptual ideal of full integration under which equity income earned in the corporate sector would be taxed to shareholders as if earned in a partnership.

Pass-through A term applied to tax preferences in a system of full integration or dividend relief. A tax preference is *passed through* to shareholders when it reduces the tax liability at the personal level as much as if the shareholders had invested directly in the activity benefiting from the tax preference.

Précompte A supplementary tax levied in France at the corporate level on any income distributed to shareholders that has not borne the full rate of French tax.

Preference income Income that is not taxed at full rates because of preferential rates, tax credits, or deductions not necessary for the determination of economic income.

Refundable income tax account (RITA) Same as Shareholder credit account.

Schachtelprivileg Under the old West German system of dividend relief, a "holding privilege" whereby dividends received by a parent corporation from a domestic corporation in which it had at least 25 percent interest were not taxable to the parent.

Shareholder credit Under the imputation system and integration, the portion of the corporation income tax that is imputed to the shareholder and treated as a withholding tax.

Shareholder credit account A device in the 1978 Ullman proposal for dividend relief under which a given percentage of corporation income tax would be entered in a shareholder credit account and shareholder credits would be limited to the amounts in such accounts. Similar to the British advance corporation tax, this is a device to limit dividend relief to taxes actually paid.

Split-rate system A method of dividend relief equivalent to the dividend-paid deduction: distributed corporate earnings are taxed at a lower rate than undistributed earnings.

Stacking of preferences The order in which preference income is assumed for tax purposes to be paid out. When preferences are *stacked first,* they are assumed to be the first income to be distributed. When preferences are *stacked last,* they are assumed to be distributed after taxable income.

Subchapter S corporation A corporation roughly similar in tax treatment to a partnership. It has up to fifteen shareholders who are individuals or estates and who have elected under the rules of subchapter S of the Internal Revenue Code not to pay corporate income tax, but rather to pay individual income taxes directly on the corporate income, whether or not it is distributed to them.

Tax preference See Preference income.

Territorial principle The method of taxation whereby a country taxes only income arising within its own borders.

Washing out preferences Preferences are treated as taxable income to the shareholder, and therefore nullified, to the extent that they are distributed.

Worldwide principle The method of taxation whereby all the income earned by a resident of a given country is taxed by that country, no matter where the income originates.

Conference Participants

with their affiliations at the time of the conference

William D. Andrews *Harvard Law School*

Hugh J. Ault *Boston College Law School*

Richard M. Bird *University of Toronto*

David F. Bradford *Princeton University*

Gerard M. Brannon *Georgetown University*

George F. Break *University of California (Berkeley)*

E. Cary Brown *Massachusetts Institute of Technology*

Edwin S. Cohen *University of Virginia Law School*

Martin S. Feldstein *Harvard University and National Bureau of Economic Research*

Joseph Gabbay *Ministry of Finance, Israel*

Harvey Galper *U.S. Treasury Department*

Martin D. Ginsburg *Weil, Gotshal and Manges*

Richard Goode *International Monetary Fund*

Harry G. Gourevitch *Library of Congress*

Michael J. Graetz *University of Southern California Law Center*

Daniel I. Halperin *U.S. Treasury Department*

Frederic W. Hickman *Hopkins, Sutter, Mulroy, Davis and Cromartie*

Daniel M. Holland *Massachusetts Institute of Technology*

William A. Klein *University of California Law School (Los Angeles)*

Richard S. Koffey *U.S. Treasury Department*

Michael E. Levy *Congressional Budget Office*

Donald C. Lubick *U.S. Treasury Department*

Paul R. McDaniel *Boston College Law School*

Charles E. McLure, Jr. *Rice University and National Bureau of Economic Research*

Kenneth Messere *Organisation for Economic Co-operation and Development*

Joseph J. Minarik *Brookings Institution*

Alicia H. Munnell *Federal Reserve Bank of Boston*

John S. Nolan *Miller and Chevalier*

Harry A. Olsher *Fund for Public Policy Research*

Joseph A. Pechman *Brookings Institution*

John M. Samuels *U.S. Treasury Department*

Carl S. Shoup *Columbia University (Emeritus)*

Lawrence M. Stone *Irell and Manella*

Emil M. Sunley, Jr. *U.S. Treasury Department*

Stanley S. Surrey *Harvard Law School*

Willard B. Taylor *Attorney at Law*

Alvin C. Warren, Jr. *University of Pennsylvania Law School*

James W. Wetzler *Joint Committee on Internal Revenue Taxation*

Bernard Wolfman *Harvard Law School*

Alexander Zakupowsky, Jr. *U.S. Treasury Department*

Index

257